AERIALIST

AERIALIST

Rebecca Truman

British Library Cataloguing-in-Publication Data
A catalogue record for this book is available from the British Library

ISBN 978-1-999632-0-3

Printed and bound in the UK by
Jellyfish Solutions

To Romana, Crispin, Nadya, Annaliese and Mum

CHAPTER 1

Skinning the Cat

> **Aerialist** – in a circus context means a performer who works in the air using a variety of techniques, which includes the trapeze.

I was a trapeze artist. Technically, I was an aerialist: I flew in the air on a variety of ropes and trapezes, on which I swung, twisted and balanced. When I was twenty-one I started an all-women trapeze company. We took our name from the traditional trapeze move 'Skinning the Cat'.

Waiting in the wings, I pace up and down. I wear my voluminous black velvet cloak with its red sparkly lining. It is edged with purple and red cockerel feathers and trails along the ground behind me. I discard it at the bottom of the rope like an unnecessary skin.

As I wait, I work through my routine in my mind, feeling it in my body at the same time; I constantly pat my resin sock into my already sticky and sweating palms. It is a wonderful feeling of fear and excitement – this time before a show, crucial for changing head space from chatting in the green room to becoming Firebird.

My years as an aerialist are divided into before and after the falls. These accidents changed everything; they made me more determined to continue the trapeze, but I was a different person, no longer carefree enough to enjoy the touring lifestyle as a free spirit. Before the falls, I was running wild and fulfilling my fantasies. Afterwards it all became too real: the near loss of life, and the shock and adjustment that followed, changed me.

I didn't think about anything but the trapeze: talking trapeze, doing trapeze and dreaming trapeze. It is an all-or-nothing profession. The skin on the palms of my hands was thick with calluses, which I habitually picked at, and my body was shaped by the trapeze: wide shoulders and athletic legs, with a deep indentation on my thigh muscles where the bar pressed into them when I hung in catcher's position. On show days, the day revolved around the show. And when we had no show, the day revolved around training and preparing for the next round of shows.

The trapeze was only one part of my aerial repertoire, there are many other shaped and configured pieces of equipment that the aerialist can work on. One of these is a single vertical rope or *corde lisse.* My corde lisse routine began with a toe climb, with a back balance as the first move. Being on a rope without bar or attachments, it is necessary to develop the strength to hold the rope out horizontally in order that the body can lie across it. Many of my moves involved wrapping the rope around a leg, knee or foot in a lock-off position, so that I could reach back, pull up the rest of the rope, and wrap it around some other part of the body to create a shape. The drops that can be done on a rope are dramatic because you can climb to the top, wrap the rope around you, and roll or slide all the way to the bottom, stopping only at the very last second before hitting the ground. It is really very hard to retain the balance of the body during a roll: either side of the wrapped rope must be kept at equal weight, which isn't easy when travelling down it at full tilt.

Complete focus on the rope;
feel it is a part of me.
I grasp it between my toes and,
as I lift myself off the ground, my second foot takes hold.
Keeping my hands close together,
I pull them towards my chest and flip upside down in one
smooth pull.
With a small bounce my body is momentarily weightless,
I bring one leg to join the rope so close that it is like an
extra strand.
I strike my first pose and acknowledge the audience.
Staring out into the spotlight,
I gesture dramatically with my free hand then suddenly
dive forward.
As I catch the rope the relief from the audience is
palpable.

The relationship between the aerialist and the audience is both distant and intimate. The audience sees the performer who is at the same time powerful and vulnerable. The act can go wrong in a heartbeat – we hide behind grand gestures and confident expressions. We allow the audience a brief glimpse into our private world; we need the audience and we also shun them; we are above them.

Sometimes I have felt the audience to be nervous of me, looking up to me, and other times I am looked down on, an outsider, a traveller with a suspect lifestyle. It is a relationship of extremes.

We never inhabit the same space. The boundaries are clearly marked, but the feeling that we exchange controls the show. The pace of the routines is punctuated by their reactions, which dictate whether to hold a pose, repeat something, slow it down or speed it up.

There are of course different types of audience, just as there are different types of performers; I have ongoing banter with my street performer friends about our values. The street performer must attract an audience, gather them together, keep them there and then extract money from them. There is a direct correlation between the show quality and the cash in the hat.

In contrast to this, our show is always pre-booked: we are planned for and paid for, however well or badly we perform, although of course there will be no repeat bookings for a bad show. There are posters and programmes advertising our show and, even if people have missed the advertising, we are so high up and big and visual that we attract people without having to work at it consciously.

As aerialists, we never speak directly to our audience; we treat them as guests watching something magical. We also have a secret that stops us speaking: most aerialists cannot act. We are gymnasts, acrobats, dancers in the air: we perform through exaggerating our own personalities and becoming part of a magnificent, gravity-defying world outside everyday experience.

As I prepare to perform, I must begin to change my focus. Sometimes this does not happen, if there are problems or distractions, rigging tangles or sound or lighting glitches – the show feels flat. Equally, if the audience feels dead and we must work really hard to get a reaction, it can become a vicious circle: the performance is forced and unnatural and the audience will not warm up. This is when it is hard to engage with the music, the trapeze, the audience, hard to act up to the lighting, other performers or the kids. This is when I believe shows become dangerous, as you don't quite care enough, can't quite concentrate enough, just want it to be over.

Sometimes we needed to set up an audience-free show for a

video or photo run, as the show lighting is set to be atmospheric and the routines are too fast moving for the camera. Photos or video taken during a live show are often murky, dark and blurred. So, we would blast the costumes with white light and hold positions until we were fit to bust for the camera. It was very hard to perform properly with no audience: we would just go through the motions, no adrenaline, no feedback, weird and flat.

But when a performance goes well you just can't beat it. It is as if you carry the audience along on a wave. You can do nothing wrong; every twitch of your hand or smile gets a reaction.

On the trapeze, I rule the world.
I am in the ring, in the air, in the spotlight,
you are outside the barrier in the darkness.
I can feel you,
a warm, breathing, reacting mass that gasps, applauds,
shouts and cheers.
I do not exist without your appreciation,
you are everything to me and nothing.

After a good show, we were on an adrenaline high. Sometimes friends or brave fans would come and talk to us. I was always disappointed if a friend said they came to the show but didn't come and say hello afterwards. We could feel cut off from the outside world and needed feedback for our egos. People see the backstage area as hallowed ground where performers need their space and respect: this is true before a show, but afterwards we wanted to glow and socialize.

I found that I subtly changed my performance character depending on the occasion: upbeat and smiley for variety shows, dramatic and exaggerated for circus, more dark and brooding for theatre and festivals. Depending on where, how and why we were working, the audiences changed and we adapted. There is the unexpected audience: this happened when we were booked for something like a dockland regeneration event or a city centre celebration. People walking around the corner to the shops, or out on their daily dog walk, would happen across us doing a trapeze show right where they usually walked. Sometimes people would stop and watch or sometimes just pass by, but either way we shared a moment of each other's lives. My favourite passing audience moment was when double decker buses went by and the top deck was on the same level as the trapeze, with rows of surprised faces gazing back at us on their way home from work.

There is the hard-core, tough weather, determined audience: normally already circus fans. When we were booked for an outdoor event, people would start arriving before the show to get the best spot at the front. If the weather was dubious, they would stand around with umbrellas while we scuttled up and down taking tarps on and off the rigging. The atmosphere would build as the crowd grew. If the weather worsened and the show was pulled, you could hear the buzz of disappointment and we would feel low and de-energised.

Then there's the open-to-enjoyment festival crowd: possibly drunk or off their heads on something, and certain to experience something other-worldly when they watch the show. A happy and relaxed vibe emanates from them: with this lot it is hard to go wrong.

There is the weekend afternoon festival audience: families with parents who are just happy to sit down for a bit while the kids are entertained, eating ice creams and drinking cups of tea. The children are open-mouthed and amazed, the adults appreciative but often distracted by the environment, which can be busy and noisy with sounds from surrounding events and passers-by.

The variety show audience: all adult and often seasoned variety theatre addicts, who know their acts and can rate them accordingly. Sometimes these people are almost part of the show, dressing up in old fashioned finery and singing along with the music hall numbers. In the case of a German variety show, people are more serious and expect a quality evening of entertainment for their money. Either way, these people are focused on what they want from the evening, and you get a measured, well-behaved reaction from them.

One of my favourite audiences is the tented circus audience: theoretically a family audience, but if you look at the ratio of adults to children there are always a lot more adults than have shares in the children, so you can only assume that adults enjoy circus too.

I love this audience because it is so comfortable with itself. There is no need to restrain reactions or discipline children's behaviour. The Big Top, and the activity within it, contains the guests in its own world. Each act brings a different atmosphere and the viewers are swept along with it. People move around, children jump out of their seats, there is laughter and exchange of banter with the clowns. I watch children dancing in the aisles, mimicking the movements in the ring in their excitement, then falling into silent awe during the darkness of a dangerous act. Even the simplest performance holds magic. Children fall around with laughter at a clown that I do not find funny at all: it is enough that a funnily dressed man falls over.

If I had to explain why being an aerialist was so good, despite being difficult, dangerous and financially unrewarding, so good that I couldn't stop even after my falls, I struggle. Because it is just inside of me, a feeling, like falling in love. There is no explanation that really makes sense, except that it is just something that I had to do. Once I discovered the trapeze, it was what I had been waiting for all my life. It meant everything to me.

CHAPTER 2

Rigging

Rigging – the verb 'to rig' describes the action of putting up trapeze equipment.

De-rigging – to take down trapeze equipment.

The rigging – is the noun which describes the equipment: ropes, trapezes, wires, etc.

The rigger – the person doing the rigging.

The top of the rigging is my private domain
On an outdoor rig you can see for miles:
wind, sun, rain – what a feeling.
Looking out over trees, towns, hills, or watching the world
in miniature below,
nobody sees me unless I drop a shackle pin on their head!

Or sweating in a tight roof space,
lying on a narrow beam,
crammed into the heat caught between the truss and the
crumbling roof plaster.
I am high above the chandeliers,
disturbing dust as thick as carpet,
It could be particles of skin from long-dead performers,
undisturbed since the theatre was built.

Lou was my best friend; she was also a member of Skinning the Cat. We share the same interests, gaudy taste in clothes and sense of humour. Lou and I loved rigging: it was part of doing the trapeze but without the stress of the show.

It was the end of the 1994 touring season and we were all completely exhausted. Lou had brought her son, Henri, on tour with her, but for this last booking we had dropped him off with his dad, Dusty. We had taken Henri on tour since he was six weeks old; this was his third year of being spoilt rotten by seven women.

A huge venue in the centre of Amsterdam. Dutch TV were setting up all around us as we ran through our act. Rigging had been a complete nightmare right from the beginning: this often happened when an agent agreed to a contract without letting us know the true technical requirements of a space. I had got used to thinking on my feet and inventing some creative solutions. In this case, the venue was about three times as high as usual and we'd been promised extra riggers, who didn't materialise.

In an extremely tight window before a live TV show, we had to sweat it out in the filthy roof space, dropping long lines down to a level where we could work in front of the cameras. We normally took our meal and tea breaks very seriously as part of the pre-show schedule, but that day we were all running non-stop between roof and floor. Lou had sent me on a tea break that day, but she hadn't taken one herself.

Lou is a one-off. She has a blinkered strength and stubbornness, which is especially activated around anything or anyone important to her. She always tried to protect me from the extreme stresses that I was often under during both the production and realisation of a show. When she became pregnant we both automatically assumed that she would bring the baby with her and stay in the company. As well as being an amazing and positive achievement, this had put our small company under a huge amount of stress: travelling with a small child is not easy. During the season that she was pregnant, she would not only volunteer for but insist on extra duties: all night driving; hammering in all the stakes; patrolling the rig all night when the security guard failed to show up. She refused to let me treat her differently or carefully. I was furious with her when, between shows, she raced off and did a bungee jump. Jumping is specifically forbidden when pregnant.

We were ready just in time for the dress rehearsal. Lou was at the top of the rig, sitting on a bit of trussing so that she could do all the technical stuff before dropping down to perform. She played an energetic character, pushing her own personality to its limits, throwing herself from side to side as she came down the rope, catching it each time with alternate hands. This was something that she could do in her sleep. But this time she missed with her right hand, and the force of her swinging pulled her legs straight off the rope. She fell head first towards the floor.

I was standing at the bottom of her rope looking up. I saw what seemed like a life-sized stuffed doll, dressed in Lou's costume, falling towards me. I was only a couple of feet away. As I heard her head hit the concrete floor, I was still wondering why this strange doll had fallen out of the sky.

I knew it was bad because I heard that noise. It sounded exactly like what it was: a skull hitting a concrete floor.

I just stood and stared. Everyone else rushed forward. An ambulance arrived. While they were putting Lou into a neck-brace, onto a stretcher and into the ambulance, I still stood there.

Skinning the Cat member Claire went in the ambulance with Lou, and I continued to prepare for the show. I assumed that the show must go on. My place as the boss was to stay and sort out the show first, before any personal feelings. After all, there was a live TV show in a couple of hours and we couldn't let the viewers down.

I knew that the other performers should not do a show after such a shock, so I approached the TV director with a proposal that I would do my solo act. The director said: 'If you could see your eyes, you would know that you are not going to be doing anything.'

Helen, our technician, and I got on with the job of de-rigging the lower sections of trapeze equipment so that they wouldn't be in the way of the cameras and the rest of the variety show. There was no way we could face going back up into the roof space to take the high rigging down.

When I finally made it to the hospital, the nurses seemed worryingly calm. They told me that the brain scanner was broken but not to worry because they just thought she had concussion. I *was* worried: they had not heard the sound of her impact. I was having a problem being taken seriously. They kept asking me what she had taken. We were foreigners in Amsterdam and Lou was dressed up in an extravagant costume. They were making assumptions to explain her increasingly bizarre behaviour.

Now I had time to ring home. Lou's partner, Dusty, was out working but Henri's babysitter said that he could ring the venue and get in touch with him. I passed on the official line, which was not to worry too much as they thought it was only concussion.

I sent Claire and Helen off to get something to eat and set about the job of removing Lou's costume and dressing her in the only spare clothes I had with me, my favourite old training clothes. Training clothes are very important to an aerialist: they must be completely comfortable, tight fitting and cover the right parts of the body to prevent rope burns. They are generally scruffy and caked in resin.

The nurses had left me alone with Lou in a curtained cubicle and instructed me not to let her lose consciousness. She was behaving very scarily, thrashing around as though she had the devil in her head, then passing out for a bit. I was extremely suspicious. I saw my dad behave like this. I had been sent upstairs when they brought him home, but I watched through the banisters. He died of a brain haemorrhage.

I couldn't keep Lou awake. I had a horrible feeling that I was watching something terrible happen and was unable to do anything about it; no one would listen. I called the nurses again and finally got a reaction. We were immediately put in an ambulance and sent to a hospital with a brain scanner. The medic told the driver to go faster, we were losing her.

At the next hospital, the surgeon explained that her brain was full of blood and they must operate immediately. Our Dutch agent had joined me by now and we were left in the waiting room to call England and tell Dusty that there had been a change for the worse. This was the hardest phone call I have ever made. I summarised the situation to Dusty then passed the phone to our agent to explain the medical details because I could not think straight.

And then we waited. Claire and Helen came back and tried to get me to eat something. I couldn't eat. I was racked with guilt: it was my company; she was my best friend; she was too busy looking after me to take care of herself. It was my fault.

After the operation I was left sitting in intensive care next to an inert Lou. My instructions were simply to keep talking to her about anything and everything that she would recognise. Until you've had to do this, you have no idea how difficult it is. I rambled on about Winnie the Pooh and Piglet, whom we had both loved as children. Lou had brought the book on tour to read to me if I was tired or nervous before a performance.

Only two things happened in the night. The rest of our rigging arrived in Intensive Care, accompanied by a huge bouquet of flowers. The lighting guys had kindly done our work for us. Years later, when I was back in Amsterdam doing my solo act, I was approached by a lighting technician who asked me please not to swing so high as last time they worked with an aerialist she fell off. It was the same men. I had never thought how it would have affected them.

The other event was that I was handed a plastic bag full of bits of scruffy fabric. It was my training clothes which they had cut off Lou in their haste to operate. I smiled to myself, thinking how pleased she would be that I had managed to remove her costume, and looked forward to ribbing her about the fate of my favourite training clothes.

Daddy sits in his favourite old flowery armchair in the sitting room. He has caught a piece of glass in his eye and is off work. We have a row. It is only the second one we've ever had; he normally takes my side on everything. So hurt and angry, I stand outside the sitting room door and think the terrible thought: 'I wish you were dead.' A week later, he dies.

I sit alone next to Lou in intensive care. The longest night of my life. She is unconscious and I struggle to keep talking. Hour after hour, no response. I feel that my efforts are pathetic and if she dies it will be all my fault for not being able to bring her back from the brink. It was my fault when Daddy died and it will be my fault if Lou dies.

It was a huge relief when I looked up and saw Dusty, who had been collected from the airport by Claire and Helen in the van. I could finally hand over the responsibility of keeping Lou alive.

> **Dusty, Lou's partner**: I'd gone out for the evening. Henri was a toddler and I'd arranged for my friend Luke to babysit. I got a phone call from Luke, saying that something had happened and you needed to speak to me. Luke said it sounded serious, because you were obviously in shock. Then you rang and assured me it was all OK and Lou was in hospital. I relaxed a bit, but when you made the next phone call you couldn't speak properly and I ended up talking to your agent Steph. Its serious, he said, you'd better get over here. There was a mounting sense of crisis: Lou was in mortal danger. I started working out how to get to Amsterdam. The earliest flight I could get was one out of New York, calling at Manchester and Amsterdam on its way to the Middle East. We set off at 2am and I landed very early in Schiphol. Claire and Helen met me in the van and told me that we were fortunate that there was a top neurosurgeon there, who had identified the problem very quickly and drilled a hole in the side of her head to relieve the pressure. It all seemed OK. When I went into the ward, you were there and Lou was looking a bit battered. I remember saying 'Squeeze my finger if you can hear me and know who I am.' It was a relief when the little squeeze came back.

When Lou could speak, she kept saying 'What's the fuss about?' We had to explain to her what had happened, over and over again. She couldn't come to terms with the reality. I ended up staying in Amsterdam for several weeks. I really didn't know whether any permanent damage had been done, or how it would change Lou. At least she seemed to be making a physical recovery. She was regaining strength slowly, but she looked quite shocking because they shaved her hair off. She was moved onto the wards and slowly we managed to persuade her to sit in a wheelchair so I could take her out.

When at last they were ready to release Lou, we considered how to get her back to England. I thought we'd do it as quickly as possible, by plane, but they said no, because of the cabin pressure. The channel tunnel didn't exist then, so we had to cross either by hovercraft or by ferry. On the morning that we were going to leave, Lou wanted to look like it was an ordinary day. She didn't want to wear bandages, and I was thinking 'No, actually I want you to look as much like a patient as possible.' I wanted to be able to say 'Look, this person has just had a head injury, please make allowances for her.' I entered into a little conspiracy with the nurses and they gave her some tranquillisers. I remember thinking 'How am I going to get her across London on the Underground?' We arrived just at the wrong time: it was 5pm and we had to negotiate the rush hour. I said to Lou, 'Take your hat off, show your bandages.' People actually steered away and gave us some breathing space.

When we got back to Bradford, we had a tearful and emotional meeting with Henri, and with Lou's parents. It was obvious to Henri that Lou wasn't well: she was absolutely exhausted and was soon lying on the sofa. There she began the process of recovery, which seemed to take forever.

I don't know if Lou has ever been the same again. Something of her was changed. It's very difficult to assign temperamental changes to the accident – who knows what somebody would have become over a period of years? I suppose a part of me does wonder if she'll ever wake up one morning and say 'My god, I feel normal again.' There's no point in waiting. What a year that was.

CHAPTER 3

Camping

Circus – a performance by clowns, trapeze acts, acrobats, tightrope walkers and jugglers, often including trained animals. The first 'modern' circus in England was opened in 1768 by Phillip Astley, an equestrian who performed his tricks riding in a circle rather than a straight line as others did, establishing the format which was later named a 'circus'.

I had what I now realise was an old-fashioned childhood. I was a child who was overwhelmed by the need to create all the time. Mum says that at the end of term other children would come out of school with a few paintings and cardboard box things, and I would return time after time for extra artefacts and paintings. She had to smuggle them out to the dustbin at regular intervals.

My other urgent impulse was to climb things and be upside down as much as possible. Mum complains that she could not walk to the corner shop without me doing 'tipperly tumbles' on every road sign. This may not sound unusual for a small child but I never grew out of it. As time passed, the road signs turned into climbing frames, to trees, to trapeze rigs, and the gymnastics to ice skating, athletics, and finally to the trapeze. The cardboard box artefacts turned into costumes, set designs, sculptures, bizarre alternative fashion, sets, props, and eventually costumes for Skinning the Cat.

My family was theatrical. Mum used to act in plays and I began my life going to rehearsals in my carrycot. Later, I remember rehearsals where my siblings and I sat silently while Mum played traumatic roles: being force-fed as Sylvia Pankhurst; hand-wringing as the Mother in *Six Characters in Search of an Author*. I hated watching her play these characters and was bored by the lack of emphasis on set and costumes, which were generally black and dull. I grew up loving theatre but hating those drab costumes and traumatized characters.

I was pretty young when I started having fantasies about the circus. I read Noel Streatfeild's *A Circus is Coming* over and over again and, from then on, nurtured secret circus dreams. My sister Nadya and I started saving up for a trampoline to start a circus act. It would have taken a long time on our pocket money, but my plans were not held back by reality.

Prior to circus dreams, when I was six, reality did hit me when I discovered that my chosen career of queen was not going to be possible, due to an accident of birth. I then announced to my parents that I would be a farmer instead. Following this, they arranged for me to go and stay on a farm for a week, on my own, to see how I liked it. Although I do remember being homesick, my memories are dominated by riding on the top of a hay lorry, making dens in hay barns and playing with wild kittens. I retained a love of farms but not of farming. Circuses often use farms for winter quarters, rehearsal or storage, so in my later life I spent much time in farmyards and always felt comfortable there.

I was second in line to my brother Crispin, with whom I have a love-hate relationship. We admire and adore each other, but competition is fierce and we constantly undermine each other's achievements. Mum referred to us as a creative team and, looking back, she was right. He would direct and I would act and make the costumes. But we rowed constantly, always vying for power and control. My path through childhood followed in his footsteps, copying his games, his friendships, his set of very strict values, interests and prejudices – and rebelling against them.

Part of the development of my 'drive' as I grew up was to try to impress my brother. After Daddy died I couldn't get through to him, he was so angry. He was very closed off and we couldn't communicate. Our competitiveness often ended in terrible rows where I would cry and he would shout.

As a family we were completely uncommercial. We knew nothing of pop music and my first memory of a television was as an adult-only thing: Daddy in the lounge watching *Top of the Pops* with the door shut. He was, apparently, watching it in order to see Pan's People dance. It was whispered about as if he were in there watching hard-core porn!

We each owned one LP. Crispin's was *The World of Steam*; mine, the soundtrack from the *Oliver Twist* musical, and my younger sister Nadya had Prokofiev's *Peter and the Wolf.* On Sunday afternoons, it would be the turn of one of us to play our LP. We had set games to accompany them. For Crispin's record we lined up chairs facing the settee, with Mum's antique gas lamp on a table at one end. This was meant to create the compartment of a steam train carriage. We wobbled up and down the imaginary corridor between the settee and chairs, almost falling over each time the soundtrack implied that we might. Yes, *The World of Steam* was literally a whole album of recordings of steam engines and we loved it.

The house we lived in was a high house, with a steep roof and big chimney stacks. I had the attic room and loved being up there. My dad had set me up a fire escape system which involved going through a small opening into the rest of the loft, running along a wooden catwalk then jumping onto and through the ceiling at the end of it. Dad had calculated that I would land on my brother's bed below. The loft had several small passages leading off it. When the gutter got blocked I was the right size to be sent along the passage to clear it. I was always proud to be the brave one helping Daddy, but I hated it when the blockages were caused by dead birds which I had to scrape out. I still have a horror of dead birds.

My favourite thing about my attic bedroom was that I could climb out of the window onto the roof and sit behind the chimney stacks. I would generally do this after I had been put to bed on summer evenings. I also used to climb out there to do a pee in the middle of the night. It saved going downstairs. Once, at dusk, I was sitting out there enjoying the evening air when Mum, who was in the garden watering some plants, happened to look up... Poor Mum.

We were not well off. If I needed or wanted something I had to find a way to earn it for myself. Mum was very proud and would never take help, but I strongly remember when I was at primary school and all the other children had progressed to doing PE in shorts and a T-shirt, I was still in my knickers and vest, which was normal then for younger children. I became desperate with embarrassment and concocted a plan to tell my grandparents about this when they came to stay, knowing for sure that they would whisk me off to the school uniform shop and buy the correct outfit. I knew that Mum would be furious, but it would be too late and it would be worth it. The plan worked like a dream, she *was* furious and yes, it *was* worth it.

Mum made clothes for us, lovingly-sewn party dresses and nighties. It was so exciting to choose the patterns and the material; the styles were a cross between Edwardian pinafores and Aladdin pants. It was only through experiences on school trips where everyone wore trendy clothes that I became embarrassed by my homemade ones and my brother's hand-me-downs. At the age of eight, I broke the house rules by secretly using my mum's sewing machine when she was out. I started to make my own clothes. She might have been furious but she was so amazed when she discovered the standard of my dressmaking that she was rendered speechless. The two best birthdays of my life were at age nine, when I was officially allowed to use Mum's sewing machine, and age twenty-one, when she bought me my own.

Mum kept off-cuts of fabric from her dressmaking in a large carved oak chest. All the bits were rolled up and tied in little neat bundles, which she says was how her grandma kept them. I was forever rooting around in this chest and begging Mum for this or that scrap of fabric. Mum tells me about my great-grandmother, who was a dressmaker and supported her family during the Depression by her sewing. When Mum visited her as a child, clothes would be hanging on the picture rail around her sitting-room. I like it that I also hang my costumes up on my picture rail, as sections are completed. Our sitting-room often looks like a music hall dressing room. I wonder what my great-grandmother would think of my costumes – all colour, sequins and feathers, very different from hers.

My dad died suddenly when I was nine and my youngest sister, Annaliese, was only nine months old. I was Daddy's best girl. We did the gardening together, him digging potatoes wearing his old red jumper and brown gardening trousers. He helped me with my art work, pom-pomming along to the radio. Best of all, in the school holidays I went with him to work to 'help'. I felt so important. He was quite a strict, traditional parent and extremely sociable, always the life and soul of their parties. Childhood memories are divided into before and after Daddy's death.

When Daddy died, I wanted to die with him, I would have liked to crawl into the earth and not come out. I felt isolated and desperate. Being alive felt like a huge effort. I tried many ways to get the attention that I imagined would alleviate this pain: truancy, petty theft, hysterics, bullying my sister... Nothing worked. Never feeling any better, I lapsed into depressed denial.

The summer after he died, we were given free use of holiday homes by kind friends. We went on a lot of holidays that year. All the places were a bit rough and run down, including one we called 'The Grotty Grotto', with peeling paintwork and terrifyingly large spiders. I can't begin to imagine how hard this time must have been for Mum, with a young baby and the rest of us moody and argumentative. I remember traipsing miserably round seaside towns, picking on Nadya, of whom I was jealous because she seemed to be attracting all the adult sympathy. Interestingly, when I ask Mum about how we were then, she says how wonderful we all were, looking after each other and helping with Annaliese. This was true, but we also took our grief out on each other. Maybe we hid this from Mum.

We went camping a lot in the following years. We all loved it. In my imagination, the camp site was a circus site and our tent the Big Top. Some of my happiest childhood memories are the camping holidays. We found a camp site in Dartmoor that we adored. We talk about it still. It was just a sloping field with a few basic toilets and a tap. There was a river running through it, where we spent a lot of our time obsessively building dams. The dams created a special pool, in which there was a large, whale-shaped rock with a baby-whale-shaped rock next to it. We loved those whales.

Nadya, sister – Our family camping holidays were an important part of our childhood. Every year we went to Dartmoor, a wild, magical place that really captured our

23

imaginations. We always went back to the same campsite because we just loved it there. It was very basic, but it had everything we wanted – a stream to mess around in, rocks to climb on, and the surrounding moors and valleys to explore. Everything was exciting: damming the stream, going to fetch milk from the farm, walking through the woods, climbing on moss-covered ruins. At night we went to sleep to the sound of the rushing stream. Most years it rained, but that didn't stop us enjoying it. We loved climbing the tors, the wind gusting around us and rain leaking through our cagoules, or sitting outside the local pub sharing a bag of crisps while Mum had a drink.

It is only now that we realise what hard work it must have been for Mum to do this holiday every year – packing a roof rack with camping gear for five people, putting up the tent in the rain and producing cooked breakfasts every morning. The car broke down more than once, and we had to push-start it down the muddy track.

There never seemed to be enough food, so I soon took over the role of sandwich-maker from Mum, as she was incapable of judging our appetites. We were all skinny children who were always hungry. One of our collective memories of Christmas day is rowing over the potatoes!

Spending time in this inspirational place gave my already overactive imagination space to blossom. Whether it was playing around the site or exploring the woods I invented my own special world:

On the bank above the river I run up and down,
clambering around tree roots and slipping down the
bluebell bank.
I am an escaping princess and,
depending on which colour dress I am wearing, I choose
my horse to match.
A dappled silver, a black-as-night stallion and a soft
coloured bay.
I choose my dress design and my horse carefully before the
start of each adventure.
Wow, but I have some pretty good dresses.

I am on an amazing adventure,
running away from an unseen danger.
I am important and precious and must not be captured.

Gradually, over the years, I found that when I was busy and creative I did not feel the sadness. Activity filled the Daddy void. This took the form of increasingly challenging projects and adrenalin sports. In the air, I was completely free and happy. I felt like a bird, without restraints, invincible, and so alive.

CHAPTER 4

Doubles Trapeze

> **Doubles trapeze** – an act where two people work together on the trapeze. This traditionally involves a catcher and a flyer. The routine often opens with the duo working above the bar performing intertwined positions and counterbalances then develops into fast-moving action, whereby the catcher swings below the bar and throws the flyer through a series of catches and shapes.

The winter season immediately following Lou's accident, my trapeze partner Rachel and I were booked to play our doubles trapeze act at the Rheinhalle in Cologne for five weeks.

I had arrived home for rehearsals later than I should have, after staying in Amsterdam long enough to see Lou stabilise. The extra time in Amsterdam had not been fun. I remember wandering around between hospital visits, feeling empty. I had to tell Lou over and over again what had happened. She just could not accept it. The first thing she said when she came round was 'Will I be ok to do the show at Halloween?' She couldn't remember what had happened last week but she knew what our next booking was. She was groggy and delicate, but alive.

My homecoming was busy and emotional. Friends, family and other Skinning the Cat members wanted to know what had happened. I remember going to our regular pub and friends telling me how lucky Lou was. But, instead of feeling happy, I felt such anger, completely freaked out. Right then, it did not feel as if either of us had survived.

We drove to Cologne that autumn, stopping off overnight with friends in Brussels for food, a bath and a good night's sleep. We were lucky to have so many friends, relatives and circus contacts dotted around Europe who would generously open their homes to us grubby women, arriving late and cluttering up their street with trucks and caravans.

The Rheinhalle is a huge venue on the bank of the Rhine. As we drove into the city, we saw that the streets were plastered with posters for the show, and the central image was me! Variety shows are much more popular in Germany than over here and there are many famous venues around the country. They can be pretty glitzy affairs. This show was no exception; the line-up was both prestigious and traditional;

The Trio Gaspar were Portuguese and we hung out a lot with their son, who was incredibly talented. They performed on the Rola Bola which involves balancing unstable cylinders on top of each other on top of high platforms. The pile got higher throughout the act, and for the highlight they would perform tricks on the top. The instability of this act horrified me: give me a nice stable trapeze any day! There was another British performer, Donimo, a white-faced clown, very cute, who had a crush on Rachel. I was told by my juggling friends back home that Bob Bramson, the German juggler, was very famous within the industry for doing clever things with hoops: he could make them dance around the stage and return to him like boomerangs. The whole show was linked together by a glamorous dance troupe, The White Diamonds. The girls strode around in stilettos and fishnet tights with plumed headdresses, the boys in white suits; you could tell that they were from East Germany by their footballers' haircuts.

The act which gave Rachel and me the most entertainment was a pair of very dramatic German illusionists. They both had beautifully-groomed long hair and pranced around the stage tossing their heads and pointing their wands, accompanied by dramatic music. Illusionists are obsessed with the secrecy of their tricks. They don't even like other performers to be backstage while they are setting up. This was a particular problem for us as, in the finale, Rachel and I were hidden in one of their magic boxes for our entrance.

There would be a tremendous artistic hubbub if the illusionists spotted anyone lurking around their props. This came to a head when a visiting friend of mine set up a camera to video our aerial performance: the pair went into a complete meltdown, thinking that it was all part of a plan to film and steal their act. I don't think they ever quite forgave me for being the main image on the poster. They got back at me by being patronising and giving me unasked for advice on how to make more of my career. They believed themselves to be superior as they were variety show artists, in their opinion way above us circus artists.

Apart from our theatre, we never discovered much life in Cologne. Rachel and I had expected a good social life but the town seemed quite conservative and the other artists mainly kept to themselves. Towards the end of the run it was my birthday; discovering this, the whole cast came out for a party and I was showered with gifts and attention. They turned out to be very friendly so we decided that next time we were on a show we would invent birthdays much earlier in the run.

Rachel and I tried to decorate our small apartment for Christmas. We discovered that the Germans don't do tacky, glittery Christmas decorations, and not one piece of tinsel could be found. There were tasteful snowflakes made out of straw, and beautifully-painted wooden nativity scenes. We were a bit frustrated by this: we craved cheap tat.

We had Christmas Eve off, as that is the German day of celebration. I took a train down to Bavaria to spend the day with my German sister-in-law, Maria, and her family. It was a beautiful twenty-four hours. Maria's family welcomed me warmly and I joined in the traditional routine of a Bavarian village. This was set in stone: carols and gluhwein at the fire station, a visit to the cemetery to take flowers to the dead relatives. and a huge extended family meal.

It was great to find myself accepted as a family member of a different culture. Maria took me to the tiny village station late at night to get my train back to Cologne. It was snowing and we sang 'White Christmas' together, giggling drunkenly. I returned on the overnight train to be back in time for the show on Christmas day. I had booked a sleeper but couldn't sleep. We stopped at every tiny village en route and I peered out each time to see the sleeping villages in the darkness.

There was no food to be had on Christmas day, so I did the shows shattered and hungry. It had been great to get away from the show for a bit, for twenty-four hours of laughing and singing.

During this time, I now realise, I was in shock following Lou's accident, and performing on the trapeze every night was not the right environment for me. Unusually, I suffered from strong feelings of homesickness, for my family and friends. There were days when I found that I just couldn't stop crying. The other and more serious symptom was severe insomnia, night after night, until climbing the rope and swinging upside down made me feel dizzy and nauseous. I had always been the older sister in my relationship with Rachel and she watched in wide eyed silence as I gradually fell apart. The person I really wanted to spend time with was Lou, who was back in England now, starting the long road of recovery.

Lou, Skinning the Cat member: It felt like the accident didn't belong to me. It was other people's accident as I had lost awareness of what was going on. I felt angry with people, I don't quite know why, maybe because I wasn't independent any more. The recovery was very difficult: sitting on that sofa, any sound really bothered me and if there was too much conversation going on I couldn't understand what people were talking about. I lost social skills. I had to have a clock next to me because I couldn't tell you if 5 hours or 5 minutes had passed; even if it was light outside, I couldn't tell you if it was night or day. I got very tired very quickly and just couldn't make sense of things. I couldn't read, couldn't physically interpret the words. I still find it difficult interpreting the words.

Dusty says that I didn't ask about Henri at all when he saw me at the hospital, I was just concerned with getting myself better. I didn't once ask, I wasn't concerned, and that hurts. Obviously he was important to me, but maybe that shows the severity of the accident. People said 'In the hospital 5 minutes later and you'd be dead.' Apparently I had the best brain surgeon in Europe, you can tell by the fact that the scar is so small. The scans are pretty impressive: the brain was pushed right over to one side.

The initial recovery was about 2 years but I'm not the same person now, it had an effect on my personality. Dusty will tell you more about that. People say 'how fantastic that you're alive, you came so close to death,' and you feel guilty for not feeling happy. Actually, I felt the opposite. I had 4 days of total amnesia and when I tried to recover that part of myself the doctors couldn't help. When I get headaches I get them on that side, so I've got a constant reminder. I still ask you and Dusty over and over again for the details of what happened, because it doesn't stay in my head. It should have been obvious I wouldn't be in Skinning the Cat any more, but it wasn't obvious to me.

My doctor at home, who was a friend and also Lou's doctor, had given me the advice to invite friends over to visit in Cologne, so that I had some support. I understand now what she meant but I took it too literally and we had a constant flow of visitors sleeping on our floor. It really just added to the stress that I was already under but, as I was not admitting that I had a problem, I treated them as guests to be entertained. I think back to that time now with horror as I struggled to function in an increasing state of anxiety and exhaustion. Lying awake every night after the show thinking: 'I must sleep or I won't be able to do the show tomorrow,' adrenalin racing through my system. We had two shows a day except Sundays.

I climbed that rope into the blackness and forced myself through the routine by sheer willpower. It never crossed my mind to tell the director of the show what had happened and that I just could not carry on.

I have a dread of making bad phone calls, the call to Dusty – Lou is okay – Lou is not okay. I suffer from guilt that I did not stay longer with Lou after the accident. I cannot shake the feeling that something awful is going to happen, I feel that I have done something so bad that there is no going back, I can see no future.

I am in fear of disappointing,
letting down or offending people.
I see myself only through the eyes of those who I assume to
judge me.
I see myself as weak and imagine that they see that too.
I imagine other people's wishes and expectations of me and
hand them the power over my life.

Jumble of bodies, ropes, trapeze bars,
all the focus is on the part which is gripping; hands, knees,
ankles –
this used to be my safe space,
the ground below is danger.

When we were teenagers we went several times on a houseboat holiday to Salcombe. The houseboats were a string of slightly dilapidated old tubs moored in the estuary. We had some fantastic times there. I remember it as always hot and sunny.

On the first day that we ever went we were hanging around the boat yard waiting to be rowed out to our mooring. There was a boy working at the yard, Michael, although he was given the name of Hobbit by our family on account of his extremely wide feet; he always went bare foot with rolled-up trouser legs. He took a fancy to me instantly, I was fourteen and this was the first real time that I returned this feeling. He took me sailing and rowing and we kissed in the boatyard behind the upturned boats. It was a sloppy affair. I hadn't realised that people opened their mouths and did stuff with tongues when they kissed. Michael seemed to have a very large mouth and had clearly tried this before. I didn't really like it, it was a bit out of my depth, but I liked him and we hung out together a lot.

We all had some great adventures on and around that estuary. We were useless at sailing and generally just got in a tangle and drifted into the path of more competent boats or got stuck on the mud and fell in trying to push off with an oar. We were desperate to be like Arthur Ransome's 'Swallows and Amazons', having adventures and being independent. Mum was always there frying eggs in the cramped galley and sunbathing on the roof of the houseboat in her embarrassing bikini.

Nadya and I had a terrifying experience one night. We were in our little cabin and were woken up by an extremely fast tide rushing past the windows. In the darkness we couldn't see the shore or any other boats, just black, frothy water rushing past us. We were sure that the high tide had pulled out the anchor and that we were rushing out to sea.

We continued to go to Salcombe as we grew up as it was a fantastic summer partying place, we would hitch hike down with friends and camp. The Hobbit would always be there, sailing all day and working in bars at night, and still happy to put his current girlfriends on the back burner to accommodate me.

In Cologne I start a recurrent nightmare based on the feeling of the houseboat in Salcombe, on that dark night when we thought we were heading out to sea: Lou is a tiny and fragile rag doll, who I hold protectively against my shoulder as the black water rushes round and around in a whirlpool and the boat with us both inside it is being sucked down.

I feel like I have lost one of my nine lives, I come to associate Cologne with death. Death is a place that I can drive away from. My love affair with the trapeze starts to go wrong after Lou's fall. There is no way I am stopping so I keep holding on, quite literally:

I feel it in the night,
the feeling of not letting go.
holding on for dear life I force myself back up,
'the show must go on',
My argument with the trapeze goes on.
I get back on the trapeze to feel alive, but I am running
out of lives.

In my dreams, I am driving away from Cologne, such dark memories of its double spired black cathedral. But I often get stuck back in the Cologne place and I am always looking for a way out.

The day we drove away from Cologne there was thick snow. I was overwhelmed by relief that I didn't have to survive the trapeze again each night. We stopped over in Brussels again and I slept a beautiful heavy sleep for the first time in weeks.

I quickly shelved this bad experience and threw myself into my work. I got busy in the Skinning the Cat office, sorting out the normal backlog of company admin and organising the coming summer tour. I spent a lot of time with Lou; she was having a difficult time recovering and was obsessed with returning to the show. I found this very difficult to deal with: I had been told by medical professionals that Lou must not work at height again as her head was very delicate. Lou was unable to accept this and the only conversation which made her happy was one which involved planning her return to the show.

This is the situation that resulted in my arranging for us both to go to Switzerland to learn the 'Perch' with Circus Krane. Lou was still very fragile and I was making bad decisions out of guilt and desperation.

CHAPTER 5

The Perch

The perch – An aerial act where one person (the base) balances an 8-metre steel pole on either their forehead or shoulder, and another person (the aerialist) climbs to the top and performs tricks. It comes with double the risk, as the aerialist could either fall off or overbalance.

At the top of the pole there is a strap for the aerialist's foot.

While learning this technique, a safety line (lunge) is attached to the aerialist and controlled by someone on the ground (the lunger).

Before working with an actual aerialist, the base must first learn to balance the perch by using sandbags tied to the top of the pole. The Perch should be practised indoors only, as the base needs to be able to focus on a point directly above, to ensure that the steel pole stays balanced.

The aerialist climbs the pole by stepping onto the back of the base's bent knee, the top of their buttock and then their shoulder, then up onto the pole. Extra care is needed for the transfer from the shoulder to the pole as this is the point in the routine where it is easiest to overbalance.

The lunger counter-weights the aerialist and ensures they do not hit the floor if they overbalance. The lunger must at all times keep the lunge almost, but not quite, taut and remain attentive to the aerialist's every changing movement. Too tight and the lunge will interfere with the aerialist's balance, too slack and it will get in the way. A pair of fingerless leather gloves will protect the lunger's hands from rope burns.

The plan was, as Lou could no longer be aerial, we would learn a piece of equipment where she could stay on the ground: she would base the perch. We were practising in an old industrial unit converted into a rehearsal space, with living quarters on a mezzanine level. This was the winter quarters of Circus Krane in Baden Baden, Switzerland.

Peter and Eva Parreiro of Circus Krane were the perfect partnership for a circus act. Eva was tiny and Peter a giant. Apart from doing the Perch with Peter, Eva's speciality was to circle the ring suspended by her hair, which was incredibly long. Peter knew the technique of weaving a special piece into her hair which attached to a swivel and a hook. The exact technique of this weaving is crucial and a closely-guarded secret, handed down through families. They were a kind and gentle team who shared their home with us and we bonded through wonderful circus discussions at every meal. No money changed hands for this training.

They took us to the most amazing steam baths. It was a natural hot spring where an indoor area had been built so that you could swim in the streams between the covered pool and the outside. We were surrounded by snow-covered mountains but our bodies and sore muscles were deliciously warm and relaxed in the hot water. I love spas and, this is the only natural one I have ever been in. It was wonderful to swim in the thick steam through the landscape.

Morning training: February, off-season and freezing. Peter, an incredibly strong man and a good tutor, was teaching us. Lou started by learning to balance with sandbags. Meanwhile, I was learning the aerial part with Peter as the base. We had been practising together for four days and the muscle aches were building up.

Lou controlled the lunge for me as I attempted, over and over again, to get to the top of the pole without overbalancing it. This is the way of our training: repeatedly attempting to do something that doesn't work, and then suddenly, when the muscles finally understand, it all comes together. What a fantastic feeling that is.

Balancing the body is an incredibly subtle thing: it can be achieved by the twitch of a fingertip or the tightening of a tiny muscle. Aerialists, even when swinging, can learn to balance on many different parts of their bodies: back, heel, shoulder, buttock. I was struggling with the critical point as I transferred from Peter's shoulders to the pole. Occasionally, I made it and shimmied up the pole feeling elated. But in the main I overbalanced and had to start again. My ankles and knees were beginning to ache from the impact of the wooden staging.

We were all getting tired, ready for lunch. But I wanted to make it up the pole just one more time before we took a break: this thing was not going to beat me. I was getting too tired to concentrate fully and, stupidly, I forgot that balancing is not a job where energy and brute force will win through. Peter again braced his right leg backward, and my bare foot pushed up off the back of his knee, onto his left buttock, and onto his right shoulder in one smooth movement. Bracing my right foot against the pole, grasping it high up with both hands, with my left foot I then shoved off from Peter's shoulder to start the pole climb. There was a split second when I thought: I'm going to make it up the pole. Then I was off again and falling; this time the lunge did not stop me. My right foot first hit the edge of the wooden staging and snapped sideways. Searing pain. I felt faint and sick. I looked down at my ankle, already the size of a watermelon. I looked up at Lou: she was holding the slack lunge rope, looking puzzled.

What followed immediately is a complete hole in my memory. But I do remember needing my mum. I rang her up for support and she shouted at me *'What are you even doing there?'* She knew that I was trying to sort out a role for Lou and not putting my own needs first. She was right of course, and I knew that she only shouted out of love and concern, but it was hard.

Eva and Peter suggested that I just return to England and get treatment there. They dosed me up with painkillers and I spent a feverish night with my foot sticking out sideways from my leg, in extreme pain. We just coped with the moment as usual, and the far-reaching repercussions of this accident, following so soon after Lou's brain haemorrhage, were not yet obvious.

I sit with Lou on a bench in the sun outside Circus Krane in Switzerland,
my smashed ankle stretched out before me.
I have a strange feeling of contentment.

Now we are both broken.

CHAPTER 6

School

> **Static trapeze/fixed trapeze** – the trapeze bar does not swing but the performers execute a range of moves that include balances, drops and hangs. One, two or sometimes even more performers turn and spin, creating shapes around both the bar and the ropes of the trapeze.

Every day when I come in from school I go to the dressing up box
and put on my princess skirt.
It is long with a slippery underskirt and a top layer of blue and silver lace.
Now I feel right.
Like some sort of woodland royalty.

I tell my friends at school about the secret tunnel between our garden and a magical world, they half believe me and I am convinced.
I weave stories about magic portals that appear randomly...
they are out of my control and clearly I can do nothing about it if they are not accessible when my friends come to play.

At school, I was only ever any good at art and sport. My brother told me that these were not proper subjects and that

I would have to do something else for a career. To Nadya and me, his word was fact. It was difficult following him through school, two years behind. He was such an academic genius and teachers were disappointed when I showed up. It didn't help at home, when Mum used to ask him to help me with my maths homework. This always ended in a row when I was called stupid.

I rebelled, ran wild, refusing to wear shoes and conquering every tree in the neighbourhood. I was of the generation of little girls inspired by the gymnast Olga Korbut: nobody had seen anything like her before. Practising gymnastics was the beginning of my physical discipline. My preferred place of practice was up on the Downs, near our house in Bristol, where I would take my sisters. They had to join in with whatever my latest craze was.

There was an Iron Age fort up by the Observatory, a flat piece of ground which provided a great natural performance space. We were able to play and practice there, imagining that we were in the Olympics. Nadya was the third and quietest child, and no wonder with Crispin and myself both bossing her around. She caught glandular fever when she was quite young and needed extra nurturing. She attracted a lot of adult attention with her blonde curls and sweet face. My grandma was always saying that she was 'the pretty one', which made us all want to vomit. From this, I drew the assumption that my brother was right when he told me that I was ugly. I played up to it, letting my brown hair grow long and tangly and scowling in photographs.

The Downs were a very important part of our childhood. There are trees to climb and woods to explore. Crispin, Nadya and I were Swallows and Amazons, tacking our sailing dinghies across the grass between rock outcrops. We searched for talking animals in the woods and built houses for Eeyore. We played on the natural slides down the cliff face, polished by generations of children's bottoms. Nadya and I had horses there: two parallel trees which grew sideways over the edge of a cliff. I still visit them and sit there when I am in Bristol. The woods were also frequented by men who stood in the bushes to show us their willies. I never thought much of this, and was surprised when I mentioned it to Mum and she called the police.

My most daring adventure was to duck under the fence which edged the Avon Gorge cliff and climb down towards the river below. It's blocked off now with a DANGER sign. I saw a TV programme recently about plants that grow there: the presenters were all rigged up in rock climbing gear! Goats live there now, too. Later, the Downs became somewhere to walk with boyfriends and abseil down the cliff face to the Avon Gorge.

They have built a playground now where we used to tack in our sailing dinghies. Why do they need a playground in such a natural children's paradise?

We had moved to Bristol following the death of my dad. I was very unhappy and lonely at this time, having lost my close relationship with my dad and moved to a new town. For all that year I stood alone at playtime, and was an object of interest to be questioned, ignored or teased.

I was noticed by the head boy, who was in the top class. He singled me out for obsessive admiration. This terrified me. He followed me round at school and called at my house every day. Not only did I not understand the vibes I was getting from him, but it was my bad luck that the head girl thought that he belonged to her. She was something of a bully, with a team of followers, so then I became a target for her anger. I tried pretending to be ill to get off school, but Mum wasn't stupid.

I was saved right at the end of the last year by Jessie, whom I idolised. She seemed so grown-up and had plenty of real friends, but still wanted to be my friend. I can still remember the glowing feeling when she first referred to herself as my friend.

I had come from a school where the standard of gymnastics was very high and found that at my new primary school I was now the best gymnast. Mr May, my gym teacher, was extremely supportive of me and of another child, Peter Gazeley, the naughtiest boy in the school. Peter was a real rebel. They couldn't control him in class but he loved gymnastics. He later found his way, like me, into the circus. His acrobatic act reflected my memories of his childhood personality, very close to the edge. He performs wearing only a sequin G-string and the finale is a lit firework protruding from his backside. He has a reputation on the circuit for being a brilliant act but very temperamental to work with. No change there then.

I was talent-spotted from Mr May's gym club and invited to a special club run by a rather frightening lady. It was said that Miss Palmer had coached Olympic gymnasts. I don't know if it was true: I wouldn't have dared to ask her. This new club involved getting two buses on my own on a Sunday morning to a school outside town.

My next craze was ice-skating. Sunday mornings became ice skating mornings. My sisters and I got up very early and walked into town for a group lesson called the Young Blades. The problem with ice skating was that, beyond the Young Blades, it got very expensive: you needed decent skates, private lessons and regular attendance. I saved up my paper-round money and eventually bought a pair of second-hand skates. I was so proud that they were white leather, not the ugly blue plastic of the hired skates.

There was quite a hierarchy at the skating rink and the mums of the more cosseted children would sit around producing flasks and warm clothes for their children after they finished their private figure-skating lessons. I don't think our mum ever came, she was too busy; anyway, she believed that we should be independent.

In between visits to the real skating rink, I invented games for Nadya and myself, based on Noel Streatfeild's skating book *White Boots*. The iron-age hill fort on the Downs changed from being an Olympic arena to being the edge of the rink from which we pushed off in our imaginary skates.

We would arrive back from the rink starving and, as there was never any food available, we got into the habit of nicking a tiny bit of Mum's private bottle of cider. She says now that she always wondered how she seemed to be drinking it so quickly!

In Bristol we lived in Clifton, which was then a slightly run-down bohemian area. It was up on a hill and had an amazing view of the city. Mum, left with the four of us and not much money after daddy died, bought a big, old, falling-down house very cheaply at auction and did it up herself. She became very tough and independent. Most people thought she was mad.

The kitchen had a massive dresser the full length of one wall; an old stone fireplace with an old-fashioned bread oven took up another wall, and all the rooms in the house had high windows with wooden shutters. Every bit of woodwork throughout the huge house had seven layers of old paint on them. We know this because Mum counted them as she stripped them with a scraper and a blow-torch. For years, the smell of burning paint was normal in that house as Mum stripped every door.

The house had ten bedrooms, so a whole floor could be let out to students and, later, actors. I remember hiding when they came up and down the stairs with their friends, worried that I would be seen on the landing in my towel or sitting on the loo with the door open. Once, when I was asleep in bed, a drunken student mistook which floor he was on and came blundering into my bedroom. He tripped and fell onto my painstakingly-made model farm. I was furious.

The best times were when the students disappeared for the summer holidays and Mum would let us stay up there with a friend, cooking for ourselves and playing at having our own place.

We loved that big, rambling house. The walls bulged and there wasn't one straight line in it. Rooms had been added over the years; part of the kitchen was an old cow shed. In the Victorian extension at the back, tiny stairs led up to what we called the maid's bedroom. This was an especially cold room and Nadya who slept there had terrible chilblains. Lying in bed in the morning, trying to work up the courage to get out of bed in cold weather, with ice on the inside of the windows, I could see my breath. I used to drag my clothes under the covers to get dressed.

When I was a teenager, I painted a rainbow on my bedroom door and murals all over the walls. I think I meant it to look like a rock star's bedroom. The front of the house was covered in Virginia creeper, which was so dense in the summer that you could hardly see my bedroom window. It felt so secret in there, like the top of a castle turret. I, of course, was the princess. Behind the house was a high-walled garden. The back wall was the side of a church, very high, with a huge rose window, making the space private, magic and special, like the secret garden in the children's book by Frances Hodgson Burnett. The layout of the house didn't make sense: I had to walk through Crispin's room, risking his irritation, to get to Nadya's room –

or I could go down the main stairs, through the kitchen and playroom and up the back stairs.

The kitchen was the best bit of the house, where we were a noisy, squabbling, starving, eating family. People were always coming and going. We were in a central part of Clifton and nobody phoned first, they just dropped in. My favourite pocket-money job was to clean the brass front doorstep. Actually, that was the only job I liked. It was the place everyone stepped over: Mum's friends, artists, musicians, neighbours; my brother's gang of hairy, smelly, beer-drinking bikers. When he played music on his stereo, the whole house would vibrate. After shouting at him repeatedly, Mum would pull out the electrical fuse.

When I moved up to big school, it was a three mile walk; my brother, and so I, chose the route over the Clifton Suspension bridge and through Ashton Court, down the hill to Bedminster. Sometimes, when the tide was out, we saw strangely-shaped bodies lying in the mud beneath the bridge and the fire service busily putting ladders across the mud to reach them. These suicides were eventually stopped by a high fence above the bridge barrier.

The walk was stunning, often freezing cold when the parklands were covered in frost. The roads nearer the school were through the old docklands. The path ran alongside the stinking river, which we named 'spit alley' because it was so disgusting.

I always had a feeling of dread as we approached the school, and I nurtured fantasies about turning around and walking in the opposite direction. This was a fantasy that I did fulfil a few times as I grew older and more rebellious. Comprehensive school was terrifying. It was enormous, and the few children from up the hill were very different and in the minority.

We didn't have Bristol accents and our middle-class parents had different priorities from those of the other children. We were called 'posh' and were constantly reminded that we were outsiders, so we had to be always on our guard to do and say the right thing in front of the rougher and tougher kids from Bedminster.

The worst fear was the toilets where the big girls were smoking and gossiping, hanging out in gangs. Sitting on the toilet was never a safe place to be. Jessie and I survived by clinging together. We had secret signs and secret words and secret games. We spent lessons passing each other coded notes about feelings, boys and plans.

My educational experience at comprehensive school was not good – except that I learned to survive. I spent years gazing out of the windows, waiting to escape. The classes were big, difficult for the teachers to control. If we ever asked a question or seemed interested in learning, we were 'posh swots'. The sciences and maths I had no understanding of at all, and I fell more and more behind. I lived in fear of being found out and had to copy Jessie in tests and homework. This meant that my ignorance went completely unnoticed.

Meanwhile, in art I was teacher's pet and always got A's. I didn't care what the other kids thought of me in art classes and took great pride in my work.

Mum and I did not get on as I became a teenager. She says that I was impossible to control and I found her annoying and unfair. She was sure that I would get pregnant and fall into bad ways. She was wrong about that: I had my own best interests at heart when it came to sex and drugs. The risks I took were more physical and social. I thought nothing of walking around late in the dark, going to strangers' houses, or jumping off cliffs.

In contrast to this, my brother and I became friends. Our age gap was mutually beneficial when it came to partying and meeting the opposite sex. I found that if I was out with Crispin, Mum stopped fussing about what time I would be home. This was amusing, as he was generally the one who drank too much and had to be carried home across town singing Queen songs. When he lost his first love and wouldn't get out of bed, I took him on camping holidays which I had planned with my friends. He tagged along unhappily, but Mum needed him out of the house as she was going on holiday with my younger sisters. I looked after him in his misery.

Having spent five years at comprehensive school, either avoiding persecution or day-dreaming out of the window, I failed my mock 'O' levels dramatically (apart from art, of course). It was then that I could no longer cover up my inability to understand anything the teachers said, and Mum found out. She was brilliant. She never said 'I told you so', which she could have done, as we'd had terrible battles over homework.

She was working at the University Drama Department where she put up notices on a board, offering a small fee for students to coach me in my subjects. This was what I needed: they went at my pace and answered my questions. I scraped through my exams. It is one of the best things she ever did for me: I needed those exams to fulfil my dream of going to Art College.

CHAPTER 7

Circus of the streets

Cupola – the crown in the roof of the big top. Constructed on the ground and attached to the king poles with the canvas of the tent laced around it, it is the central point and the strength of the tent. We hang our rigging off it, then it is winched up to the top of the king poles pulling up the tent and rigging with it.

Rachel and I, plus our doubles trapeze, joined the *Circus of the Streets* in Sheffield. The use of the word 'streets' was a reference to the streetwise style, not the venue. The venue was a large and beautiful red-and-white big top, illuminated magically by strings of lights at night.

Doubles trapeze was my favourite aerial discipline. I loved the hours of practice, working together, going over and over our moves, perfecting and trying out different possibilities, until we were too tired to climb the rope. A traditional routine involves the 'base' or 'catcher' hanging in 'catcher's position' which requires enormous strength in the knees. The lighter partner, the 'flyer' moves between the bar above the catcher and swings below the catcher in a wrist-to-wrist grip. To hold a partner wrist-to-wrist, it is crucial to wear wrist tapes covered with resin, otherwise the sweaty and slippery surface of the skin makes it impossible to maintain a grip. From this position, the flyer can be dropped and caught by different bits of the body (ankles, armpits, toes, back) or can twist, turn and swing in the catcher's grasp.

We drove to each new site on a Sunday and, the next morning, we would watch from the warmth of our caravan as the big top went up. When the cupola was set up at head height, we would emerge from our caravan to fix our rigging and then hang around and watch as the crew did most of the hard work to pull up the tent. This was the life!

We appeared with the rest of the cast in the opening of the show, performed our doubles trapeze in the second half and then took part in the finale. I found it necessary to eat my evening meal in two halves, so that I was never too full to be upside down. I was extremely happy at this time, having a regular routine and mixing domesticity in my beautiful chrome-covered caravan, Wanda, with our daily shows. We visited towns where friends lived, so there were endless rounds of visitors. They would watch the show and afterwards I would invite them in to have tea and admire Wanda's glittering interior splendour.

The circus proprietor, Tony Hopkins, was a strong personality. It is a tough life and he was running two shows at the same time, touring for about ten months of the year and, as often as not, doing a Christmas show as well. We grew to respect each other and established a long-term friendship.

At the back of the ring was a small hidden space where we did a last-minute warm up in the cold, and from which we could peep through a crack in the canvas to see what stage the show had reached and make sure to be there on cue. Our act was the 'Warrior Princesses'. We would arrive in the ring swinging flaming torches and doing some home-made martial arts moves. The music was an eerie chanting, with a strong beat. Wearing our raunchy leather and feather costumes, we executed our doubles trapeze routine. It began with me toe-climbing up to the trapeze and then rolling Rachel up the rope to join me. The first half of our routine was mainly balances and moves where we interlocked and entwined together. The second half was fast moving, swinging under the bar, incorporating drops and catches. Our finale was the neck-to-neck spin.

Hanging under the bar in 'catcher's', I place a short velvet-covered loop around my neck; it is joined to another loop by a swivel which I pass up to Rachel on the bar above me and she places this around her neck.

We draw the keepers down to fit snugly in front of our faces, placing the loop across the back of the neck and down past the cheeks, thus preventing strangulation.

I lift Rachel off the bar in both arms and carefully manoeuvre her so that she is hanging below me. Taking her hands, I push her strongly clockwise then let go. She takes her hands behind her back and crosses her ankles to become as small as possible. She spins at top speed.

We are alone together in our connection.

All around is blackness. My neck gyrates with the strain. When I cannot stand her weight any more, the signal to stop is a sharp clap from me and we re-join hands on the next rotation.

CHAPTER 8

The Unicorn Theatre

Swinging trapeze – where the aerialist swings back and forth gathering the momentum needed for tricks. Not to be confused with flying trapeze, since the performers – solo or doubles – do not leave the trapeze for another. The tricks are executed at the peak of the swing and as the performer jumps or drops they always return to the same bar.

When I was about six, our whole family travelled to Turkey in a Ford Cortina with stick-on flowers over the rust patches. My dad was working there and so we all went. We had travelled abroad before, camping in France and visiting friends in Sweden but this was long distance and we were on a shoestring. The back seats of the car were flattened and Mum made a big mattress to spread over the resulting space and there we kids slept, played and fought.

It took about a week. We ate whatever was available en route or cooked on our camping stove by the roadside. Eating scrambled eggs in a lay-by in Yugoslavia, egg ran down my fingers and froze, putting me off scrambled egg for years. In the cheap hotels there were signs saying 'no eating in rooms'. We could not afford to eat in restaurants, so we smuggled the camping stove into our hotel room and cooked baked beans secretly. I was terrified that we'd be caught and thrown out. After we had spent all our money and missed the last ferry, we watched as the cafe in the terminal closed and the leftover food was thrown out. Torture.

I am reminded of Turkey sometimes by smells: the odd whiff of floor wax or natural yoghurt. The town of Izmit was a riot for the senses: busy market stalls, men running pulling carts like taxis, brightly dressed women and the delicious sickly taste of Baklava. I was traumatised by the poverty: men with no legs and without crutches shuffling around, often with milky-coloured unseeing eyes, hands outstretched. There was a family just like ours, from the tiny girl up to the mother holding the baby in her arms, lined along the street, all begging. I wanted to take them all home and feed them.

There was a children's playground next to where we were staying and we stood in a row along its fence and watched the big black powerful steam trains taking people to work. The local school teacher taught classes in the playground: there was no actual school building.

These family trips were the beginning of a love of travelling that I share with my siblings. Travelling or working abroad has been a big part of all our adult life. The trips were probably adventure enough, but we children made another layer of secret adventure underneath the adults' knowledge.

We had special places, of which we took imaginative ownership. A family friend, Jane Straker, had a house called 'Pinecroft', just outside Bristol. She was a character who fed my imagination, a cosmopolitan and a linguist, coming and going in our lives from her worldwide travels: Mexico, South America, Chile. Jane was a strong character and an individual. Jane was not somebody's wife or somebody's mother but just herself, doing her own thing in her own way. In my imagination, she was a romantic and fascinating figure like Gum from Noel Streatfeild's *Ballet Shoes*. She wore large pearl earrings and an unusual pendant, a round puffer fish that looked like a foreign treasure. She dressed to suit, wearing a brightly patterned Indian poncho and a Mexican bowler hat. The house was decorated with foreign artefacts, South American masks, Mexican bark paintings and oriental fabrics.

Her sometimes home, Pinecroft was halfway up a very steep hill, standing at the top of a long flight of stone steps and surrounded by a beautiful garden. It was like a mini estate, with overgrown flowering shrubs, a small orchard and a field, surrounded by steep banks which were brilliant for rolling down. We could put up our little ridge tent and camp the night in the orchard. We always looked after things that we owned very carefully. Often we were given a group family Christmas present like a sledge or a tent, and these things were named and cared for like family members. We loved our tent, we named it 'Wren' and kept it brushed and cleaned out. When it rained, we spent more time outside adjusting guy lines for maximum perfection than inside sheltering.

Jane was away abroad a lot, so we could spend some happy holidays at Pinecroft as if it were our own. At the side of the house lived Mr Hedges, the gardener – that really was his name. We never spoke to him and treated him like the enemy, running away and hiding as soon as he appeared. His existence did not suit our fantasies of exploration and independence in our imaginary realm.

Stretching up the hillside behind the house was bracken-covered moorland. We burrowed into the highest bracken, flattening and shaping the stems to build houses. Then we set up our house, weaving bracken bowls and plates together. Mum tells me that Pinecroft has been sold now and that there are houses built all the way up the hill where the garden was. I never want to see that.

Sometimes, when Mum finished a job or a show, people would make drawings, models or paintings of her. She is always depicted dressed in red with patterned scarves and large dangly and decorative earrings, perhaps on her bike, taking wood for the fires at the women's peace camp at Greenham Common. Mum held the family together. She had to work but always made sure that she was there at the end of the school day with a pot of tea and a homemade cake. She batch-cooked cakes, but never had quite the time for details like taking them out of the oven before they burned or removing them from the freezer in time to eat them. Looking back, she was a seriously cool mum, but I didn't see it at the time.

At one time, she ran the Bristol Craft Centre, where artists and craftspeople worked. When I was fifteen, she got me a job there helping the leather man, Dick, who made belts and handbags. My job was bevelling edges, stamping patterns, dying and polishing. Even now, I still love the smell of leather and polish. It was really satisfying work. The leather polished up like shiny conkers. When a big pile was assembled, the buckles and leather gleamed. Then Dick would head off to Saint Nicholas's market with huge armfuls of them.

I remember being poorly as not all bad: after we had got through the messy bit of vomiting or whatever, there was the cosy convalescent stage. Mum would take away the sick bowl and wheel in the 'poorly table' which enabled us to sit up in bed and have a pile of jigsaws and Lego. Mum would leave us with everything we needed and go off to work, but she would pedal home at lunch time up the steep Bristol hills to check on us, with a Beano comic.

I was always making. If we didn't have it, we made it. Nadya and I constructed a boat out of twigs, in the cellar. We didn't have anywhere to float it, but that did not stop us from making a boat. I was desperate for adventure, could not endure ordinary day-to-day life, so I imagined that we were going to sail our boat like the Swallows and Amazons. I dreamed and planned islands and camping trips. Jessie's dad took us for a picnic to a river one day. I borrowed my brother's compass and made a survival kit in an old tobacco tin: safety pin, sugar lump, Oxo cube, small bandage, plastic bag, small blade... I planned to take our homemade boat to float it there. I don't think he ever took us there again, but we were happy just dreaming about it in the cellar.

Although I would try my hand with any materials, fabric was the one that I was most at home with. My dolls and stuffed toys had an impressive range of clothes and bedding: dreaming up new things for them got me through the school day. The dolls also had daily essentials made for them: writing kits, illustrated sheets of paper, tiny envelopes in a little folder with a corner for the even tinier stamps. I have some of this stuff still, in a big wooden box under my bed. It is one of my daughter's favourite pastimes to rummage through it and ask me questions. There is a box of love letters from my first boyfriend; random articles made for toys; blue teddy's rucksack containing a plastic bag tent and full camping essentials; drawers made out of After Eight boxes covered in wrapping paper (with some of the dolls' kitchenware still inside); my dad's pipes (the smell still reminds me of him); diaries; notes that Jessie and I passed to each other under the table at school; special cards; gymnastic certificates; icing sugar figures that grandma gave me, from Mummy and Daddy's wedding cake.

Nadya and I had some beautiful rag dolls. We preferred them to plastic dolls because they were specially made and cuddly. I had won Matilda at a school fair by guessing her birthday. Lucy was a doll I had visited in a toy shop, month after month, admiring her beauty and her dress while I saved up my pocket money.

Matilda and Lucy wrote letters to Nadya's doll, Olga. They had tea parties and balls to go to, for all of which I needed to make the correct clothes.

When my daughter Romana was born, I made her a rag doll, putting into her all the love and care that I had felt from my childhood. She has a beautiful dress with sparkly buttons, petticoat and drawers, and special pyjamas with animal buttons. Oh boy, I enjoyed doing that! I am so thrilled to see her having tea parties with my old dolls and sharing their bunk beds and clothes.

Eventually, I moved on to making the actual toys. The first few were strangely-shaped as I experimented with three-dimensional shapes, making the legs all in one and then hacking them up the middle into two legs. Then I realised I needed to make an insert to create three-dimensional legs. When I had perfected my technique, I took a bag of my finished products around some local shops. I managed to get one, Rainbow, to stock my rabbits, kangaroos and owls. They sold like hot cakes! This was my first business. I think I was about twelve. Secretly, all the toys had small pink satin hearts inside them. My brother loved them and named the first large rabbit 'Shirley'. When I had made enough for each delivery to the shop, Crispin lined them up: armies of owls, cats, rabbits and mice.

Crispin was a great organiser of people and games, with me beside him to adore and challenge him. We had a long-standing family club which we used to allow Mum's friends to join for a fee. We created hand-written magazines full of stories, puzzles and competitions. I still have a load of them in the box under my bed. In order to get us to write enough for each episode, Crispin had to get very officious. Nadya and I were never quite good enough, and every club meeting we would make him angry by losing our badges. We would scuttle around our rooms in a panic, looking for the cardboard badges with safety pins on the back. I am afraid that I wasn't above finding Nadya's and pretending it was mine.

The club was called 'The Tracking Troupe'. We had a mascot, 'Tracker Jim'. My brother made up a theme song for him; I can still remember the words and the tune. We got old clothes and smeared them with grass and mud to go tracking in. I don't know what the tracking thing was about: it was something Crispin came up with. We had meetings in the tool shed with the guinea pig. This tool shed was also where I went when I felt that I had been hard done by in the house, to sit and cuddle the guinea pig. He understood me. I had a long run of guinea pigs. They often came to a sticky end with foxes or simply died of cold. We believed that it was better for them to be running free and have a shorter life than live in a cage and be safe.

We had a Pollock's toy theatre with cardboard cut-out stages and a set of plays with cardboard characters on bits of wire, with which to slide them on and off the stage. The longest and most boring of these was the *High Toby*. For some reason, it was I who had to perform this and I always got in a muddle as the bits of wire tangled on the stage. Long-suffering neighbours and Mum used to sit through these productions. We would always run late, getting into a mess with music on the cassette player, or the battery light bulb would blow. Mum would start singing 'Oh why are we waiting', which really wound us up.

The biggest events we ran were our theatre productions. They started with just our family when we were very young. We were 'The Unicorn Theatre' and as we got older we involved children from other families. I made all the costumes for our productions, out of loo roll cylinders, egg boxes and old curtains.

Crispin, brother – Our Unicorn Theatre was conceived, set up and run by children, using only our own ideas and resources and a playroom for a venue, and no adults, except those who paid to be in the audience. We made our own costumes, scenery, programmes and publicity, directed and rehearsed and ran highly successful performances of Alice in Wonderland (1978) and Toad of Toad Hall (1979), amongst other productions. Fifteen children, four or five families all working together over several months to reach the climax of three performances with a maximum audience of ten; the borrowed red velvet curtains on which the spotlight (OK that was provided by a parent) would finally fall when all was ready.

On the night, the reporter from the Bedtimes newspaper would await, parents and friends clutched their paid-for individually felt-penned programmes (a cardboard template ensured brand uniformity), and the bedroom – connected to the stage by a crucial set of back stairs – was filled with the true excitement of the theatre dressing room. Who knows how good the performances really were, or why you could never remember your lines, but the RNLI were always pleased when the annual donation raised from ticket sales arrived.

And where are they now, the company and cast of the Unicorn Theatre? Some would say that their very careers were shaped and spurred on by those great and early performances. There's a lighting designer now at the BBC who once lit our six-foot-square stage. He was also one of the many who painted the three or four backdrops with water paints on glued-together sugar paper. There's an internationally-known women's aerial theatre group whose director and owner once made the costumes for Unicorn from the contents of her family dressing up

box. And there's a successful paediatric consultant who…
never went near the theatre again.

Rehearsals sometimes ended in fights and tears. I could never remember my lines and Crispin had yet to perfect his directorial skills. My youngest sister, Annaliese, by then a toddler, was finally allowed to join the cast for *Toad of Toad Hall*, the last production we did. She was, I think, a squirrel who had one word to say in the court scene. She always had to be kicked, to remind her.

CHAPTER 9

Art College

> **Flying trapeze** – the aerialist known as the 'flyer' jumps from a high platform to create and build up a swing. In flying trapeze, the tricks involve the flyer leaving one trapeze bar and being caught by the 'catcher' who is hanging from their knees (the position known as catcher's), either swinging on another trapeze or static in a 'cradle'. The tricks happen at the peak of the forward swing as the flyer passes from the trapeze to the catcher's hands.

People ask me how I come up with designs. I don't really know, it just happens, presumably the same way that people who are good at maths see everything numerically. My mind constantly collects images, creating a library of colour schemes: patterns and shapes, characters, textures, the way things move or catch the light, the way one object is placed in relation to another, emotions, words, anything. Everything. It can be as simple as seeing some fabrics that work together sparking off an idea in my head.

Wandering up and down the aisles in the Bombay stores,
my eyes dart around looking for fabric which captures the
feeling that I have envisaged.
I pile pieces together,
pulling out bolts of cloth side by side and laying coloured
jewels and lengths of sequins on top of them.
My mouth practically begins to water as the right matches
come together.
My heart beats double quick,
I am in a paradise of sequins,
patterns and colour.

Maybe all those years daydreaming out of the school window weren't wasted after all. Daydreaming has trained me how to search for ideas, stimulation and solutions. My mind can entertain itself happily playing with an idea. I like to have a starting point, a brief or a problem, then I daydream about it. Walking on the moors, sitting on trains, looking out of my kitchen window as I wash up.

First, fragmented images, feelings, things I have seen in the past and stored. Then questions: how will it be strong enough, light up, fit in the van? Then the search for materials: skips, fabric shops, lifting tackle warehouses. I collect materials which make sense of the feeling that I have found. Depending on what I come across, the piece can be several different versions of the same feeling. How do the materials attach to one another, how do they contrast and set each other's colours off, how do they move, reflect, stand up, support each other?

I talk about a feeling rather than a vision or a design because that is what it is like. The emotional attachment to an idea is key to its success. As I ponder on this feeling, it starts to have a visual image, then, while I am working with materials, the piece comes alive.

Mum once called me 'creatively arrogant'. It is just that once I believe in an idea I don't have any doubts. This ability to think creatively is the most precious part of what I am.

I met my first love when I was fifteen. He sang in a band that I had been invited to see by a friend and he sang all his songs to me, then offered to walk me home. He was so cool, only a year older than me but he seemed much more worldly and grown up. I was completely smitten. We were together for a year before he got the offer to go and play football in America. It was a good first love experience. We tried everything out together: parties, camping, rock concerts and sex. I was devastated for a few weeks after he went to America, but found when he returned a year later that I had become a different person from the one he remembered. I had grown more confident and wanted more than early marriage and the job in a bank that his bank manager dad offered to help get me.

I changed schools at sixth form. Jessie and I were drifting apart. We still got on well, but I wanted to meet different people and experience different places whereas Jessie was shy and refused to come with me to youth clubs and discos. I was forced to hunt for more outgoing friends. My new school was up the hill in a much posher part of town. It was a relief to no longer have to watch my back in the corridors but I didn't click with my new art teacher. I found school art lessons very restrictive. We were repeatedly presented with still-life arrangements of rubber plants and household items or sent out to draw views of the school buildings.

I was looked down on at my new school for being uneducated, from a tough working-class school. This was a complete turnaround. They were 'scared' of me, coming from my rough school, and I was not accepted. There was a cliquey hierarchy who had already decided who was the best in the art class, and it was not I. I began to lose my belief in myself and to be bored by what I was doing. I tried my hand at stone carving and lino printing, but when it was time for college interviews for my art foundation year, I had no confidence in my portfolio.

My first art college was my foundation art year in Bath. Living in digs away from home was fantastic. I missed home, though, and got low at weekends, feeling lonely. But it was not far from Bristol and Mum came to visit with Annaliese and we went to a delicious vegetarian cafe for tea. Bath was full of trendy cafes and bars and I easily got part-time work to help subsidise my grant. I always got jobs as a pizza waitress and had to wear miniskirts and be quick off the mark with cocktail orders and extra toppings.

I really enjoyed the pace of life, working hard at college all day, straight to happy hour to drink half price cocktails or to do an evening shift waitressing. I'd finish work around midnight and then go clubbing to Moles. Moles was a tiny underground club, at the time frequented by the Stranglers. I was extremely sociable and enjoyed small alternative clubs. In Bristol, I went to the Dugout club. It was a low-ceilinged basement filled with smoke and Rastafarians. Someone peered at you through a tiny window in a small door before letting you in. It was quite cool for me, as a white girl, to be there.

I struggled with my artistic style during my foundation art year, but settled on trying everything. Coming from the oppressiveness of school art lessons and suddenly expected to become a real artist, I panicked at first, looking at what everyone else was doing and copying bits here and there. I felt insecure. I had always thought that I was a good artist but suddenly, amongst artists who all thought they were good, I wasn't so sure.

As my confidence grew, I felt I had been released. I really became myself, no longer pretending to be like the people at either of my schools. I became completely oblivious to other people's opinions, happy to look different and experiment with that. I cut up jackets and re-sewed them with contrasting fabrics and jewellery all over, multiple coloured scarves, necklaces, chains, bangles, large earrings, theatrical rings with big glass gems. I plaited hair extensions in, weaving lace and ribbon into my hair. Lou tells me that the first time she saw me, when I was talking to Dusty, she was so jealous that he knew someone who dressed like that. This is quite funny, as she had blue hair and the most bizarre sense of dress that I have ever come across. I may well have looked ridiculous a lot of the time but I felt great.

My first end-of-term show was a weak display of attempts to be what everyone else was, until a friend pointed out that the reason my show was no good was because I was wearing everything that should be in it. I had numerous different styles, sometimes copying things I had seen, or utilising fabrics I got hold of cheaply. A furnishing shop had old books of swatches which I patchworked together for skirts and jackets. I made a ball gown from an old bedspread and recycled net curtains.

Bath Academy of Art had its home in two huge Georgian houses which had been joined together to make print rooms, life drawing rooms and fine art studios. In the attic was a labyrinth of small rooms where we could make our own studios.

My new friend Sarah and I created art installations in our attic studio. We made furniture out of a broken toilet and old bath; stuffed and painted washing-up gloves came out of walls; we aerosolled a street art set (I had a friend in the wild bunch in Bristol who came over to teach me graffiti art). With this my confidence grew as I found my own way.

Every term, I went to stay with Crispin at Oxford University. He was so bright that, despite our struggling comprehensive education, he had sailed through school straight to the top. I always went to visit when he was having a party, and what a good time I had! He was at a college where there were only two girls, so when I arrived dressed in my chamois leather leopard-print dress I received an enormous amount of attention.

It was during this time that I was introduced to dope smoking. I wasn't very good at it. Sarah had to teach me to smoke and I never could draw properly to keep a spliff alight. I also tried magic mushrooms at one of Crispin's parties and just felt a bit dizzy. One time, in a London club, I sniffed something and passed out on the toilet floor. I never touched drugs again. I was just no good at it. My friends at art college often took e's and stayed up all night watching rainbows. I refused to partake: my imagination is already quite extreme and I was scared what drugs might do to it.

I had first spotted Sarah in the life drawing class. She says that I looked arrogant and I thought she looked scarily confident. We are both tall and able to put on a loud and confident show and we bonded immediately. Sarah became both my artistic collaborator and my travelling companion during the holidays. We would work for half the summer, waitressing pizzas to save up money to buy an Inter-rail ticket. This cost around £100 and you could travel around Europe on it for one month.

We would set off with our backpacks with no real idea where we wanted to go. Once we were on the backpacking circuit, we found out about the cheap places to sleep and headed off. Venice station platform was well known, as was a beach in Antibes. When we arrived, there would be plenty of other packers sleeping rough and the social scene was guaranteed. We did get moved on by the police, but the more times a night this happened, the cooler you were as you bonded with other packers the next day. We'd sleep anywhere on our beach mats, in sleeping bags with our home-made pouches containing money, passport and Inter-rail ticket clutched to our chest. We'd stay for a few days, living off French bread and cheese, then move on when we heard of a good scene somewhere else.

I became tolerant about travelling. The journey is part of the score. Sitting around ferry ports and train stations is all about socialising with the peer group. Those were brilliant times. Of course, we didn't appreciate it fully at the time: we were too taken up with insecurities and boyfriend issues. But the energy, freedom and lack of responsibility, I now look back on with envy.

CHAPTER 10

Bradford

> **Drop** – this describes a move where the flyer goes through a controlled fall but is caught at the last moment by the wrists, toes or ankles.

I struggled to find the right college to take my degree in art because I wanted to combine disciplines. My work, although theatrical, was too experimental to fit into a theatre design course. Then I discovered that Bradford College was running an innovative course for what they described as 'true generalists'.

I changed trains at Leeds and arrived in Bradford Interchange on the small train: chugging and clattering like a clockwork toy it deposited me in a whole new world. The very atmosphere was different from what I was used to. It felt poor, grey and unloved, a city without frills. I was used to the bohemian nature of Bristol's poverty and the affluent café culture and boutiques of Bath. Bradford had pie and peas and bargain shops. Bradford is a town of depth, culturally, socially and artistically but this vibrancy was not instantly clear to me. Dressed in my homemade clothes, I had cut my matching jacket and trousers from upholstery fabric, with a purple satin shirt and amber diamante jewellery. I was hoping to look like an eccentric fashion designer, maybe Vivienne Westwood or perhaps a rock star, Prince cross-dressed with Madonna. I could not have looked less like a local as I hauled my large art portfolio off the train.

I had come up on spec on the interview day as, typically for me, my paperwork had got lost in the system. They had told me that they would see me at the end of the day, if they had time. I sat in the corridor all day. As with all the main decisions in my life, I never had a doubt that this was the right place to be. When they eventually called me in, there were four art tutors on the panel, long haired, intimidating and chain-smoking. Luckily, they loved my eclectic mix of toilet sculptures, jewellery made from melted rubbish and a musical instrument made from scrap plumbing materials.

It was initially difficult to move from the Bristol and Bath scene to Bradford. At that time, there was no obvious trendy cafe environment in Bradford and the clubbing scene seemed very mainstream. For the first week I couldn't even meet anyone, as I was staying with the daughter of a friend of mum's while I looked for digs.

I couldn't live in student halls as they wouldn't allow in my big black cat, Oberon, who had been given to me in Bath, as a kitten. He came everywhere with me. When we travelled on the train to Bristol, he would sit on a seat politely and behave impeccably. He was an intelligent cat: he learned to break into any fridge and steal cheese, which he loved.

Once our course started I soon made friends, found digs and got sociable. There was a small club, Pickwick's, where I soon became a regular. I found a pizza restaurant where I got a job as a waitress. I missed home a lot but it was a long way away, so I never popped back for weekends. When I started at Bradford the art college was in the Grove building, which had huge high-ceilinged studios. Years later, I watched a man gouging out the carved letters, 'Bradford Art College', and filling them in with cement. The building was turned into a library. That hurt.

The tutors were sometimes amazing and sometimes dreadful. What a bunch of characters! We all moaned about them, as they were so hard to pin down for help with our work. They were all too busy being dysfunctional artists themselves. I didn't know it then, but this sort of tutor was a dying breed, not acceptable in our current, more business-like art college environment. They seemed to spend most of their time in the pub, often giving individual tutorials there. They chain-smoked, drank too much and took the pick of each new student intake for girlfriends. The art history academics were proper dusty looking; the 3-D tutor with fingers all different lengths from accidents in the machine workshop; the print makers, covered in ink, bending over the multiple tiny drawers of precisely laid out printing blocks.

The Community Arts tutor: tall, intellectual with his classic artist's long, lank hair and handmade stripy suits, always with a cigarette on the go whether he was smoking it or not, the ash burning away so that it hung in a long line teetering over someone's precious artwork. He was passionate about art and its place in society; he encouraged us to get involved with community arts projects. He had a real social conscience and a world-weary cynical outlook.

The Textiles tutor always wore a large fur hat, whatever the time of year, high heeled boots, theatrical makeup and decoratively bejewelled tops and skirts: a sort of good and beautiful version of Cruella de Vil. She held herself and spoke with the authority of art royalty. She is retired now and I teach at the art college. Every year, when we do our end-of-year degree show, she arrives bedecked in the same glory and we give her a royal tour. She still makes her stunning textiles and has the same stylish air.

The course head, bald except for a halo of tufts, had a long and forward protruding neck which earned him the nickname of E.T. He was a father figure in a cable-knit pullover who was genuinely committed to the generalist approach of our course. He told us that we would make friends there that would stay with us for the rest of our lives, and he was right.

The Painting tutor was articulate, talented and educated, an ego-driven surrealist painter. He could be cruel; his critiques were brutal. He didn't really like me: I didn't flirt with him and I wasn't a traditional fine artist. He would hover beside me in my art space, take a long sniff, 'no oil paint'... and move on to talk to a 'real' artist, leaving me to mess around with bits of fabric, rubber and plaster.

Head of School: so serious, tiny and wiry. She was dignified and caring but tough. She calmly managed everything while everyone else was busy being creative or falling apart. She was the sanity in an ocean of madness. I found out later that she had fought hard for me to be allowed to do my Trapeze Performance instead of a conventional degree show, and she kept a poster size photograph of me on the trapeze to remind her, she said, 'of what could be achieved'. After college, we remained friends; it turned out that she was a gypsy and had been brought up in a proper horse-drawn wagon. Now I have photographs of her on my wall, in her beautiful wooden gypsy wagon.

We were all scared of being thrown off the course, which happened to weaker or unpopular students at the end of each year. Group tutorials could be humiliating: the tutors tore our efforts to shreds to enable us to find ourselves artistically. I could use the different departments to create sculptures, set designs, costumes and performances, without anyone trying to keep me within boundaries. I loved every minute of it.

I soon developed the confidence to pretty well ignore the briefs we were given and do my own thing. The tutors were happy with this, as I produced huge amounts of work and always managed to justify what I was doing. I never confined myself to one department, but used textile facilities combined with 3-D and print-making. I found that if you looked around you could find what you needed somewhere. I dyed multi-coloured sand for a sculpture in textiles when I should have been in 3-D, and used a printer I found in 2-D to emboss fabric when I should have been making posters. The best policy is to always make friends with the technicians: they are the ones who really know how to use materials and equipment. And they weren't in the pub.

There was a good gang in our shared house. We cooked huge vegetarian slops every night and squabbled about the washing-up. My main friend was a girl called Bob. She was a tomboy, brilliant at community arts and always on hand with her tool kit to build giant props or stages. In the second year she came out as a lesbian which was no real surprise. She was always falling disastrously in love with completely unsuitable people (me at one point, which took a bit of working through). I had arrived still attached to a boyfriend in Bath and soon ditched him for a Bradford student. I changed boyfriends every time I changed courses or social scenes.

The other thing that was great about Bradford College was that they encouraged students to work with external organisations. In my first year I made a good relationship with a small local theatre, Theatre in the Mill, and worked on several bizarre performance pieces with their Fellow in Music. More than once, I stayed up on my own during the holidays, working on productions extra to my college projects.

Ruth Caswell, 1st year tutor: You had been given a brief to make a costume piece that was based on a painting. I was talking to all the good kids upstairs and I said 'Where's this Becky Truman, does she ever come in?' They told me that you were in all the time, working in a room on your own in another part of the building. I went down the back steps of the mill and when I opened the door to your room the smell of latex and resin could have blown you up! The scene was like some mad science fiction film: you had a big bucket of resin and you were dipping fabric, lace and yarn into it and stretching them out into sculptural costumes. You were so involved with the materials' possibilities and what happened with them; you didn't know where the idea was going, returning to try something else when you were not satisfied with the result, engaging with what you had created and allowing it to suggest different possibilities to you. That relationship with your work was truly creative.

You had a photocopy of Max Ernst's 'Red Horse Blue Horse' and you weren't just making one costume, you were making the whole tableau. You must have been using hundreds of pounds' worth of materials but nobody interfered. I used to pop in and look at it when you weren't there but, other than fact that you might die of resin fumes, you were best left to it.

It was a sort of restlessness that I got from you right from the start: you were pushing it somewhere else and you weren't doing it in a prescribed way, you were always pushing it much further than was required. What was really exciting was that even as a first year you were fulfilling your own brief, because it had to satisfy you. What amazes me is that you created something that was totally subjective because it came from inside; it was a total thing that you were making, not just a skin that you put on. You intuitively found a medium for performing because you couldn't be static, you had to be part of the manifestation of the work and that is not the same as being a costume designer. It's the totality of what you did; you animated your whole body to 'transform people into something'.

In our second year, Bob and I got part time jobs as 'Bradford's Bouncing Back Bears' – a campaign designed to boost the profile of Bradford. We often found ourselves, bear costumes and all, at important events. Through it, I met local councillors and community groups. The bear costumes were huge padded structures. Sometimes there was free wine available at the launches and events we attended and we soon discovered that by removing the padding you could hide several bottles of spare wine inside the stomach cavity. Visibility was not good, so we would always have a minder to lead us by the paw. There were times when the job was hazardous: in the less salubrious districts of Bradford, we were targets. It was nerve-racking to be inside a bear costume, unable to see, weighed down by wine bottles, when suddenly the minders disappeared and the children's war cry rang out: 'Get the bear!' Tom Clinton, the man who ran the campaign, was the first person who believed in me enough to divert some money towards my own first production.

When I lived in Bristol I had modelled in some local fashion design shows. The designers there were innovative and theatrical. I idolised a lady whose designer name was 'Mary Hell'. The clothes she created were more costume than fashion and, inspired by her, I dressed more and more dramatically. I had noticed that there didn't seem to be any sort of promotion or community of designers in Bradford, so I had proposed to Tom Clinton that his campaign should fund me to put on a fashion show with a difference. The clothes/costumes were worn by performers rather than models: they were mainly dancers, but we had some cabaret acts in the show too. I called it a fashion cabaret and it was the first time I experienced the whole package that is involved in running a show.

The fashion cabaret got me noticed by two key artistic motivators in Bradford. Alan Brack, who was organising a small festival at South Square Arts Centre, asked me to do a performance there. The theme was China, and the plan was to change the whole environment into Chinatown for the weekend. I made a performance with theatrically-styled Chinese costumes. The other person who introduced himself to me was Dusty Rhodes. He was looking for artists to be involved in his events and asked me to do a performance.

Dusty led a large group of people who would squat buildings temporarily and turn them into theatrical events. A team of artists and enthusiasts would work, without pay, for weeks, making art out of found objects and rubbish. They were wonderful events. Cars were chopped in half and suspended as if driving through the wall; scaffolding towers and catwalks were erected for performances and art works; there were welded life-size rhinoceroses, giant spiders, even a human-sized hamster wheel. Each event had a theme, such as 'The Ark' or 'Movie Stars', and on the night both artists and audience dressed up. The efforts people made were amazing. They queued up and were put through a series of games, perhaps a love scene with a dummy, or being winched up in the air or taking a turn on the giant hamster wheel.

Dusty, friend, Lou's partner, artistic director – I had done a lot of music and street theatre while at university and now I started to dream about putting on large-scale outdoor events. It has always been a passion of mine. I have a combination of skills, music, theatre and an eye for producing shows and spectacles. I was doing building work to earn a living so I was able to knock seven bells out of things and build large structures and I was surrounded by a mixture of people who combined everything from building and joinery skills to artists, sculptors and musicians.

It started low key: there was a derelict house next door and I knocked a hole in the wall and we did a party through a cupboard; we called it 'Through the Wardrobe'. That was successful and somebody said please do it again and we started making it more and more artistic, using that combination of building skills and artistry and the sense that it was open to anyone. There was a freedom associated with it that people felt, there was a good energy, when you bear in mind that all of this was happening on a volunteer level. We mobilised hundreds of people to do things for the love of it, for the crack, for the good time, for the experience of sharing and doing it together.

Next, I persuaded the landlord of the Alfresco garage at the end of the Norman Arch to let us have it for free, with the ruse was that we were testing the waters to see whether it was possible to set up a film studio in Bradford. We got a whole load of scrap cars and did a sculptural piece with a car that crashed into the middle of the dance floor, a cascade of cars as a central piece, based on the idea of *The Italian Job*. It was a great party and at the end of it everybody said 'let's do another one', so we did another one where people dressed up as film extras and we were the film crew. When the police arrived at four in the morning there was a nun dancing with an aboriginal in the middle of the dance floor; they were completely baffled and walked off.

The Estate Agents got wind of it later and said 'we understand you had one hell of a party' and we said 'yes well, you know, it was the party at the end of filming.' By then we were attracting crowds of five or six hundred people. An artistic community was being created, and at the next party at Fettle works over one thousand people came. The energy levels were fantastic.

The first time that I was involved in one of Dusty's events, where I was doing a dance piece in one of my bizarre costumes, I met Jimmy Iqbal. Jimmy (stage name Raven James) was striking, with long black slicked-back hair mixed with feathers, a furry gorilla-type jacket, black leather trousers and high black boots. His profile was hawk-like and the effect of this, with the feathers in his hair, was very Native American. He performed on the trapeze and, being powerfully built, he executed an extremely macho and impressive routine. We chatted backstage and he offered to teach me trapeze. I readily accepted. This would prove to be a life-changing decision.

My first impression of Bradford had been of a tired, grey city, but I grew to love its majestic industrial landscape: rows of mills with enormous gateways into cobbled yards; Lister Mill in Manningham standing like a palace on the skyline, catching the sunset right through both sets of windows, lit up and visible from all around the city. Bradford turned out to have a rich culture and a thriving and grass-roots artistic community. This was a true lesson in not taking things at face value.

CHAPTER 11

Training

> **A doubles trapeze bar** – has internal dimensions of the same width as the catcher's bottom, plus the space for a hand hold on either side. Unlike a solo trapeze, the bar protrudes beyond the trapeze padding, just enough for another pair of hands to grip. This extension allows for two pairs of hands/ knees to be on the bar at once.
>
> Welded to the bar are two metal thimbles, each having 25mm cotton rope spliced onto it; the length of the ropes is determined by the taller partner's height. The free ends of the ropes are also spliced around metal thimbles.
>
> The splice which goes around the bar is whipped securely with strong string to ensure that the ropes cannot slip off the thimble. On top of this, a tightly-packed layer of padding further keeps the splice in position, and also provides protection for parts of the body which strain against it.

Jimmy had a trapeze rig set up in a sports centre just off Covent Garden in London. His method of teaching was very traditional: either you climbed straight up to the high trapeze to learn, with no safety line, or you didn't bother. There was no other approach.

I was completely terrified. Despite good gymnastic training, my palms were soft and my arms and hands were not built up to take the strain. The trapeze looked very high. Even to get on it to practice, I had to climb up the rope. This meant that my grip and arms felt weak even before I reached across for the trapeze bar. I soon developed an open wound where the rope dug into my leg as I climbed. I had impressive bruises behind my knees. I was not naturally fearless on the trapeze but learned slowly, by repetition of the exercises and moves. This gave me strength and confidence. I stuck with it, terrified but addicted.

After my lessons I hung around the street performers in Covent Garden, feeling happy to be still alive. I admired the street show performers, who had to be tough, engaging and loud. I soaked up inspiration from everything I saw, like a sponge.

I went to London at weekends. Jimmy was working with Circus Senso, which was one of the early alternative circuses. He introduced me to the idea of combining circus skills with visual art. I saw Cirque Imaginaire, Victoria Chaplin's show. It was so gentle. The skills were not presented like tricks, with drum rolls and clapping, but combined the quiet quality of mime characters, props and costumes. I had found my art form.

Jimmy taught me to make my own equipment. From him I learned to splice and how to calculate the width between the metal thimbles that are welded onto a trapeze bar. He showed me where to buy the lifting tackle from which to hang the trapeze, how to cover a trapeze with soft padding around the welds, and which tape to use for the bar. This information is crucial to an aerialist: you must be responsible for your own equipment, to rig it, check it, test it. Circus rigging is outside the boundaries of the understanding of health and safety inspectors

Back in Bradford during the week, I knew that I loved trapeze but was terrified as my arms and grip were too weak to be safe. I made the decision to change that. Every morning I got up extra early and cycled to the local sports centre where there was a wall bar. I worked hard at 'chin ups' and 'leg ups' until my hands got calloused and my muscles developed. This was the beginning of a constant challenge in my life: how to fit in both physical training for the trapeze and make the art to accompany it. Travelling to work with Jimmy at the weekends, and training on the trapeze before and after college, was pretty full-on.

The combination of making art and having found the physical freedom with which to express it was perfection for me. Discovering trapeze was like finding a part of me that had been missing, it was my soul mate. It gave my life meaning, structure, freedom, space, air, light and confidence. It enabled me to express the dreams that I had been envisioning all my life through the characters in my favourite story books. It was the beginning of an adventurous love affair, the only one that I was truly faithful to.

CHAPTER 12

Circus workshop

> **Velvets** – The part of the trapeze where the ropes are spliced around the metal thimble.* To make them look good and to protect our skin from the sharp welds, we cover this part in velvet.
>
> *Thimble – a teardrop-shaped insert for wire or rope that is clamped, spliced or welded to form a fixing point.

As I gained confidence with Jimmy, I needed to set up my trapeze somewhere in Bradford where I could practise. On hearing that there was a circus workshop at a sports centre in Manningham, I thought that might be a good starting-point. I arrived during the workshop on a Friday night and spoke to the manager, who gave me permission to put up my equipment. I spent the next twenty years training in this space whenever we were off tour.

The circus workshop consisted of a disparate bunch of professionals and amateur jugglers and unicyclists. I added trapeze to the mix and settled in very easily. The characters at the workshop were to provide me with a strong group of lifelong friends.

People took their children with them, so a new generation of circus enthusiasts was learning the skills as well. Some of these children became Skinning the Cat fans and friends as they grew up. I was teaching trapeze to a couple of local people, so that they could take part in the aerial performance that I was planning for the show at the end of my art and design degree.

I met Sam at circus workshop. It transpired that he had introduced my trapeze teacher, Jimmy, to circus skills. I was still a student when first we met, and I admired him and his transient lifestyle. We have woven in and out of each other's lives, meeting by chance and picking up as if nothing had happened in between.

After Lou's accident, I used to go and sit in the comfort of Sam's kitchen on his rocking chair and unburden my feelings of guilt, responsibility and shock. He loved to cook for me and often fed me, as he admitted, to keep me there longer. Having always had a large appetite, I was very happy and grateful.

Another important friend was Anne Nicholls, an amateur juggler who later became our company administrator. A key element of the workshop was to go to the pub and have a curry afterwards. I started a happy relationship with these Friday nights. When Skinning the Cat got to the stage of busy tours and there was any chance of getting back to Bradford to the pub before the lock-in, we would race up the motorway and arrive to bang on the pub window. Plans were made, relationships started and ended, gossip was shared.

Johnny, company friend – I first met Becky when I was 6 or 7 at the juggling workshop held every Friday at the Manningham Sports Centre. I went to the workshop with my dad most weeks for about 2 years. He would juggle with his mates while me and my friends would throw balls to each other and dive around on crash mats. We used to watch in awe as Becky and Lou practised and offered tips to beginners on the trapeze. What remains vivid after nearly 20 years are the clouds of chalk used for grip, the grubby strapping bound round ankles and wrists, the elegance of the deliberate falls into the safety net, the enormity of Becky's thighs tamed by leopard print leggings and the smell of both fresh and stale sweat.

When I was about 8, a travelling family attended the workshop for about 6 months. Each member specialised in a certain circus discipline. Becky spent hours on the trapeze with the youngest daughter, Kimberly, who was almost 3 years younger than me. I remember Becky consoling me after Kimberly beat me in an arm wrestle in front of a large audience after the workshop. The crowd had all laughed and, although I felt embarrassed in defeat, I felt far less foolish for having lost to a girl, given Becky's obvious strength.

Every week as we entered the sports hall Becky would come over for a chat. She would smile and make an effort to engage me in conversation. I was quite shy around adults and a little intimidated by Becky's physical power and social confidence. Though I found her presence warm and comforting, when the attention was directed towards me I counted the seconds until it passed.

I have a strong memory of meeting Becky after her show at the Festival Mela: she was still in costume and heavy make-up, out of breath and probably still high from the performance. It had been a year or two since I'd last seen her and although, besides the make-up, she looked physically the same. I couldn't believe the contrast between the softness I remembered from Manningham Sports Centre and the animalistic ferocity she emitted on stage. She said hello with the same kindness she always showed, and I could do nothing but look at the ground.

The Bavaria pub, affectionately known as 'The Bav', became an extension of my home. Essentially a gay pub, it also incorporated the more bohemian aspect of the Bradford community. It was the centre of social activity for the Manningham area, and played an important part in the community. At the weekends, it was packed.

On Friday nights, a large crowd would arrive early to the Bav, straight from circus workshop, bringing children and bags of smelly training clothes and juggling clubs and trapeze rigging. Sometimes, as the early crowd and younger members left, we would take a break and go for a curry and return later. Other times, we would just stay until we were the worse for wear from drinking beer on an empty stomach. I had quite a high capacity for alcohol at that time. The long evening generally ended with a whisky chaser and often we would adjourn to someone's house for yet more socialising. As well as being fun, it was where people met and planned projects. Often, we were visited by people from other circus groups. The outcome of these casual meetings and conversations could be far-reaching, resulting in different combinations of groups becoming professional, Skinning the Cat, Snapdragon Circus, and the Wonderboys, to name but a few.

The Bav was run by John and Kevin, who were everyone's best friends and confidantes. Friday was Kevin's disco night. He would sit in the corner and play 80's music, and by the end of the night I would inevitably be found squashed into the corner, dancing to the Weather Girls.

We went in regularly on week nights when it was quiet, using it like our own front room, with the added bonus that we could have a drink and meet members of our outer circle. It was great to have a place where everyone you knew and wanted to see could be found at some point during the week. The Bav was burnt out during the riots of 2001.

After I'd made an unsuccessful attempt to live with my boyfriend, Julia (Joolz) moved into my little house on the corner of Skinner Lane in Manningham. She was working on the education programme for Bradford Festival. Joolz was a very tidy person and I drove her mad. I would race in from training, dump bags and training clothes, grab food without washing up and race out again.

Julia liked a nice orderly house and an orderly routine. She tolerated my eclectic taste in décor and only moaned sometimes about my mess. She would come in exhausted from a day's work, collapse onto the settee and bribe me to fetch her fish and chips by paying for mine. She came from a very close Bradford family who kindly adopted me, as my family was so far away. I got on well with them because they were similar to my own family. There was lots of micky-taking, banter and rowdiness.

Every Sunday, we went for dinner at one or other of their houses. They still include me, thirty years later! Joolz and I were living together when we both broke up with our long-term boyfriends. We went a bit wild after that, going out a lot and having gangs of friends back after the pub. Julia soon got together with one of the jugglers and went on to marry him, which broke up our happy living style. I continued in my wild behaviour without a thought for the future.

My next housemate was Lizzie. Lizzie and I moved into a house round the corner from the Bav. She was a photographer I had met through Bradford Festival. We were both tall with dark brown hair, which we hennaed to make a rich dark red. Lizzie was very big on kitsch. She collected plastic snowstorms.

Wherever I travelled, I looked out for one for her, despite the fact that they drove me mad. They covered every surface, including the edges of the stairs. Dusting would have been impossible, so it was just as well that neither of us was keen on it.

We filled the house with decorations: mine were gold and brightly coloured. There was a wall-sized golden gryphon that I had made at Art College, and drapes of Asian fabric. My favourite object was a gold plastic clock surrounded by a winged unicorn, with plastic roses inside the face. It took pride of place after the gryphon. Lizzie liked religious kitsch, such as plastic Virgin Marys, as well as anything to do with Elvis Presley. We shared a love of animal print fabric.

Lizzie had health problems at the time, so when I was not working away I supported her as best as I could. We shared boyfriend disasters, work stresses and flu germs. We cooked and socialised together and shared an ever-increasing strong network of friends. We were pretty close.

Living in multi-cultural Manningham was a great experience for us. Our local Asian shop on Oak Lane displayed a sea of vegetables, including some unusual shapes. Thick bunches of herbs, bulk packets of spices and super-sized tins of ghee lined the shelves of the no-frills interior. Behind the counter hung some just-in-case wedding decorations and random boxes of henna powder. We could buy fistfuls of fresh coriander and just about anything else we needed.

The local curry houses were many and varied. Our favourite was the Silver Jubilee, which was very basic: just rows of canteen-style tables, it was the sort of comfortable place that you could easily drop in and sit for a curry by yourself on the way home, or take up the full length of a table with a large gang from the pub.

The other important eatery in our lives was the Italia café in Great Horton, run by an effervescent Italian family who seemed to know everyone in Bradford. Loud Italian voices over the noise and steam of the coffee machine, a pool table where people hung around and chatted after they had eaten, buzzing and sociable. We were always sure to meet friends there, on purpose or by chance. The food was simple and delicious: big plates of chips or vegetable stew, always accompanied by a pile of doorsteps of white bread. It was an early doors cafe, somewhere to go for an early tea straight from work.

At home, Lizzie and I cooked huge piles of vegetable stir-fry. We were both vegetarians and Lizzie was often on strange health diets. A typical meal would consist of a bag of vegetables from the Asian supermarket, fried up in the wok with some tofu and a pile of rice. Lizzie had a cheeky sense of humour and referred to me as 'bucket of chips Truman' due to my huge appetite for carbohydrates. She also gleaned much amusement from the regular phone calls from what she called my 'foreign liaisons' when a foreign male would ring or visit, following a tour.

The problem with being two young women living alone was that some of the locals assumed that we must be prostitutes, partly because that was not an uncommon profession in Manningham and partly because it was an explanation for unmarried women. One evening I was in alone, waiting for the landlord to come and collect the rent. He passed the cash back to me, wanting sexual services instead. I was scared and explained that I was not interested. He was surprised but not aggressive. I went straight to the Bav, where Lizzie and our friends were having an early evening drink. I was never alone again when he came for the rent.

CHAPTER 13

Bradford Festival

Hocks position – knees over the trapeze bar, toes together and pointed firmly down towards the ground.

I first worked for Bradford Festival when I was still a student. I got a job helping look after the artists, accompanying them to their pitches and setting up a board with show information. I spent some time as assistant to an escapologist, learning how to tense my body while the chains were being secured around me. Bradford Festival was being regenerated, initially by artist Alan Brack, who was later joined by event organiser Dusty Rhodes. They were a passionate team who combined importing inspirational foreign companies with strong and multi-cultural community participants.

The highlight of the two weeks was the Asian Mela: music, rhythm, colour, stages with dancers, bhangra bands, circus performances, outdoor theatre companies, stalls and street vendors. Artists from around the corner, artists from around the world. By Sunday evening the park was knee deep in half eaten samosas, raita and happy tired people. The mixture of people and performers, the colours, the smells – it was a beautiful mess,

During that weekend, it felt as if you would bump into literally everyone you knew: the world and his wife and his cousin once removed, the next door neighbour, the neighbours you hardly knew, the colleagues from work that you don't normally see, the best friend who'd moved away, all sitting on a rug eating bhajis while the kids ran wild. If Bradford is the world in one city, the Mela was that city in a field.

The year I finished college, I managed to persuade Alan Brack, the director of the festival, to fund me to put on a cabaret at one of the main venues, the Bradford Wool Exchange. My newly formed aerial company (not yet named) would of course be the star. I had a small track record already, having produced and performed in cabarets while I was still at college and was getting to know a bit about raising funding.

We spent the summer prior to the festival incarcerated in Dusty's warehouse with a small team of artists, making the set for the Wool Exchange. I rigged the trapeze above the glue pots and paint and we rehearsed whenever we could find the time.

The Wool Exchange was a vast and beautiful building with a vaulted ceiling, pillars with arches between, and hanging lanterns. I was asked to design a set which would not only work for our cabaret but would look good for all the events to be held in there. I decided to design work to complement what was already there, making multi-coloured drapes adorned with gold swirls to reach from the top of the hall to the edges, enhancing the vaulted beams still visible between them. The marble pillars were wrapped in the same fabric; the lanterns, made of clear glass, were covered in lighting gels, giving a Moroccan effect. The main feature was the four gold gryphons, which were a larger and more theatrical version of the small stone carved ones in the roof.

The get-in for the set took longer than it should have and we worked through several nights to install it. In order to attach the drapes to a wooden frame suspended in the centre at the top of the hall, we had to run an electric cable to the top of the seventy-foot-high scaffolding, pull up my sewing machine and sew the seams up there. This was my ultimate comfort zone: high in the air with my sewing machine and a load of gold swirly fabric.

The show was a great success. I had been offered some work doing something similar in Brighton but, when I chatted to Alan Brack about where to base myself, he said: 'Why do it for someone else in Brighton when you can do it for yourself here?' That suggestion and the support and network I already had in Bradford made my decision for me.

We became a women's company. This was not the overt political statement that people sometimes imagined but the outcome of my experiences of men. I felt safe with women and I also liked doing the jobs that men generally expect to do. I love driving big trucks, and reversing caravans into tight spots is highly satisfying. And, of course, I love rigging.

My first attempt at working with a male trapeze partner was a disaster. He started to believe that I belonged to him, turning up uninvited at social events and acting the dominant male. It got quite nasty and I felt uncomfortable working physically with him. On the trapeze, we touch each other on many parts of the body. Normally this feels professional; even when the routine looks sensual, it is not. This man's touch started to feel sexual. I could not work with him any more.

I had some shows coming up and called Jimmy in a crisis to come and work with me. He did so and saved the day, but it was never going to work long term because Jimmy was a very traditional male. He did all the rigging and the act took on the traditional male/female trapeze act style. So, when one of the performers that I had taught at circus workshop was available, she became my first female partner. After this, it seemed quite normal to look for a female rigger and technician. I don't think that we ever sat down and made the decision to employ an all-female company: it just felt right.

The stage on the lake in Lister Park was Dusty's vision for Bradford Festival. He built it with the scaffolding feet in the lake so that the stage appeared to float on the water, with reflections mirroring the performances. The shores of the lake, where the hill sloped down to the water's edge, provided a natural amphitheatre.

Dusty, friend, Lou's partner and artistic director – I wanted to build a stage on the lake for several reasons. I thought it was a wonderful environment, with the capacity for a reasonably-sized audience and a backdrop of trees; sound travels wonderfully across water. There's something very magical about a particular moment in the evening where the wind drops and there's stillness on the water: we could play with that combination of water, reflections, the land and the trees.

The same spirit that had developed for the parties started to be applied. I had in mind a finale to the festival that would incorporate a lot of elements. I didn't know what the story line would be; in fact I ended up writing the story line on a scrap of paper on the afternoon of the event. We created lots of pieces. Malcolm the Mechanic got a scrap car he'd taken the wheels off; he'd welded together a pair of 45 gallon oil drums so there was this car that looked like a car from the outside but was able to float on water, driven with some outboard motors. Then we converted a bicycle so that it could float and had little paddles to cycle across the lake, and you'd agreed to come along and do a Skinning the Cat piece.

Sarah Worrel and Jill Forester dressed as dragonflies with little gossamer wings and they paddled around on the lake in a pair of canoes. When they got to the bottom of the stage, you took over and got hoisted on winches up the side of the stage, and by the time you got up to the top we'd released two other people on aerial runways dressed as birds; the birds flew across the lake on the cables. The juggling convention was there, so they had a mass juggle with fire on the stage, while fire sculptures floated on the lake. It was incredibly alive and organic. So many people were enjoying it on a participatory level. I look back at bits of video clip and see that it was not very sophisticated, but that wasn't the point.

It was a tremendously exciting time. I remember you as a young artist emerging from art college with an idea, and you got the opportunity not only to do a show in an iconic building like the Wool Exchange but also to direct a huge part of the operation. You had not only the budget to do it with but also a whole back up of people who know how to get up 70-80 foot in the air and attach things. It was incredible.

The festival finale was planned around the lake. That year, as well as the usual local artists and community groups, the Eleventh European juggling convention formed part of the festival. The juggling convention was organised by a contingent from our Friday night circus workshop. In September 1987 Sam and Steve of the Bradford-based Saroste jugglers returned from the European Juggling Convention in Saintes with the news that the Convention was to be held the following year in England – in Bradford, actually, and the Circus Workshop members were going to organise it.

It all made perfect sense: Bradford Festival was keen to have the Convention as part of the programme and Manningham Sports Centre was thrilled. A group of about six jugglers quickly formed the core organising group which involved about 1,000 jugglers, unicyclists and acrobats from all over the world coming to Bradford for the best part of a week in September.

In addition to this, my friend Bob from college, now a maker of giant puppets, had organised a visit from the large Spanish group the Diablos Del Clot. These two large contingents were fantastically and creatively unruly and were incorporated into the finale along with us locals. The stage on the lake in its setting was stunning and Dusty had planned an adventurous finale, which included *Skinning the Cat*, around it.

We rehearsed the finale in the middle of the previous night. There were large numbers of people whom Dusty tried to coordinate on walkie-talkies. There were artists in the lake, on the lake, on the land, on the stage, in the air. A bicycle crossed the lake on floats. Unfortunately, it started sinking during the rehearsal because someone had misjudged the weight. This prompted the cyclist to cycle harder and that made the back wheels sink down more... Meanwhile, I was suspended from a tower at the side of the stage, hooked up to an electric winch that took me down from the top of the tower, dangled me just above the lake and then back up again. Unfortunately, the operator of my winch got distracted and forgot to stop the winch. I got a dunking in the lake, which I have never been allowed to forget.

Bob, art college friend – 'Los Diables Del Clot' (the Devils of Del Clot), had gone all out on their dragon, which was probably 25ft long and 8ft high. He was quite cute, until he started shooting fireworks from his mouth. The devils hold a metal spike, onto which fireworks are mounted, and wear fireproof capes; they are accompanied by drummers, who also wear fireproof capes! The Finale was amazing, Fire Jugglers, the stage growing into a sculpture, the firework platform, a few leaking rowing boats containing giant puppets. What was meant to happen was that as the jugglers created a dance of fire on the stage, the stage sculpture would grow and the giant puppets would glide elegantly across the front of the stage, taking the audiences eyes to the pyrotechnic stage, then the firework display would start and the devils would do their show amongst and around the audience.

It was a windy night and the sinking rowing boats were blown past the stage and towards the pyros, to the terror of the pyrotechnician. So, trying to avoid the fireworks, we punted furiously back into the wind and landed back in front of the stage. When the devils broke through the crowd they saw me struggling in a boat and started aiming their fireworks at us. I remember saying to Elaine Airth 'we're getting out of here', to which came a faint answer of 'I can't move'. She was paralysed with fear.

CHAPTER 14

Setting up Skinning the Cat

> **The rig** – the metal structure which we must erect to have something from which to hang the rigging.

After the excitement of performing our first year at Bradford Festival was over, we were faced with the reality of needing to raise some money to buy a van to tour in and an aerial rig to perform on. The rig can be a simple tall, metal, goal post shape about nine metres high, held up with cables and staked into the ground, or a multi-posted and differently-shaped structure, depending on the show and imagination. I wished to make a very theatrical show, which told a simple story with a set design and props, costumes, and special effects. Possessing our own outdoor rig would avoid having to cope with the restrictions of height that venues often present. An added bonus would be the settings in which we erected it, often with the moon and dark scudding clouds or sunsets behind us.

I started looking into loans and funding. When I first had a meeting with The Prince's Youth Business Trust, I was irritated to find that they did not simply hand out money: applicants had to do a ten-week business course, submit a business plan, and only then, and only if it was good enough, could you get an interest-free loan and a small grant. I had naively thought that, as I had created a successful product, that was enough. Why would I need to waste time on a business course? I only started the course for the money that I hoped to get at the end of it. However, it turned out to be some of the most useful time I ever spent.

The course was run by an energetic and inspirational character called George and consisted of a mixture of young people with a range of business ideas. I remember a team whom we nicknamed the Tofu Twins. They were planning to sell veggie burgers at festivals. In addition, there was a band, an accountant, and us. George taught us about cash flow projections, marketing and business plans. These skills turned out to be crucial and also got us our first bank loan.

My friend Sam has recently asked me why I set up a whole aerial show instead of just becoming an individual aerialist or performer, as he did. There are lots of reasons. I had an exciting vision and wanted to have artistic control over the whole show and not just a small element of it; I had numerous ideas which needed more than one person to realise; I wanted to create a whole magical world for the audience to lose themselves in; I am a creative control freak who does not like being told what to do. The only way to really fulfil my dreams was to make my own company and have the final say on everything. I am not a designer who can work to somebody else's idea – it's my way or no way at all!

Also, there was also an element of insecurity behind my plans. I never thought that I was good enough and had to hide behind costumes, make up and props. Just maybe, if it was all over-the-top fancy, glittery and bright enough, no one would notice that it was only me underneath.

But it wasn't just for creative reasons that the company grew: there are many practical considerations which dictated the size of Skinning the Cat. As an aerialist you are bound by rigging points, which means you must work in a big top or a venue unless you design your own structure to rig off. This means that you are self-sufficient and can be booked for any event, regardless of whether they have the rigging points that you need.

Consequently, you have a structure to erect and to transport. For this you need a minimum team, depending on the size of the structure and the show performed on it. You need trucks and people to help and you need enough performers to create a show of the length that you are selling to the booker. So, basically, once you want to do it all your own way, you are obliged to become a company. Once you are a company, you have overheads to cover, office space, insurance, vehicle costs, publicity... and a responsibility to keep people in work for the season: you cannot just have the odd 'gig', you need to provide a whole tour. You start with an exciting idea of something that you want to create and end up running a company.

Skinning the Cat took on a flexible format. In the summer, we produced a complete show, working on our own rig and travelling to wherever we could get bookings. Often, we drove crazy distances and had not enough time to sleep. In the winter months, I would work indoor venues, performing my solo show *Firebird* or doing a doubles trapeze act with Rachel. We would slot into a circus, cabaret, variety show, pantomime or corporate entertainment.

It was an exciting time, setting up Skinning the Cat. Initially, I worked with Emma who had stage-managed my show in Bradford Festival. She was highly efficient and had impressed me with her enthusiasm by stopping me in the street before we had met and asking me for a job on the show. She was going to manage and administrate the company. Then I found my first female trapeze partner at circus workshop and she joined us and added her enthusiasm. Initially we had only bits and pieces of work, so we spent time dreaming, planning and practising our trapeze routine. We went on short courses to learn Peking opera and Tai Chi. We met many other performers on these courses and began to set up a network of inspiring contacts, who showed interest in what we were doing.

We had no vehicle to begin with but whizzed around Bradford's steep hills on our bikes, setting up meetings with arts organisations and performing in sports centres for children's Christmas parties. It was so exciting when we got our first van, driving it home with our Simply Red cassette blasting out. We were all set to conquer the world!

Cycling to trapeze training one afternoon, I stopped at an Asian fabric shop, attracted like a child to sweets by the wonderful fabrics on display. The man was friendly and talked about the beautiful clothes he could run up for me if I chose a fabric. I wasn't really interested, because I made all my own clothes, but I chatted to him pleasantly about it anyway. He persuaded me to go behind a screen to be measured. I went out of politeness: he was so friendly. Still making conversation with me, he went through the motions of measuring, but inside my clothes and right into parts of me which did not need measuring. I just stood there, frozen and polite, while he acted as if this was perfectly normal. I thanked him as if nothing strange had happened and cycled off to my training session on the trapeze.

This was not the first time something like this had happened. But this time I was older. I got home and rang my mum, howling. I didn't want to go to the police but I had to regain some self-respect: this was not ok. I talked to a prominent member of the Asian community and decided that he would speak to the man. We went together to the shop and I pointed the man out and left. He broke down, terrified that we would go to the police. He apologised, which should have made me feel better – but it did not change how I felt inside.

Externally, I was so confident with men, but bad childhood experience with my grandpa had left me feeling guilt; this had never eased. I carried this curse into all my friendships and relationships, believing that everything that went wrong was my fault and that I am essentially bad.

A game, special for us while the other children are downstairs.
Desperate to get away,
desperate for the time to get the train home,
guilt, secret, never tell.
My fault for misunderstanding the game,
just 'a bit of fun'.
My responsibility to keep this secret all these years,
don't destroy the family, rob the others of their grandpa.

But I've never felt a penis before,
I am dirty, guilty, bad.

CHAPTER 15

Double swan

> **The double swan** – a trapeze move where the base hangs in catcher's position and the flyer is suspended by the catcher. Both are upside down and facing in the same direction. The flyer wraps the legs around the torso of the catcher and crosses the ankles with flexed feet in order to create a lock, clamping the thighs strongly. Both performers have arms free to pose in the position.

There was an agent, Shirley Hayter, who had all the main circus and street theatre acts on her books. She got us our first booking at Glastonbury festival. I think that probably the only reason that we got the booking, with no track record, was that no one had heard of anything quite like us before. Now the heat was on to get our outdoor rig built.

Our first experience with an aerial rig nearly finished us before we started. We had invited a friend who had some experience of rig design, and with whom we had recently spent time on a flying trapeze course. He came to stay and we made plans and discussed designs with Les, our welder. Les was a master welder: he had made the doors for the Channel Tunnel and welded up our trapeze bars. We planned to make the uprights of our rig out of gas tubing and the cross beam out of a scaffolding ladder truss. We collected some materials from scrap yards and lovingly rubbed, primed and painted them gold. Somewhere along the way, we hadn't completely understood some important details.

The day we put it up was terrifying. Winching up an eight-metre structure for the first time was difficult enough. But as it went up the joints buckled at the knees, and the ladder truss at the top twisted dangerously. Pulling up rigs is a skill which takes a lot of practice at the best of times. This structure had basic faults that meant it was never going to work. The ladder truss at the top was too heavy for the gauge of the gas piping we had chosen for the uprights. The sleeves which joined the middle of the uprights were loose. I was too inexperienced to have understood this in advance.

We were devastated. We had a booking at Glastonbury the next week and had spent all our money on this dodgy steel monstrosity. In a confidence born of despair, I rang up a company who made aluminium lighting trussing. I explained what had happened and that lightweight trussing would be a perfect solution to our problems. They said, 'come down and we will see what we can do for you.' I had struck lucky with Optikinetics: it was run by a rock musician who was sympathetic to our plight. They provided us with lightweight trussing, which was much more suitable than the heavy old steel, at an extremely reasonable rate. All the attachments and equipment from the disastrous rig transferred onto it very well. We had a beautiful rig in time for our bookings.

This terrifying early experience of how *not* to build a rig taught me a lot. Through watching the way that lengths of metal move and how the tensioning points affect them, I began my interest in rig designing. Over years of installing rigs and rigging, I was to develop a vast understanding of the practical side of engineering. Gradually, I was able to design bigger, better and more adventurous rigs.

I find this interesting now, as I try to teach my students, many of whom struggle with academic work but have no problem with three-dimensional, practical and artistic challenges. How did someone like me, who can hardly add up, let alone do a stress or load-bearing calculation, become an expert in the field of rig design? Seeing a calculation on paper makes no sense at all to me and my brain turns into knots if someone tries to explain it. But if I watch how something moves or feels or, even better, I climb or swing on something and feel its movement, it is absolutely clear to me how it should work.

I always thought that I was so stupid at school: when nothing on paper made any sense, my brain would glaze over. Now I realise that I just understand things in a very different way. The shame of it is that I spent all those years at school gazing out of the window and feeling thick. If only I could have been learning in a way that worked for me.

Ba, company technician – I remember standing around on a beautiful evening in the circus field at Glastonbury… There was a simple structure made of silver trussing. The show itself was a simple series of sections, predominantly aerial work, a bit of single trapeze, a bit of single web, a bit of doubles web, a bit of free form swinging trapeze, a bit of fire clubs, cloud swing and it ultimately culminated in a really dynamic doubles trapeze routine – all under some really basic lighting and an intriguing layering of music and atmosphere.

The result was something pretty exciting. There was a lot of energy and passion in the show, the doubles trapeze routine was brilliant and worked fantastically with the music and the fire was mesmerising. I was actually really surprised later when I saw how amazing the costumes and make up looked in the light of day as I hadn't noticed them in that first show: the basic lighting flattened them out completely.

We rehearsed over the winter devising the new show in the Skinning the Cat space in Dusty's warehouse, making the set and I remember your house being a sweatshop for the fantastic trademark costumes, usually overflowing with feathers and Lycra. I was the happy recipient of a long-coveted Becky-created jacket, on the premise that as technician I would be the only member not to have a Skinning the Cat costume. That jacket was fantastic and made me so happy.

It hadn't been part of the original plan or budget, but I rattled on so much about getting a better lighting rig that you finally found a wee budget to shut me up. Subsequently I put together the most comprehensive, cheapest lighting rig and sound system that the budget wouldn't stretch to. I enjoyed the challenge of blagging much of this for next to nothing, haggling hard and finding some creative ways around not having enough money for such a thing. This did mean that the resulting LX rig was more than a little 'unconventional' in places!

Our first show was called *Snakes and Ladders*. It was very simply a series of routines strung together with ethereal music and mystical-looking costumes. We played characters which evolved from our own personalities: myself, long, lean and fluid, moving slowly like a giant stick insect; my trapeze partner, short sharp and angular, her style was darting movements like a lizard on a hot rock. Lou lay across the top of the rig, sloth-like, dropping trapezes in and out, lazily coiling and uncoiling the ropes before dropping down and acting like a maniac; Ba on the ground passing fire clubs and equipment up to us in the air.

Up and down the rig,
up and down the ropes,
on and off the trapeze.
Slipping sliding dropping slithering,
we are on a giant games board.

We appeared at Glastonbury festival about eight times over the years. Everybody loved it. The booker for the circus field, Arabella Churchill, was a friendly yet forbidding character. She was extremely good at getting everyone to drop their price in the knowledge that it was the favourite booking of the season. We looked forward to going as a meeting place for performers as well as to see everybody else's shows. I made it to the pyramid stage once in all those years. I used to forget it was a music festival: for me the main action was in the circus field.

The build-up of excitement began on the approaching motorways, as we came across more and more hitch-hikers and interesting-looking vehicles. We would generally try to fit in some extra people for the last part of the journey. When my mum lived in Bristol we often spent the previous night with her or, having arrived back from the continent late at night, would park up outside the locked festival gates until morning.

There was a feeling of artists, travellers and friends coming together. I am afraid that we were not above smuggling in the odd friend, hidden underneath the caravan seats or in the back of the truck with the equipment. It was a slow passage in for the last few miles, and we had to arrive in time to get rigged before the festival started. But that did not seem to matter as we bumped into more and more friends.

Once we had played there a few times, I would greet the Site Manager of the Circus Field like an old friend and together we would sort out the best spot for us. Rigging at Glastonbury was a long drawn-out affair as every few minutes one member, or all members, would have to stop to greet a passing friend. It was sometimes a hard job for me to remind the team that we were there to work.

We were often on the other side of the hedge from the acoustic stage and we were surrounded by sound systems and shows. Sometimes, I fought my way through the crowds to the green field for some tranquillity. But generally I loved the buzz of being in the centre of all the activity. During the day, we sat around our enclosure watching different walkabout acts rambling past and seeing the punters have a go on the flying trapeze rig, which was next to us. I hardly needed to move in order to be entertained, unless there was a particular show that I wanted to see. The day started early when the sound systems woke us up and ended late after our midnight shows and a last stroll around. It was at this time of night that Glastonbury was at its best: fires lit everywhere, impromptu drumming and dancing as people got creative in the small hours.

There was a downside to Glastonbury: the toilets. So many people were using them that they would be full before the festival opened. After that it went from bad to worse. One year, the toilets collapsed into the pits and we heard that a woman had fallen in. A couple of years later, a new member of Skinning the Cat told us that she was that woman!

There were rainy years: one particular year, our arena became an island in the middle of a lake. All the shows were cancelled and people had to find alternative ways of entertaining themselves. A company member from our neighbouring show 'Le La Les' got his canoe out and paddled along the water-filled tractor trenches. He later balanced some chairs to quite a height on top of his truck and proceeded to play the trombone naked, while balancing on top of it all. I have a great photograph of him.

Ba, company technician – It had been raining pretty heavily in the week leading up to our arrival at Glastonbury, and was raining heavily when we arrived and throughout the building of the rig. The electricity was late being provided and it seemed like the whole weekend would be wet, wet, wet…. but, on the Friday the rain stopped, the sun came out and the site dried out a lot.

I had become addicted to a Shawn Colvin album that had been given to me by a friend of Lou's who stage-managed Shawn, and I used this tape as the pre-show music. It was happy and jiggy and did a really good job of attracting people over to the rig leading up to the show. By the time we were ready to start there was a massive audience gathered, huge actually, and by the end there was an even bigger audience. It was really exciting, they loved it. Afterwards lots of friends and relatives and other circus performers came back stage buzzing about the show and it was a really great feeling. Everything had come together, better costumes, better rig/set, better performances, better show really – with LX and sound rigs, showing it all off to its best.

After the show we all set off through a gap in a hedge to get to the temporary wooden bar, complete with fairy lights and grand piano! That was a good evening.

The last time I went to Glastonbury the magic was wearing off for me. They had erected a fence to keep out the travellers, which made for a very different festival. Only people who could afford it got in, which kept out many of the artists who had made it the great creative festival that it was. As I got increasingly burned out from touring, I found that Glastonbury felt too much for me. The full-on surround sound, the hundreds of friends, thousands of punters, mud, toilet squalor.... I began to feel claustrophobic and, whenever I had time, I would fight my way out of the central area to the peace of the green field area.

CHAPTER 16

Berlin

> **Splicing** – is the term which describes the joining of pieces of rope in order to create a loop, a join, an eye in which to insert metal thimbles, or simply to make a neat end to a rope. A splice is formed by partly untwisting the strands and then interweaving them back into the main rope.

It was during our first summer season that we received a letter from two German girls, Tanya and Freida. Another aerialist had recommended us to teach them some doubles trapeze. This was at a time when circus schools were few and far between and it was more normal to learn with another artist, as I had done myself. We wrote back to say that would be fine but they would have to follow us round our bookings and learn in between shows.

Tanya and Frieda were excellent gymnasts who already had some aerial skills, so teaching them was rewarding and fun. They helped out a lot and we all became good friends. In many ways they encapsulate my happy memories of the early days. We all had youth, energy and passion; we didn't have so much work and the show was in its infancy; we had the time to experiment and discuss trapeze moves and creative ideas for the show. We came up with some good stuff as well as plenty of wild ideas, which turned out to be completely impractical but were fun at the time. It was all part of bonding and growing as a group and, in the hectic years that followed, it seemed like a special, innocent time. We didn't earn much but we didn't spend much; we had casual staff (I think we gave them about £20 a show). We were all happy just to be doing it.

The following winter, Tanya and Frieda invited us to stay with them in Berlin where they now had their own training space. My trapeze partner and I, along with my boyfriend, and part-time company member, Hilda, all decided to go. By pure coincidence, the week before we went the Berlin wall came down and we found ourselves in the most exciting and desirable place in Europe. It was a wonderful experience. We walked around the wall, and collected souvenir pieces. Seeing it in ruins and watching the crowds of people crossing from East Germany, I felt like a part of history.

It was different for the Germans of West Berlin. They suddenly found their city invaded by East Berliners and were not completely happy about this. You could spot an East Berliner a mile off: footballers' hairstyles and clothes which were very old-fashioned compared to those of the trendy West Berliners, and all clutching their newly-purchased electrical items.

We went to huge flea markets where, in addition to the official stalls, people sold small wares placed on plastic bags on top of the ice and snow. All the people we met furnished and clothed their lives from such flea markets. Using old or salvaged items was normal for them and it created a very alternative, European look, a style I loved.

I found myself in a difficult position. Two of us stayed at Frieda's flat and two at Tanya's. My trapeze partner really wanted me to spend all my time with her. We were training on the trapeze together, so I prioritised her feelings and we stayed at Tanya's together. This really annoyed my boyfriend and I experienced for the first time the tug between relationship and trapeze that was to be a recurring theme in my life.

My relationships began to follow a pattern. Initially I would be put on a pedestal, everything about Skinning the Cat and my lifestyle would be cool and awe-inspiring. Slowly, resentment would set in: my life was full and busy; I was away a lot; I was passionate about what I did; I prioritised the work elements of my life above the personal; I could reverse a truck and caravan around a tight bend better than any man I knew. I could not stand it when men started to get clingy and I would back off.

Gradually, my relationships got shorter and shorter as I spotted the warning signs faster. I started to have casual relationships that never got too close. This worked just fine for many years, until I became burnt out by touring and started to yearn for stability and home. I had never planned anything ahead, except for the next show and the next tour – my personal life was on the back burner. People often asked me what I would do when I was too old to trapeze. That's a bit like asking a teenager how they plan to spend old age. It just doesn't figure, doesn't exist in the imagination. I could only see today.

CHAPTER 17

The Half Angel

The Half-Angel – is a drop from sitting on the bar. A brief moment of balance is required as one arm extends above the head and only one hand is holding the bar. A quick flip off backwards. The foot must change from pointed to flexed during the fall backwards, so that it catches around the velvet padding at the side of the trapeze. At the same time as falling, twist the body in a half turn so that the back is arched, the extended leg is hanging down straight almost in splits and the free arm is posing.

I was in my early twenties and believed myself to be invincible, never scared and full of contempt for newspaper reporters who always asked me: 'Aren't you scared of falling?'

It was during a show and my concentration was wandering. The fairground next to our pitch was so loud that, although our audience could hear our music, once up in the air I could hear the fairground clearly but my own music only faintly.

The music is very important for the beat and timing cues and also it helps me to become my aerial personality. I was feeling extremely wound up. Before I knew it, I had flipped myself off the trapeze backwards into a half angel drop, completely missed catching the side of the trapeze with my right foot and hurled myself twenty feet onto the hard ground.

I felt no initial pain, just extreme surprise to find myself on the ground so suddenly with all the audience holding their breath.

I re-climbed to the trapeze as fast as possible and finished the show.

This was in our early touring days when conditions were pretty rough. I slept a damp night in a leaking tent feeling increasingly traumatised.

In those days, we'd put up with pretty well any conditions just to get the work. We couldn't afford extra vehicles to tow caravans, so we camped, slept on people's floors in rows or, if we were lucky, stayed in cheap bed and breakfasts.

Ba, company technician – That B&B in Whitley Bay! It was like a train corridor sleeper section, like that scene in *Some Like it Hot* but without the curtains. Do you remember? 2 bunk beds head to foot, so small that only one person could really stand in the room at any one time and everyone else had to sit on their bed. I remember arriving late-ish and warming up our customary one pot slop that one of us would prepare on rotation. I think that night it was my dreadful fish slop and we covertly heated it up on a camping stove in the B&B, hoping it wouldn't set off the fire alarm.

We did a show the next day when it was extremely hot; afterwards, Lou went for a swim in the sea and returned with blue hair dye dripping down her face, I remember her joking about being a sea monster. Then we took the rig down and packed the van. The organisers couldn't believe that it had all fitted in, and there was still enough room for all 4 of us too! That was one neat pack! But we did have to draw straws for the back seats.

I had compacted my upper spine. From then on, in every country we visited I was frequently on the hunt for osteopaths. Although often I could not understand their language, I understood their meaning when they held up my x-rays to the light, sucked in their breath and tutted slowly and shook their heads before clunking me around a bit and sending me away. The problem with a touring lifestyle is that there is no continuity of medical care. You slip through the net as far as seeing specialists and general health checks are concerned. As a result, my compacted back injury was only crisis-managed.

I felt a terror that my bad back would stop me performing on the trapeze. That was all that mattered. Life revolved around this need to be on the trapeze. Common sense did not enter the equation. Following this fall, I found sometimes that I would experience random feelings of vertigo halfway through a routine.

The ground below me suddenly drops away,
the air around me changes and feels threatening.
My head feels light and my hands grope for something
solid to hold.

Mum recently sent me this poem that she wrote when she heard of my fall but didn't dare show me at the time. It makes me want to cry now when I think what I put her through. I would disappear for weeks on end and she had no way of finding out how or where I was: no website, mobile phones or e-mails, just the odd phone call from a foreign hotel.

AT DAYBREAK
The taste of her tears
Was bitter beyond bearing.
And all the dead women,
The ancestors, heard:

112

Yes, yes, we remember, remember.
The pain cracks our hearts;
Our cries tear the velvet night.
We know, know
What cold shadow awaits
The laughing girl
Swinging in the topmost branches.
All our remembering,
All our knowing,
All our love,
Cannot cradle her falling.

Jill Truman

CHAPTER 18

Manningham sports Centre

> *Corde Lisse* – the name given to a routine performed on a vertical rope. The beauty of the *corde lisse* is the simplicity of one single rope on which you can work, moving between the highest and lowest point on the rope. The rope can be wrapped around the body in an infinite combination of moves, rolled down, slid on or spun. There are no rules for it. My favourite type of rope for *corde lisse* is 3-strand, where the ridges of the strands can be used to hook into with the toes and fingers.

Although we were getting work all over Europe, it continued to be important to be based in Bradford. We always returned there for the winter. During these off-season months we would train and prepare the next season's tour, run local workshops and Christmas parties. The council ran Christmas events for children in the local sports centres, where we would perform for them and then hold a workshop for the children.

In Bradford, we became a bit of a novelty, whizzing around in our truck and doing shows. One year, Bradford Festival did a touring parks programme. That is, as well as events in the main venues, a smaller festival toured lesser-known parks and areas which were perhaps more deprived. We performed in five different parks on five consecutive days. That's five hours to put the rig up, one hour to install the soft rigging, two hours of show preparation, two shows, and then three or four hours to de-rig. As a result, everybody in Bradford saw our show but oh my god we nearly died!

From the very early days we always got a contribution of £500 from Bradford Council towards our running costs. However, the year that Barry Thorne became Lord Mayor was also the year that Linda became our first ever administrator. Finally, we didn't have to do every single thing ourselves. She started putting pressure on them to help us out more. We desperately needed another van, so a plan was put together to lobby the council for money. With the support of some council officers, we dressed up in our costumes and ambushed Barry in his office. Acorn Video, a local documentary company, put together an appeal video to show snippets of show footage interspersed with interviews in which we explained what unique ambassadors we were for Bradford and what great work we were doing with our schools' workshops.

Barry Thorne really became involved. We set up a publicity stunt in which he agreed to be dressed up as a Skinning the Cat member, strapped into a safety harness and hauled up on the trapeze for a press call. He was not a slight man and we could not fit him into our costumes, so I made him a feathery headdress. It took several of us on the end of the block and tackle to get him into the air. He really entered into the spirit of it. Following these efforts, the council came up with an annual sum of £10,000. This was the nearest that we ever got to financial security: it paid for our rehearsal costs, which we had previously managed on an annual overdraft.

Manningham Sports Centre was still a crucial part of our existence. They tolerated increasing amounts of aerial equipment in their roof space and only charged us the 35p entrance fee. It was the kind of sports centre that was open to whatever the local community wanted to do, so we were there every day when we weren't performing. We would run routines and try new moves, while underneath us were baton-twirlers and football matches. We were part of the scenery. It was normal for the footballers to look up and watch our antics while they waited to play. Nobody questioned it, and nobody ever mentioned health and safety.

The physical satisfaction of a good training session,
muscles stretched and tired,
dried sweat,
hands sticky with resin,
palms rough with callouses.
The whole body pumped up and elongated
so strongly and now so relaxed.
We lie exhausted on the crash mats under the rigging
discussing trapeze moves,
our love lives,
what we are going to cook for tea...

CHAPTER 19

Teething Problems

> **Wrist strap** – a long strip of cotton tape, approximately 2 cm wide and 50 cm long, wrapped firmly around each wrist of both catcher and flyer, then tucked into itself. Heavily covered in resin and never washed: the more impregnated the resin is, the more effective the grip. This enables the wrist-to-wrist grip to grip tape instead of sweaty, slippery skin.

My trapeze partner and I were living together, working together, socialising together and touring together; I suppose it was only a matter of time before something went wrong.

We had had many late-night conversations where she discussed all the damage the world had done to her. She had had a raw deal out of life. There wasn't one friend, boyfriend, employer or family member who hadn't wronged her terribly and I was horrified at what they had put her through. I understood why she felt damaged, and was determined not to be another person to hurt her.

I began to find that she had dark moods. As we got closer, they were increasingly aimed at me. The show was the greatest trigger because it was of my making and the costumes were mine – these earned a lot of praise. I began to dread the time immediately after a show, when people would come backstage and praise things that I had made or conceived. As people repeated, over and over again: 'I love the costumes', her face would blacken.

She told me that I was taking all the glory. So I slowly withdrew. She would become furious when I spoke to people, especially men. She told me that I was pushing myself forward at her expense. I began to fear speaking. I dreaded the moods, the sulking, and the efforts that I had to make to get back in the good books. Every time she threw a mood, I would tiptoe around, creeping and crawling, until she had punished me enough. It was horrible, but as I believed so deeply that I was bad, I completely agreed that everything was my fault. I was pushy, I was arrogant, I grabbed all the attention, I didn't let her follow her dreams, I flirted with all the men...

This was not the first or the last time that some of these criticisms were made of me. And over the years I have learned from this and, I hope, now give other people more space. But, at that time, I was the one with the vision that had made a show which was becoming increasingly successful. I was bright (literally: I dressed like a rainbow) and extrovert. It was my energy, drive and artistic arrogance that had made Skinning the Cat a reality.

Our relationship became destructive for both of us. I became unhappy: living the dream but not enjoying it. I was consumed with guilt and confusion. I was torn between keeping her trust, and desperation to get free and be myself again. But that would make me the next person to damage her.

I had been to Paris for a week, visiting my Spanish acrobat boyfriend, Salvador. Being away for a week made me realise that I just had to get out of this situation. But still I didn't want to hurt her. Things had got so bad between us that she was not training with me and the last show had felt dangerous. I returned, having decided to walk away from Skinning the Cat and leave her to it. I would start another project and be happy.

But I hadn't reckoned with the rest of the company, which by then had become a strong team. Lou, Ba, Linda, and stage manager Jo. Linda had changed the organisational face of Skinning the Cat and we could not risk losing her. On my return, I found that Linda was also unhappy about the way this member was treating her and she, being older and wiser than me, wasn't having any of it: she was threatening to leave. When we finally discussed the situation openly, I discovered that Ba was also having a hard time. In a small company, it takes only one person who doesn't fit in and everyone's life is a misery. We called an emergency meeting and discussed the problem, asking her to leave. I was massively relieved but also guilt-ridden, as I knew that we were repeating the pattern of her life. It was very nasty and I was mainly blamed.

Ba, company technician – I could probably list a hundred reasons why I think this happened, holding my hands up to a hundred crimes and blaming other people for a hundred more, but it would only be supposition. She never shared with me what had led to the breakdown in our friendship, or what had made her so unhappy and cross. Initially I was starting to feel isolated, until talking to you it was a great relief when the bubble burst. The situation made both you and I – and probably herself – pretty miserable.

That Cardiff show was the final straw. The atmosphere in the van was horrible, the atmosphere building up the rig was horrible and the atmosphere leading up to the show was horrible. The show was really dreadful, she was only just making it round on her flips, looked to be quite unfit and a little too heavy and, as you and she weren't talking at all, I can only wonder what it was like for both of you doing that doubles routine!

I was scared for her in that show, I wasn't in the company when you had that fall from the trapeze but it stuck in my mind, and I was scared that there would be a really nasty accident. I was constantly evaluating whether we should stop the show. Afterwards, this fear turned to embarrassment as people had paid good money for us to perform and it was a pretty poor standard. I do remember everyone ending up in four separate corners at the end of the day and a lot of tears.

It was really emotional... it was so obvious that she was not fit enough to do the show and didn't seem to like any of us. It was totally clear that we couldn't continue.

We had the meeting at your house. I think it was just the four of us. You and I did most of the talking and generally it was a very civilised meeting as I recall, tense, a bit grumpy but very civilised. I know we talked about the fitness issue and she was openly relieved, saying she didn't think she was up to it. We did also say that our personal relationships were making us miserable and that we couldn't see how we could carry on. I think we said there were two options: she could have Skinning the Cat without us, or she could leave.

Once the decision was made that she would leave we carried on talking for quite a while, more amicable than we had been for some time. Maybe I was naïve, because I was actually really surprised to find out the following day that we were public enemy number 1. It was never going be easy for her to hear what we said and I don't believe we were bad, but I do understand that she may have needed to think that we were bad.

I learned a lot of things from this experience, not all good. Afterwards, I never got too close to my trapeze partners again, but would move between about three different flyers for different types of work. Also, I did not want to have a business partner again. I never again wanted to feel that I could not control the destiny of my work and that guilt might lead me to have to walk away from it. We were a team but I was very firmly the leader. We always interviewed new members carefully, but I realised that people say what you want to hear in an interview. Subsequently, we did make the odd misjudgement about company members, but they would be on seasonal contracts, so if they had a problem with me or just did not fit into the team I didn't renew their contract.

There is no ideal situation. As the boss in a small team that could be touring abroad for months on end, I often felt isolated, and in some instances ganged-up against. But, in spite of the grief these situations caused me, I preferred it to the utter misery of living in a dysfunctional relationship

I have the odd dream about her: in one, I find that she has managed to get back into the company without my noticing and I suddenly realise with horror that I must walk on eggshells forever. In another, I recognise the friendship that we had and we talk through what happened and manage to move on from the guilt – we are both so happy to be friends again.

CHAPTER 20

The Hate Campaign

> **Contemporary Circus** – uses traditional circus skills to convey a story or theme. Developed in the late 20th century, this approach tends to focus more attention on character and story development, and on the use of lighting design, original music, and costume design.

This all came to a head right at the beginning of our second tour. We had a lot of work coming up. Knowing it was the end-of-term show at the small circus school in Bristol, I raced down to watch the show in the hope of finding a new company member. Mum came with me and we both immediately spotted Lucie. She stood out from among the other students, both for her level of skill and her stage presence. I approached her after the show and before she knew it, she was in Bradford, rehearsing in Manningham Sports Centre.

We often gave trapeze lessons to would-be professionals or people who just wanted to try something different. One of these participants offered to help out on tour as a volunteer and, as this had worked well with art college students on placement, I gladly accepted the offer. She didn't fit in with the group and parted company from us pretty crossly when we wouldn't allow her a part in the show. It was a brief arrangement which had not worked out and I would not have thought any more about it except that, unfortunately for me, she teamed up with my still-fuming former trapeze partner.

Both considering themselves to have been victimised by me, they formed what they called a 'hate campaign'. They gathered together a gang of friends who sat drinking beer and jeering at us all day as we rigged in Bradford's Lister Park and then stood in the front row during the show, laughing and shouting. The strain that this put me under while rigging and performing made me feel ill. For the next two weeks, I had to lie down in the caravan between shows, feeling weak and sick from stress.

I heard reports of this gang over the next couple of years. The worst time was when I found a drawing attached to my rigging, of a cat hanging from a noose with its guts spilling out. The caption read 'There's more than one way to...' I understood it as a real safety threat and we always checked our rigging carefully when they were around. I have wondered since why I did not just call security and have them removed. It was all tied up with guilt. This horrible experience added to my childhood feeling of badness and has influenced my trust and decisions about how and with whom I work.

I get fixated on a point in time that has traumatized me. In the pit of my stomach I feel like I have done something so bad. Grandpa? Dad? The hate campaign? Relationships with people scare me; however right I think I am – I am still wrong.

'The dreadful thing' is going to happen,
it wakes me in the night,
it is in my dreams,
it is there in the morning when I wake up.
What is wrong with me?
Why do I let this stuff happen?
It is all my fault.
I am not a monster.

This was the first time that I had actually felt ill from extreme stress. I was quite frightened by it and went to the doctor to have tests done on my general health. I had decided that I had some awful disease as I didn't see how the extreme weakness that I was experiencing could be caused merely by upset. This was the beginning of a slow deterioration in my health. Tests showed that I was low in iron and B12, but unfortunately there were no further explorations. I recovered and put it behind me with no real explanation, although the doctor had said that I was artistic and lots of artists suffered from stress, which is why they so often turn to drugs or alcohol. Over the next few years, I seemed to get stomach upsets and colds more often and for longer than everyone else. I started to accept this as just something that I had to live with.

I had come up with the vision of Skinning the Cat out of my own imagination. At the time I started there were no other narrative-based aerial shows in the UK, and nothing in the same style. There was a small movement, of which we felt part, initially known as 'new circus'. It later became 'contemporary circus'. It was mainly jugglers and a few aerialists, but no aerial groups. Contemporary circus brought a new wave of people, from all levels of society, into the circus industry. Circus began emerging in schools, sports centres and parks. Now anyone could learn circus skills and some became professional, bringing new methods and ideas to the culture. Circus has always appeared as part of theatre and dance, but contemporary circus artists have developed new styles and added and extended to other art forms through circus skills. When we started working on the continent, I realised that the UK was way behind the rest of Europe, where all circus and outdoor art forms crossed with visual art, puppetry, physical and outdoor theatre to produce a style of performance which was energetic, exciting and fresh. There was no distinction between contemporary or traditional circus.

I found that each country had its own style. The French and Spanish specialise in anarchy, creating companies like Archaos, Malabar and Royale Deluxe. These shows were wild and exciting, using circus skills in a way that we had never dreamt of. The Dutch and Germans are very inventive, creating more organised, cleaner work with a high skill level, and often using vintage circus and the beautiful old-fashioned fairground style, like Circus Gosh and Circus Roncali.

I was in awe of some of these companies. There were plenty of good shows and talent but, luckily for us, Skinning the Cat was quite different from any of those. I think that we were gentler, more mystical and, of course, though I say it myself, our costumes were second to none! I had conceived us in isolation. Perhaps we started an English style. I have noticed many similar UK aerial companies starting up since. I considered Skinning the Cat to be an art form, as are all circus acts.

The overheads of running a touring company, especially one with high technical specifications, are enormous. We were top-bracket insurance, together with steeplejacks and deep sea divers. Even our driving insurance was astronomical, because of the show biz lifestyle we were assumed to be leading. The work that we did just about covered our overheads but, like many arts companies, we were looking for funding to help us develop.

We were unable to get funding from the Arts Council as we were not recognised as an art form. At that time, they considered all circus as purely 'entertainment'. We spent weeks on a grant application and made a trip to visit them in London, only to be told that there was not a department into which we fitted. This was very disheartening, as we saw other arts companies in Bradford that had started about the same time as us, become regularly-funded organisations. While I believe that any type of company should be able to earn its own living, we needed help to produce the original artistic product.

We had got our first break on the continent when our agent Shirley got us a trial show in Gelsenkirchen with a big German agent, Achim Rhode. He loved our work and booked us for the following year for a major tour. The problem with this tour was that, never having done anything on this scale, we had no idea how to schedule the shows, the rigging and the travelling to actually include time for sleep. We accepted Achim's plan and it turned out to be gruelling. One booking actually had to be cancelled at the last minute because getting there in time was a physical impossibility.

The problem was made worse as Ba had terrible problems with her knees. She was the technician, so the show was not affected. But trying to relieve her of some of her share of rigging and van loading work put us all under strain. Ba also, of course, was upset and worried. We were not able to access medical help and she sat around getting depressed and smoking too much.

On this tour we were sharing the bill with an Australian company called 'Stalker Stilt Theatre'. They were an extremely efficient organisation that found the time to do yoga and meditation in their hotel rooms while we were still rigging. We got into a touring rhythm with them and particularly befriended a half Dutch, half Spanish musician from Amsterdam called Pino.

Pino, Spanish drummer friend – There was never a dull moment with The Girls. I became very fond of them all, always happy to see each other where ever we met on our tours. Becky and Lou the big heart of Skinning the Cat, we became friends in a drumbeat. I had great admiration for them, as it was hard work on and off stage, the amount of physical rigging and de-rigging they had to do blew my mind every time. Wind, rain or sun there they were!

I lived in the heart of Amsterdam so when the girls where having a few days off and were in the neighbourhood they came to visit and then we went wandering the streets. I lived in the 4711 factory at the Frans Halsstraat near the Albert Cuyp market. Sometimes we started off there; it was a great market, a heaven for Becky to find the right material, for the ever-so-fabulous costumes she designed herself. Just walking and talking and laughing all at the same time, five, six or sometimes seven women all chatty and giddy we did sometimes cause a short traffic jam.

Working in Germany is a very efficient experience. Their favourite phrase, used so often that it began to make us all laugh, is 'alles klaar'. This phrase, spoken so confidently, encapsulated how very organised they were. You would never catch a Spanish performer or event's organiser expressing this feeling. I really loved being part of their cultural network, going from one event to another. There is great respect for circus and the performing arts in Germany, which is reflected by the financial input of each city. Even the tiniest village has a programme of summer events, paid for by the town hall. We often played in the central market place or park, where the whole area would be decorated with bunting and fancy lamppost covers, banners and flags. There was always a street market, and of course, the event always ended with a cover band and a good German beer festival. We did many a de-rig to the sound of Beatles tribute bands, surrounded by cheery drunken Germans.

These ersatz Beatles were very popular in Germany. They did a pretty good impression on stage with mannerisms and haircuts to match. Off stage, they looked a bit odd with their Beatles 'look'. One group came to a party in our caravan, and we were horrified to discover that they called each other by their Beatles names offstage. They also seemed to expect the adoration that the real Beatles had attracted. I am afraid that afterwards they were the butt of a few jokes!

Joking and messing around was hugely important. It helped us cope with the intensity of being together and the exhausting workload. We gave every single object we worked with a name which was funny only to us. For example, our tape measure, given to us by agent Achim, was called 'Achim's granny'. I can't remember why, but it will have been funny at the time. This made it difficult for the casual staff who were provided by the booker to help us with the workload: they never knew what we were talking about. We must have been highly irritating. I'm sure this is normal: if we had carried on working together forever we would have developed a whole new language.

My favourite German Festival was Augsburg. It is a small town, just outside Munich, which has a long and diverse summer arts programme. We made such good friends amongst the staff that we would stop off whenever we were in the area and, often, our good friends Thomas and Günther would come to visit when they heard that we were in Germany.

It was in Augsburg that I had my only terrifying experience of the rig falling. When a rig is being winched up or down it is as vulnerable as a large piece of tissue paper in the wind – but heavier, if it fell on your head. It was during pull-down that I failed to notice that one of the side cables had become caught in a nearby tree. As I continued to lower, one side of the rig stayed static and the whole thing tipped off the props. As it fell it twisted, ripped apart in two places, and crashed to the ground, followed by the heavy steel props. This rig was our livelihood. Without it, we were nothing. It was an extremely expensive piece of equipment and not easily replaced. We had a big tour to do and we needed to earn the money.

We dismantled the rig and found that, apart from the two sections which had ripped clean through, it was amazingly undamaged. Thomas, who knew all the local tradesmen, drove me around with the injured bits of rig and found the right welders who did a beautiful job for us, extremely cheaply. We went on our way shaken but none the worse for wear.

> **Thomas, German technician friend** – At the end of the festival, the rig fell down. This was a big shock for you all. Apparently it was the first time something like this happened to you. You felt more responsible than all the others. The first time I saw you in a situation of stress, you took things on your own shoulders as if it was only your mistakes, which was not true.
>
> I followed you around all those years, there was Kehl, Nürnberg and Meiningen. One time when you had to travel overnight, I came and drove the truck for you. Claire did not trust me driving and stayed up all the night while the others were sleeping in the back. Ulm, and a little festival along the River Donau, Manchester with the burnt caravan and the South of France, the holiday place for you circus people. Everything was a bit temporary, but this was exactly what you were used to.

Thomas became my German boyfriend. He was lovely, far too nice to be treated so casually by me. He was my boyfriend when I was in Germany. To me that was simple. He bore it well. Not only did he have to put up with my comings and goings but I would generally bring the whole gang with me, using his flat as a base between shows to fix equipment, sleep and socialise.

I know that he loved us all and we became part of his social network and his family too.

It was typical of Claire to sit up with Thomas to make sure he drove safely. She was a highly responsible member of the company and a great support to me. Claire had English parents but had been brought up in France in an amazing alternative community. The heart of the community was her mum's sisters and their children. Claire's family had built their homes from derelict farm cottages which were up a steep hill in some woods in the Ariège, only accessible by foot. We stayed there a couple of times on our travels and had an insight into Claire's childhood with her welcoming and extended family.

One of Claire's cousins was working in Germany and we were invited to stay at the same place as him. This turned out to be the home and music studio of a man called Michael Jackson. He called himself Mick and wasn't actually 'the' Michael Jackson but was a successful song writer/record producer. Bizarrely, he had written the Michael Jackson hit 'Don't blame it on the Sunshine'. He had sung it himself initially and it was a minor hit before he let it go to the famous pop star.

Mick turned into a good friend and we stayed there quite a few times. This was when the fame of the Spice Girls was at its peak and Mick had decided to try and produce a girl band of his own. Impressed by how I managed my own group of women, he offered me a job getting his group into shape. It sounded like a bit of fun and certainly a change. But I was completely dedicated to Skinning the Cat and couldn't see how I could do both. I have no idea what happened to his band.

CHAPTER 21

Driving

> **The Cradle** – A piece of equipment that is tensioned – as opposed to swinging – so that the catcher's body swings from their knees like a hinge and the flyer jumps on and off the catcher from standing on top of the cradle, rather than from a trapeze. The problem for the catcher is that the knee joints are constantly under terrible strain.

The nomadic life suited me well and we repeatedly travelled certain routes that I loved. I couldn't get enough of roaming around Europe, each country with its different atmosphere, smells, scenery, language and culture. My favourite journeys always involved mountains. Switzerland, where even the landscape looks luxurious and wealthy: driving our dusty and travel-weary convoy between lushly green, steep slopes, the mountains look as though they have been planned by an architect, so beautifully triangulated and coiffured. Along well-maintained motorways we were led through gently curving tunnels which seem to go on forever.

France: long straight roads flanked elegantly with well-spaced trees provide cool rest from the heat. The Pyrenees, where France turns into Spain: the green of the French side turning into the arid, brown Spanish landscape. No tunnels here, so the trucks often overheated as they struggled to tow the trailers up and down the steep inclines.

Even the service stations felt completely different. In France, they were air-conditioned, clean and efficient, in Spain hotter, rougher and more than likely staffed by one man who might also be running a slightly grubby tapas bar. We knew certain routes intimately: which Belgian roads had deep tyre ruts that made the caravan weave; which of the service stations had showers; how to plan to reach the Paris Périphérique at night to avoid the traffic jams.

Journeys were harder work once Lou's son Henri was born. He would be lulled to sleep by the engine but would often wake if someone needed a toilet stop. When we were driving in the van behind his vehicle, we tried to hold our bladders for as long as possible, knowing that once we all stopped, the people in the cab with Henri would be condemned to playing 'I'll drop it and you pick it up' for the next few hours. Lou loved driving, and even more so once Henri was born. She said it gave her a break from him, but of course when he slept in the truck all day he would be awake all night!

My favourite times during a driving day were mealtimes. As the journeys got longer, frequently down as far as Portugal, we developed more and more extravagant snacks to relieve the boredom. Helen, who became our technician after Ba's knees failed completely, was my favourite co-driver. About eleven o'clock in the morning, she would pass me a banana and after each bite I would pass it back to her, so that she could re-apply a dollop of chocolate spread for the next bite.

I first met Helen when I was performing at Leeds City Varieties, where she was crewing. It is unusual to meet a female crew member at a theatre who also knows about teching, especially one that you get on with. Long black hair, heavy black eyeliner, slightly gothy-looking and always dressed in black, as all technicians are. Helen had never worked in circus before but seemed keen to take on the challenge. She has an incredible memory for dates, names, events and times which often all merge together for me into a general memory mush. The other thing that stands out to me about Helen's character is her sense of ownership and loyalty. Once she is part of a group, friendship or show she takes it on completely, always referring to 'we' and becoming completely involved in everyone's lives.

At lunchtimes, I would shout through the hatch with a long order of contents for my sandwich, which I had been planning since banana break: perhaps Marmite, smoked cheese, mayonnaise, lettuce, tomato, avocado and vegetarian salami on German black bread. When you drive from nine in the morning until midnight you run out of things to think about.

We had a cassette player in the truck, although we often struggled to hear the music over the roar of the engine. The cassettes got a real bashing, and all our favourites died eventually from engine heat or getting snarled up in the cheap tape player. But, as we all brought our favourite mixes along, we got to know lots of different music. Often the tapes weren't marked, so there are many songs to which I know all the words but am not sure who's playing the music.

Helen read book after book, having ordered a whole series from her book club before we went away. I could never read for long in the van, it made me feel sick. I would enjoy the rare stretches of personal headspace that travelling time offers. I did all my best planning, dreaming and scheming: about the clothes I was going to make for myself when I had time, the characters and their costumes for the new show, new trapeze moves and routines, and romantic fantasies about relationships.

If I love a book I will read it over and over again. The Narnia books were important to my childhood fantasies, and I felt their effect into adulthood. I especially loved the ones that involved a journey. *The Voyage of the Dawn Treader* was my favourite, and *Prince Caspian,* when they are walking across Narnia.

Stories are crucial for feeding my imagination. I hear a story and immediately see it visually, as pictures or action for a show. The characters I read about feed into characters that I meet and I extend them into the realms of my imagination. Helen and I would often look at each other as we drove through mountainous landscapes far from home and say 'further up and further in', which is a quote from the Narnia books. This line captures the feeling of excitement and adventure that travelling gave me. When I am walking in the mountains, I am not just out for that particular walk, I am scrambling down a steep incline of scrubby bushes and rocks, grabbing onto plants to stop myself falling into the valley which contains a sleeping dragon guarding his gold treasures, seeing in my mind's eye an illustration in *The Voyage of the Dawn Treader* that always makes me feel like this.

One year when the tour dates were slow in coming in, I got very low, taking it personally of course with a sense of failure. In reality there were often external reasons that affected our bookings: post year 2000 slump, recession, the World Cup... Anyway, we had huge gaps in the tour schedule that I couldn't fill despite my best efforts. Still at home, I retreated to an old comfort zone and re-read the whole of the Narnia series. I needed to re-establish the magic in my life, getting back to the roots of my need for adventure.

During one ten-day gap that I had desperately tried to fill, we headed for the nearest circus park-up in Paris. I had some great chats with the proprietor of the big top, who taught me some good rigging techniques. It felt great and reminded me that my life was not just about being successful and cramming it with tour dates to earn money: it was about the bits in between and the experiences we had when we got the space.

Administrator Jan was sharing the worry about money with me, so I rang her on a local payphone, pumping in change when the beeps kept going, I tried to explain that it was all right, and the experience was more important than the money. I have no idea if, stuck in the office on her own worrying about paying the bills, this was the helpful phone call that it was meant to be.

The evening meal would be the best, because we would actually stop to cook and stretch our legs. If I wasn't driving after dinner, I could also enjoy a gin and tonic from our bar. I remember experiencing one of those pure happiness moments one driving day: we had pulled up at a truck stop in Spain and Rachel, our resident Rock Chick – due to her general behaviour, clothing and hair style – had put Nirvana loudly on the player. I was standing by the open truck door swigging beer and looking generally wild, and feeling 'Right, this is where I want to be, this is what I want to be doing and these are the people I want to be doing it with.' It is a memory snapshot I will never forget.

By the time we stopped to park up at midnight, people would be feeling cramped and crabby. The business of preparing for our night stop, downing caravan legs and converting tables and sofas into beds, could not happen fast enough. Finding a favourite space to sleep was the nearest we got to personal space on a driving day: Claire preferred to make a bed in the truck cab, just to be alone. Usually, we simply parked up in a truckers' car park wherever we found ourselves. On the continent this is normal: there are no signs saying No Overnight Parking; showers, toilets and cafés are provided. Much more civilised than the UK. Our trucks, with 'Skinning the Cat' painted on the side, would of course be the truck-stop novelty, but we were used to that. Whenever I smell stale pee I am transported back to those trucker's park-ups.

It was always a problem organising a tour so that we could get from *a* to *b* in time. One year, we had initially turned down the offer of some work in Italy, as it involved driving across Europe through the night and getting no sleep. We had stopped doing that because it made the shows too risky. The Italian agent was very persuasive and suggested that she could find a driver for one of our vehicles, our stage manager could drive the other one, and the performers could take an overnight train with a couchette. The plan was extremely successful and our Italian driver, Osvaldo, soon became a regular team member, allowing us to take on extra work. Every time an overnight journey was involved we'd contact 'Os' to tell him which country to meet us in. He was a great character, a tiny Italian man amongst a gang of Amazons.

It was always difficult to get everyone moving in the morning on travelling days. We would be a bit brain-dead from driving the day before and I would get frustrated with the amount of time it took us to get on the road. This was always hardest with new members who didn't understand our tight domestic system. Australian Zoe would sit on her bed for ages with clothes everywhere, unable to decide what to wear. Jackie wandering off for a lengthy and invigorating shower in the service station without packing her bed away first, when you can't set up the table for breakfast in a caravan until the beds are packed away. This all sounds petty, but multiply it by seven and add a baby into the equation and we would be late to start rigging – which meant skipping on technicalities pre-show, which meant potential danger, as the one immoveable time is show time. As a result I would start worrying about everyone's safety as soon as they started their ablutions for the day!

For the first few years of our European touring, there was a system for moving goods around, called Carnet. It was a complete nightmare: we had to know our routes in advance so that we had the correct paperwork to be stamped at each border. Sometimes it was difficult to convince Border Control that we were not importing and exporting goods. This was not only time-consuming but meant there was no option to change routes or fit in last-minute bookings. The main responsibility for this fell to our tour manager, Jo, who would disappear into the control office for ages while they interrogated her about the goods we were carrying, in languages she didn't speak. I think she often got the papers stamped only through a mixture of charm and the fact that they did not know what else to do with us!

When we had more than one night to spare, we would stop over with a circus. Once, when we were sleeping outside a Big Top in the outskirts of Paris, Lou took Henri to the doctor, as a mosquito bite on his ear had gone septic. She was a bit upset because the doctor told her off about Henri's finger nails being so dirty.

Cleanliness was not always easy on site and on the road. That same night, our technician and I, in bed in the little yellow caravan, found it impossible to sleep because of the number of noisy, biting mosquitoes flying around our heads. We decided to pitch a little tent and seal ourselves up in it before they had a chance to get in. We had installed ourselves with all our bedding and were just settling down to get some sleep, when some rats came sniffing around the tent. We were back in the caravan with the mosquitoes like a shot.

Depending on the nature of the booking, we might be supplied with hotel accommodation. We always carried the trunk containing the costumes, which looked like a large coffin, into hotels. This was because the costumes and the rig (which had once been stolen for its value as scrap aluminium) were the two things that were most individual to us and hardest to replace.

Dusty tells a funny story about lying in bed with Lou one night after we had returned home late. The costumes were parked up outside her house in the van. I rang them at some ridiculous hour to say that I couldn't sleep because we had forgotten to take the costumes out of the van. Dusty says that, instead of cursing me for my neurotic behaviour, Lou jumped out of bed to go and get the costumes, exclaiming 'Oh, poor Becky!' She was great. No one in Manningham actually wanted a load of smelly costumes, but it was not many years later that the vehicles in that street were burnt out in the riots.

I was constantly on edge in case the rig was stolen again for scrap metal. Once we were staying in a flat in central Paris and the rig was strapped to the roof of the truck. Two of us decided to sleep the night in the caravan, and I fastened a chain round the rig with a large padlock, with the other end dangling through the skylight of the caravan. If anyone had tampered with the rig, the rattling of the chain would have woken me. It was a life without any insurance. We had to live on our wits.

> **Ba, company technician** – It was a tight turn around, two one-nighters back to back: one in central Germany, one in Morlaix, France. The only way to pull it off was to drive two-thirds of the way overnight, then get up very early the following morning and do the last haul hopefully in time to put up the rig and do a show for that evening. We hit Paris very late and there was so much traffic. I remember us musing whether it was the Tour de France, had there had been an accident, or was it just some really bad road works. We queued for an eternity

and then suddenly the traffic started moving and we passed out of Paris with no sign of any of the above.

Anyway, we pushed on to approximately half way between Paris and Morlaix and started to look for somewhere we could park up for the night. Jo was driving and saw a country road that she thought was a likely candidate, so we drove down this track for a short while then stopped. It was a truly spooky spot, we could hear large dogs barking in the distance, obviously straining on chains or held in a compound. They sounded pretty ferocious.

I remember having really freaky feelings and a Hammer House of Horror image in my head. Every time I went round to the rear of the van to get something for the camp, I expected to return and find someone missing as if we were being picked off by some unseen assailant one… by… one. I didn't say anything that evening, and we all pretty quickly laid the camp, got in our sleeping bags and I for one fell asleep immediately.

We woke up to a gloriously sunny morning to find that our makeshift camp site was in a graveyard that we hadn't been able to see in the night, but we had sensed it was there. The next day we chatted about it and you said that you had felt almost exactly the same as I did. Next to the graveyard was the most amazing field of sunflowers all saluting the morning glory. Lou took a photo of you, Lucie, Jo and me, with our faces turned to the sun amongst the sunflowers. Priceless.

Arriving brain-numbed and stiff after a long drive, we would generally get lost finding the site. Owing to driving round one-way systems which weren't marked on the map, or just our inability to read foreign signs, we would be late to meet the on-site manager. I came to never trust directions from people who said 'you can't miss it'. In general, we would be made welcome and formed a friendly bond with the promoter and the team of helpers who were provided for us.

CHAPTER 22

Rigging

> **Pull-up** – when the whole rig with its props, cables and stakes has been laid out correctly on the ground, it is pulled up to vertical using a Tirfor, a winching device which moves the cable through self-gripping jaws and allows one person to lift several tons in weight.

On arrival on-site, the first job is to decide on the position of the rig: checking the slope and evenness of the ground; no power lines overhead to cause obstruction; no tree branches where cables might get caught; no gas pipes or electrical supply lines under the ground – this last often involved extensive wandering around with site plans and council men scratching their heads. Using our pre-measured lengths of string and scruffy old tape measure (Achim's granny) Helen and I would mark out the line of the rig and the staking points. The barrier had to be set up, to protect the public from our working area and to give us a sense of ownership of our space. No-one can really get started until all this is done.

Then the rest of the gang would change into rigging boots and work clothes. Being a bunch of female performers, all with individual styles, this involved an eclectic assortment of coloured overalls and differently-patterned boots.

Steel toe-capped and heavy,
pulling on my rigger boots I feel strong.

The smell of the rigging,
oil from shackles on my hands and musty rope smell in
my nostrils.
I stomp around coiling and uncoiling,
clanging piles of metalwork, pulleys, cables and swivels.
Measuring for staking points,
looking up to consider angles for tensioning lines and
examining fixing points.

I feel confident and in control of my environment.
Nobody can get this quite as right as me,
Nobody can tell me what to do,
this is my life on the line,
I am in charge.

We stored most equipment in metal ammunition trunks bought from the army surplus stores. Lightweight flight cases on wheels would have been more appropriate but were too expensive. Ammo trunks were strong and heavy and, once emptied of equipment, had many uses, such as propping up bits of rig, as steps up to a rostrum during a show, or simply as seats. The only drawback, apart from their weight, was that they would rust up a bit when we packed up in the rain. We also sported a bunch of old suitcases bought from Oxfam. These all acquired different names, ranging from 'the 'rigging suitcase' to 'that big bastard'.

After unloading the equipment and laying out the rig in place, this large metal structure had to be bolted together. I found this job extremely boring and always ensured that I had something 'more important' to do. All the cables, which are attached to the structure, had to be unrolled and the long webbings shackled on and laid out. The most important cable was the control pull-up, which went through a Tirfor: that works like a winch but is more controlled and slow. I operated it with a scaffolding pole lever and shouted orders to everyone holding support cables to keep the rig level as it went up. This central pull-up cable passed through a high scaffolding prop, called a goat, which falls down when the cable lifts out of it once the rig gets to about two-thirds of the way up.

The tea station had to be set up as soon as we could access the trestle table. It had a very important role during the eight hours rigging time. Everyone had different tastes, ranging from decaf tea with goats' milk, to very strong tea with one sugar and a tiny splash of cow's milk or very weak tea with loads of soya milk. Making a round of tea became so complicated that it was much easier to get a big pump flask of hot water so people could help themselves. Though we did like to make new members make a round, just to see them suffer!

When we reached the point at which all was ready for pull-up, someone would lay out the trestle table with lunch, and we would take a re-fuelling break. If I didn't eat before pull-up it would take me longer to tension the rig correctly. I never could think straight on an empty stomach. Pulling up the rig never ceased to be nerve-racking. A rig is only strong once it is precisely upright and tensioned off. On its way up, there is eight to fifteen metres of unwieldy metal structure propped in the middle by scaffolding. If one person on a side cable pulls too enthusiastically the whole thing can slip. The others would start unloading the stage while I went round the rig with a spirit level, tweaking and tightening the ratchets, click by click, until I was sure that it was safe to work on. I was proud of my expertise.

I have learnt to design and install rigging through experience. I think that once something interests you and is necessary to your life, you take every opportunity to learn about it. I had become so interested in rigging that I almost preferred to watch a company set up a show than perform it. In circus and outdoor theatre, people create some extremely innovative props and equipment. I was always keen to see how these worked and found people very helpful in explaining their systems to me. I watched, copied and re-invented techniques, often more by trial and error than anything else.

Then we split into teams: the stage, the props, the soft rigging. Everyone did their jobs like clockwork. Backstage would be set up, the dressing-room caravan towed into place, the truck was driven between the cables so the backdrop could be hung from it. We took turns cooking an early evening meal, although our favourite cooks would get pressurised into cooking more frequently. We operated within this space as precisely as people do in their homes: everything had its place and everything had its time span. In warm weather, we would eat outside around the trestle table. In wet and windy weather, we would squash round the caravan table, climbing over each other to reach stuff.

Thomas, German technician friend – My first impression with you was amazing, incredible, beautiful, or maybe just strange-appearing women, with sport clothes that had a lot of holes. You were like a street gang, there was this energy, the vagabonds that make a place feel home once they have set up their stuff. Everything had to be exactly the way you wanted it, you were the pros that just needed a helping hand. I felt quite insecure, with all your self-confidence.

You guided the audience into a different world that was fascinating. A world that was very much a reality, that you lived even after the show. People felt that. I think in the end there was a dream they took with them, for the coming Monday of an everyday life.

What I appreciated very much those days was this warm kind of family feeling I had with you all, I was a technician working for the Augsburg Festival but I felt included and liked for myself.

CHAPTER 23

Staking

Sledging – the action of wielding a sledge hammer in order to bang in one of the 1.5 metre steel stakes which secure the rig to the ground. To sledge efficiently, you should use the weight of the hammer head, not muscle power, to strike the stake head.

Even with good technique, sledging needs a strong sledger, so we had to be careful to share the load, as it could exhaust the aerialist's grip on a show day. Staking points are vital to the security and safety of a rig. The ideal ground for staking is soft but firm, not too wet or boggy nor too dry and dusty. If it is too much one way or the other, you have to use a different staking pattern. Nine times out of ten, it was not ideal. A normal staking pattern is two stakes, one just over a foot behind the other, both slanted slightly away from the direction in which the cable tension is pulling. Then the stakes are roped tightly together so that if the first stake pulls out of the ground when under tension, the back-up stake catches it. In bad ground, you simply add more back-up stakes in an ever-increasing pattern behind the original stake. With a tightrope – which pulls four times as much tension as a trapeze rig – I have had to put up to ten stakes in soggy ground.

Stakes stick out just at mid-shin level so, if you are sensible, you put covers on them when they are in place, otherwise you walk into them in the dark. We sometimes remembered the covers but mostly just collected nasty stake-head-sized scars on our shins. Despite them being two-inch diameter steel, it is easy to bend stakes by hammering them into tree roots or rocks, so there was always a pile of bent stakes waiting to go to the metal workers to be straightened.

Once the rig is up, there can be some settling into the earth of both the stakes and the rig feet, so it is a good safety precaution to check that everything is tight before the show. It is possible to drive stakes into tarmac, which is actually quite soft for 'hard' ground, though an absolute nightmare to get out because it is so sticky. When we were on a tarmac site, I would arrange for a forklift truck to be there at de-rig, as it was the only way to get the stakes out.

We often performed in German market squares, which are frequently paved with cobble stones. I became an expert at removing these to reach the soft earth underneath. It is quite a delicate technique. You have to mark them all with chalk so that you can replace them correctly afterwards then, in order not to damage them, you first have to scrape earth from around the edges, then wiggle the stone gently. Next, you jam a screwdriver down the edge and wiggle some more until the stone is free.

There is something incredibly satisfying about sitting on the ground in a marketplace, chipping away at cobbles with the German public looking on. They are dying to tell us off but cannot, as we are there under the jurisdiction of the Town Hall. I imagine that we provoked a lot of tutting around dinner tables.

Under the cobbles should be a thin layer of sand then, if you are lucky, soft ground to drive the stakes into. A similar technique can be used for paving stones: it just needs more people and crowbars instead of screwdrivers. The biggest nightmare is hardcore sites. Sometimes these are disguised with earth and grass on top, which lulls you into a false sense of security. But underneath is tons of impenetrable rubble which damages stakes, splits sledge hammer handles and busts our backs. The worst misunderstanding that we ever had about staking was in Holland. The agent had assured the booker that we could stake into sand on the beach and didn't mention this to me. It seems all too obvious to me what would happen to a stake if you banged it into soft sand then tensioned it to half a ton.

The last resort technique for securing a rig doesn't use stakes at all but attaches to weights or existing fixing points. With weights, it is simple: when I have marked out the fixing points, a lorry with a hydraulic arm arrives and lifts the weights into position. They are generally either the concrete blocks used to balance a crane or skips full of sand or rubble. I have found that although on a fixed point the rig pulls only half a ton, a weight, with its potential slippage, has to be two tons.

Once we had to set up in a really posh town square in Italy, which had a marble floor. The skips full of sand arrived, but with every attempt to tighten a cable, the skips pulled along the slippery marble. Someone came up with the idea of calling the fire service to wet the sand and thus double the weights. It was exciting for us when the Italian fire brigade turned up!

Sometimes, when the site manager does not want any risk of damage to the ground at all, it is possible to fix a rig using street furniture, such as lamp posts, railings or pillars. I have even run cables between drain covers. When we played in Covent Garden, the back cables were attached to the pillars of the St Paul's, the actors' church and the front ones stretched right over the audience to the railings of the opera house opposite.

CHAPTER 24

Firebird

> **Spreader bar** – because all tents and venues are different heights and because each act has an ideal height to work at, it is often necessary to rig a spreader bar. This is a short length of steel or trussing suspended at the exact height at which the aerialist wishes to fix the rigging. The bar must be static and so needs to be tensioned off, either with cables and wagon ratchets or block and tackle, to four points lower than the bar itself. Once this is achieved, the trapeze and ropes can hang, swing or turn from this fixed point.

My solo act was called Firebird. I dressed in my favourite costume in my favourite colours, red and purple, covered in swirls of gold and sequins and bedecked with feathers. My face was painted with exaggerated eyebrows and glittery gold. At one point, I made a costume for Firebird which was one hundred percent head to toe sequins. It was like chain mail and weighed a ton, making the act harder work for my grip, and the sequins cut my skin, so I only wore this for special occasions.

Firebird was handy for off-season because it was a lot less effort to hop on an aeroplane alone with a suitcase full of rigging and costume than to organise our main show. I performed this regularly at Leeds City Varieties, a beautiful old music hall. The age and condition of the building meant that it was an extremely dodgy rigging job. I had to go up to the attic, thirty feet above the stage, move all the dusty old props and sets out of the way and pull up the floorboards so that I could peer through the small holes in the plaster ceiling of the auditorium and identify the ones which were just above the front of the stage. Then I had to drop a line, very gingerly, through the two holes (which were only a few inches wide), trying not to not damage the ancient and decorative plaster work. Next, I had to lay a piece of trussing across the beams to spread the load, as no one beam looked strong enough on its own. It was lucky that Health and Safety never got as far as the attic. Then, I would haul up the rigging which I had previously laid out on the theatre seats below. The spreader bar was tensioned off to the handrails of the upper balcony. I was never sure that the rails wouldn't come loose as I put them under enormous strain at the peak of my swing.

My solo show was a piece of equipment called the cloud swing. I used to swing above the audience in front of the stage, as there was more height there. They had to move the first two rows during my act or the audience would have been smacked in the face by my rope.

I had to have an assistant, to pull the rope to start my swing, return it to me and pull it to stop me when I needed to dismount. Lizzie, my housemate, was very happy to help, dressed in her sparkly waistcoat and putting on her showbiz smile. The first time she did this she underestimated the speed at which I was travelling after my highest swing and got pulled off the stage and into the orchestra pit. We never let her forget that.

As I perform my throw-out, the big dive off the rope. I am so close to their upturned faces beneath me that I can see their fear as I swing over them. I hit my head on the velvet pelmet at the top of the proscenium arch: it doesn't hurt but deadens the swing and makes it difficult to pull myself out of the dive.

I swing at the same height as the audience in the top balconies on either side. When I am upright I can smile and gesture to them. It feels great, personal, performing so close.

Ascend rope,
throw one leg over to sit on the cloud swing,
trap the climb-up rope between legs and signal for Lizzie
to swing,
forward one time and back,
two times and back,
three and release rope.
Slide back to hocks,
swing, swing,
sit forward,
pose.

Rope scraping across skin,
stomach lifting when the swing peaks,
heart beating double time as the air races past my face;
slide back to knees,
swing, swing,
back balance,
drop to knee catch,
re-catch cloud-swing with hands,
swing, swing,
pull sideways with legs straddled,
hold in star position for 2 swings,
drop backwards and catch rope with one knee,
hold for 2 swings,
pull to standing,
swing, swing,
wrap both ankles around cloud swing,
dive forward up and out,
swoop down underneath and back to re-catch,
swing, swing,

jump off at front of swing with arms straight out in crucifix position
catch rope in armpits,
catch climb-up rope with feet and descend.

Jill, Mum – I saw that cloud swing several times, at Leeds City Varieties and Glastonbury, and maybe in Bradford as well. It was astonishing and terrifying, especially in the theatre. The entire audience faced upwards, gasping. My heart stood still. Thank god I was unaware of the complicated rigging.

The show at the City Varieties was called 'The Good Old Days'. Here I was privileged to work with some proper old fashioned variety stars, the likes of Danny La Rue, Dora Bryan and Barry Cryer. Backstage was a comedy of divas. Danny La Rue had the ugliest little poodle I have ever seen. It was a special breed that didn't have any hair and was much fussed over. Danny's personal assistant scampered around preparing frocks and looking after Danny's ego. He sat in the Green Room between acts, in corset and stockings, with no wig but full make-up and eyelashes, holding court as only an old-fashioned star can.

CHAPTER 25

Cloud swing

Cloud swing – a piece of equipment for solo performance. The artiste swings until she is parallel with the ceiling, on an 8-metre length of rope with a swivel spliced at each end to prevent it twisting. The swivels are attached, approximately 4.5 metres apart, to the spreader bar. This creates a wide loop of rope for swinging on.

There must be space above the spreader bar so that there is no chance that the artiste will hit her head as she dives off at the peak of the swing.

The repetition of training for and performing in trapeze shows had a profound and lasting effect on both my mind and body. It is the deep imprint made by each aerial move that keeps us safe in the air. Security and body memory go hand in hand. Rachel and I once went to some contemporary dance classes to help our movement technique. We were like the comedy duo, heading off all over the place and getting the routines wrong. Dancers are trained to pick up routines quickly, but an aerialist will practise the same move over and over and over, maybe for months, even years, before it goes into the routine. Consequently, we are slow-brained but, once the move is understood, the whole body knows it without question or conscious thought: it has become an everyday movement, just like picking up a cup of tea.

Years after my retirement as an aerialist I am still affected, I still regularly do my pre-show preparation stretching but it lacks the satisfaction of the end result.

I go through my routines in my dreams, checking everything over and over again, curving my body, placing my foot, my grip... Sometimes I have nightmares in which I am going through them just before a show and then I suddenly remember that I haven't practised for ten years and I don't know if I can pull it off. I am terrified. The question goes round and round in my mind: how much memory remains in my body and how much do I need pure muscle strength?

Visiting the circus, I venture into the ring during practice time. Holding the bar like a long lost friend I try to go through my moves. I find that, while there are plenty that are strength-dependent which I can't do any more, my body automatically remembers the techniques... if I do them one at a time.

Cloud Swing can be one of the more potentially dangerous pieces of aerial equipment as it has a very high, long, wide swing, which means there is no chance to land on a crash mat and, at that time, there was no option to wear a safety-line. When I learned cloud swing we only used a safety line during rehearsal. But in recent, more safety conscious days, I see that they are using a lunge during performance too.

To do tricks on the cloud swing, the artist must re-build the swing constantly. Tricks only work at the peak of a swing which has reached the correct height, and each trick reduces the height of the swing. It always shocks trainee cloud swingers to discover how exhausting and powerful that swing must be; the forearms get extremely pumped up.

The moves performed on a cloud swing take the form of balances, drops, rolls and turns. The high point of the performance is the 'throw out' which can be done either forwards or backwards. It is an extremely dramatic and impressive move. Pulling out of it takes a great deal of strength. The best cloud swingers can do several throw outs in a row without a break.

I was taught cloud swing by aerialist Isobel from the French circus Archaos. I did a short apprenticeship with her very early on in my career. She was an extremely intimidating personality, traditionally triangular-shaped as aerialists become, with broad shoulders and small bum. She could do eight throw-outs in a row and had absolutely no sympathy for me: when the back of my knees bled from rope friction, she continued, relentlessly, to send me up to practice, her face completely expressionless, I'm not sure she ever bothered to learn my name. I was terrified but continued because I loved it. And she was not a woman whom you said 'no' to.

My happiest memories of cloud swinging are of when we were working in the open air. I used it as a way to test the stability of the rig, or just to wake me up in the morning. Any excuse to get up there and swing away in the wind or the sun. The best ever was when we set up the rig to rehearse on the edge of a valley in the south of France; I could swing away in the sunshine overlooking the stunning scenery. It doesn't get much better than that.

People ask me how I felt. I don't seem to have the words to describe it because a feeling is just a feeling sometimes... The best description was my mum's poem where she calls me 'the laughing girl, swinging in the topmost branches.' That's how it was for me, that's how it felt inside, just laughing and swinging.

Tuck, push forward, tuck, straight, tuck, forward, tuck,
straight...
Point toes,
Tempo back and up.
Feeling free and safe in my own little world.

There was a farm in France that we loved. Marleychard, we called it the circus farm. It was a wild and derelict place, with a small lake where you could swim naked, unseen. It was owned by a circus entrepreneur, Alistair. He was extremely tall, an amiable giant with a prominent nose, sticking-out ears and an alternative sense of dress. He was always to be found in the yard, hosing down bits of tenting and loading or unloading trucks for his various jobs.

Alistair had an extensive extended family who came and went. The youngest son was called Willow; we had first met them at Glastonbury and, as Lou pointed out, 'you know you're at Glastonbury Festival when the kids are called Willow.' Everyone there lived in caravans, arranged in a jumble around the farmyard with tarpaulins and fairy lights stretched between them.

Performers, passing on the way to Spain, or with time off in that area, would park up and spend time relaxing there. We used to pass as much time there as we could manage. It was a haven after the madness of a summer circuit. We spent long days swimming and lying in hammocks, followed by getting together to cook a huge al fresco meal, eaten at long trestle tables. Sometimes, we would dress up in our glad rags and everybody would pile into the back of a truck and head out to an auberge to eat.

If we were there for any amount of time, we would have a party: food, dancing and music, all around the caravans in the candle-light. I remember one particularly sweltering summer, when the weather suddenly exploded into an enormous tropical storm. It was such a relief after the heat that Lou and I danced around outside getting happily soaked. Afterwards we sat cosily in the caravan, cooking porridge in the middle of the day!

One day, when we were sunning ourselves by the lake, we suddenly spotted a herd of cows at the top of the hill. They must have just been let into the field and were charging headlong down towards the lake for a drink. We were right in their path and dived into the lake at top speed. It was like a comedy film.

There was a man there called Jim, who built and painted gypsy caravans: old-fashioned barrel tops with intricate woodwork and bright colours. He was one of a gang of regular friends that we made there. I spent lovely times sitting in his caravan or around his camp fire, chatting, or just being. Jim had a painting of me on my rope on the side of one of his trucks. He had copied it from a photograph and set the scene above the lake on the farm, surrounded by woodland.

The painting makes me feel like a fairy-tale character, twisting and turning on my rope above the water like a spider on its web. This is how I feel when practising on the side of the valley with no-one watching, just performing for myself.

This place had everything that I loved: circus people, trapeze, caravans, beautiful scenery, outdoor living and sunshine. I often thought about re-locating Skinning the Cat there. But every year when we got back to Bradford for the winter, the reality hit me of what it would be like to run a company in France in the winter – a country where I did not know the system and without the help of our Bradford-based team.

Helen and I climb the track to Marleychard: Alistair has sold it. The yard is now empty of people. All the old caravans and trailers, some of them such beautiful traditional wooden ones with paintwork done so lovingly, are now rotting and overgrown, their coloured paintwork faded. It is full of the ghosts of the people who had left and of such happy times. We don't stay long.

Not far from the circus farm is a small town called Aurillac, which comes alive each year when it hosts a very prestigious street theatre and circus festival. All the bookers and agents go there and it was a great place for networking and seeing everyone's shows. We used to stay at the farm on the way to the festival, so by the time we were on our way we had developed an entourage of other performers and artists who decided to come with us; including, of course, Jim and his beautiful barrel-topped gypsy wagon.

The festival has a main programme and a fringe programme. The first time we went we were on the main programme, which was a great achievement for a small English company. I was excited and overwhelmed. All the giants of the European circuit were there – I felt as if I was surrounded by gods. Every corner I turned, I would see another legendary company rigging up their shows for me to watch. There were amazing tents, structures, hydraulic stages, building-sized puppets... The atmosphere was electric.

Anyone who was anyone was there. When I was not working I could wander between shows, talking to people and lapping up inspiration. To my delight I found myself right next to Circue Perrillos, a Spanish company I had long idolised from afar. We sat outside late at night, chatting and drinking, I became firm friends with Adalaida and Jordy, the couple at the heart of the company. Perillos have a beautiful and remote home in the mountains outside Barcelona. We soon adopted this as another of our stop-off places when driving between France and Spain.

On the side of the mountain, they had an aerial rig permanently set up and a dusty ring for practising with the horse. I loved having a turn on the horse, riding bareback round and round until my legs got tired and I fell off into the gorse bushes. The horse was called Sirius. In between shows he would amble around the mountain side, sneak up behind people when they weren't looking and push them over with his head. That was his trick in the show and he expected a reward for it. Sometimes we would go to visit friends and return at night, riding Sirius in the dark through the mountains.

CHAPTER 26

The Sprite owners club

> **Cotton Rope** – Aerialists work on cotton rope. Hemp or man-made fibres rip the skin. The rope is called 3-strand which means that there are three sections of rope twisted together. The twist of the rope, how tight or loose, is called the lay.

During a few days off in the south of France, Helen and I had split off from the rest of the company to go to the circus farm. We were heading back up the French motorway towards the ferry to meet the others, when we noticed smoke coming out of the caravan. We pulled over to put the fire out but couldn't find it. The smoke was coming from inside the caravan walls. We squirted a fire extinguisher through a gap in the inner wall and set off again. It wasn't long before we noticed more smoke and stopped again. This time we ripped out the inside wall of the caravan. The smoke seemed to be coming from the electrics in one corner. By this time, we had really messed up the caravan and, when we got to the ferry port, we had to sleep amongst the debris.

The next day, we drove onto the ferry. I spent the whole crossing feeling uneasy because we had not properly found the source of the fire. We looked forward to getting back to England and scrapping the caravan as it was getting too old anyway. As we were sitting and waiting to drive off the ferry, having a laugh at the funny side of the situation now that it was nearly over, a man knocked on the van window. We thought he had seen more smoke but no, he was a caravan enthusiast from the Sprite Owners Club and had noted that our caravan was a Sprite. He wished to enrol us, so that we could join them at rallies. We nodded politely, not liking to tell him that we were planning to dump it.

We had many beloved motors, all with individual names, and a high turnover of caravans as they never lasted long, bouncing along behind heavy, equipment-laden vehicles. A typical journey would begin with loading the truck, stocking up the fridge and the sandwich box and an early morning dash down to the ferry. Keeping Skinning the Cat fed was an enormous job. We used up a lot of energy; for this reason an evening meal formed part of our contract. We would always have our own early dinner before the show and the contracted dinner in a restaurant later. Helen was our favourite shopper – she became expert on who liked what and who had which dietary requirements. We were outside rigging in the fresh air and doing two shows a day, so we burned off calories and refuelled constantly.

We used the time on ferry crossings to have group meetings and discuss tour dates or problems with the show. The meeting would be followed by a good meal at the café, the sort of food that we wouldn't see for a while, if we were heading abroad or, if returning, hadn't experienced for ages. We would stuff ourselves with a good fry-up. This would be followed by a trip to the duty-free shop. In the group meeting, we would have decided who would buy what, to stock up the Skinning the Cat bar. The truck bar had become a crucial part of our existence because we were often the finale act; by the time we had finished, the real bar would be closed and the socialising over. Needing to come down from our after-show high, we took the stocking of our bar extremely seriously – and we became well known for our caravan parties.

Our favourite truck of all time was called Gloria. She was an old furniture removal van and, as well as the equipment storage space, she had a living space with bunks and cooking facilities. This was a revolution in long-distance touring as we could sleep en route, which we could not do in a caravan. There was room for three in the cab and about four in the live-in space. You could shout through the gap in the back of the cab for a cup of tea.

It was always funny to see the faces of the customs officials when they demanded to see the passengers. The side door would open, steps dropped down, and everyone would pile out, normally half asleep. We were frequently stopped and searched at borders or randomly stopped by the Spanish 'flying customs'. Did we look suspect? Luckily, when they saw the amount of equipment stuffed inside the vehicles, they often limited themselves to ripping open any pre-rolled cigarettes and feeling down the seams of the costumes.

The furthest that we ever drove was Portugal, which took about three days at our towing pace. I had a particularly scary experience descending a mountain in Portugal, just outside Lisbon, towing a caravan down a steep and seemingly never-ending slope. I put my foot on the brake and nothing happened. I tried again: still nothing. Towing a caravan downhill, the caravan can actually want to go faster than the truck and, if you try to brake, it starts to weave unnervingly, which can lead to jack-knifing. The best thing to do if you start weaving is accelerate, pull out of the weave and gradually slow down in a controlled fashion. All this is impossible if the caravan is already pushing you down the hill faster than you can drive. We were extremely lucky in this case because we were near the foot of the mountain, so I was able, eventually, to slow down enough to pull onto the hard shoulder. I found that if I stopped for a while, then drove for a while, I could regain some braking power. In this way we limped into Lisbon, where we were due to perform. It is not something that I wish to repeat.

We had two weeks of shows in the area; there had been some dreadful contractual errors due to linguistic misunderstandings between our office and the Portuguese agents. We had arrived expecting to do one show and they were expecting a different one. We pulled it off, with some pretty fast rehearsing for one aerialist who hadn't done a particular role before. Our visit to Lisbon was rounded off nicely when we were stranded there for a further two weeks while we argued with mechanics and waited for a new part for the truck to make its way from Spain. Two unexpected weeks in Portugal sounds like fun, but it was extremely stressful because we were worried about when the truck part would arrive and whether we would have to cancel more work. The experience cost us a fortune.

To add to our mad Portuguese experiences, we were offered a corporate hospitality performance in Portugal while still in Holland, which conveniently fitted into a gap when we would be driving between sites. As we were always struggling to balance the books, we accepted. The plan was for Lucie and me to be dropped off at an airport, fly to Portugal, do the evening show and fly back in the morning. The others would drive to the next site, set up the rig, then pick us up at an airport near to the next site in time for that evening's performance. It was a tight schedule, but, apart from needing the money, I enjoyed a challenge.

We arrived in Portugal as planned, only to discover that we were expected to rig our trapeze on a boat in the harbour. They had built a 9-metre-high structure for us above the roof of the boat which was already standing about 7 metres out of the water. The roof of the boat was glass, and the plan was that the audience (some sort of champagne-and-canapés crowd) could watch us through it. It is quite difficult to rig a trapeze on a boat which gently sways in the water: by the time that gentle movement has moved up to the top, it has become a violent rocking motion. Added to this, there was a strong sea wind blasting through the harbour.

Having finally accepted that the trapeze was going to be slightly wonky whatever we did, we went to get changed and made up. It was only when we returned for the entrance of our show that we saw, to our horror, that most of the audience were standing on one side of the boat and the trapeze was hanging at a horrible slant. Lucie and I carefully picked our way through our trapeze routine silently communicating to each other which of the balances were not going to be possible. Following the trapeze I was scheduled to do my cloud swing act. My stomach churned as I swung wonkily to and fro across the glass roof, passing over the murky water 9 meters below at the far end of my swing. I decided that, if I came off, I'd rather go through the glass roof than confront the deep dark water.

We made it safely through the performance and thought that we could relax, de-rig and fly back to join the others. But we had not allowed for the Portuguese party spirit which caused our agents to sleep through their promise to pick us up and take us to the airport. By the time we realised this and had ordered a taxi, we were running late for the flight. We left the hotel in a stressful flurry and it was only when we were trying to check in for our flight that we realised that we had forgotten to reclaim our passports (hotels used to retain them in case you ran up bills then did a runner). There was nothing for it but to wait for our agent to arrive with our passports and get on a later plane.

We finally arrived at Schiphol airport in Amsterdam, late, exhausted and relieved to be met by the worried faces of Lou and the team. Unfortunately, it transpired that our baggage, containing the crucial trapeze and costumes, had fallen off the baggage wagon when we changed planes in Milan. We were told not to worry: if we just waited for the next flight to arrive it should be on it, though they couldn't be completely sure of that – it could be tomorrow.

We were already running late for our evening show. We had no choice but to leave in the hope that the luggage would arrive in time by courier. It was about twenty minutes before the show that a motorbike arrived with these crucial items. I'm not sure at which point in our touring lifetime we began to refer to ourselves as 'The Skin of our Teeth.'

CHAPTER 27

Rehearsal Time

Neck spin – a short loop of webbing attached to a swivel by a keeper. Place loop of webbing around the neck so that it sits at the base of the skull at the back. This must be secured by a keeper.

Neck spins can be done from a static point or from a spinning rope or hanging from a partner's neck.

During our off-season training sessions at Manningham sports centre, we practised new moves and shaped up routines. About one month before the start of a tour we put all the elements of the show together. At this point we had to put the whole rig structure up, get all the different members of the company together and work on links, narrative and characters. Finding a place big enough for this (9 metres high with plenty of floor space), was always a problem. If you rent a commercial unit of this size it costs a fortune per square metre. I was always looking out for spaces which were 'between users'. We rehearsed in the Bradford Wool Exchange before it became a book shop; the Windsor Baths before it got cut up into pubs; a disused car warehouse before it was knocked down and, finally, the enormous St Margaret's church in Leeds, where the walls were so thick that it was ice-cold, even on a warm spring day.

Spaces were loaned to us unofficially and we had to move on as soon as the building was needed. For the last week, we would put the rig up outside. It was important for us to become accustomed to working with the elements as it brings different challenges to performing. Sometimes it would rain heavily or even snow during this week, which would mean that the show would start the season under-rehearsed.

This period was also important for breaking in new company members, who needed to learn the sequence of rigging events. A new member would pale when she saw the volume of equipment being loaded into the truck. But we soon toughened them up.

Hilary, American clown – On my arrival in Bradford, I found it to be a bit dreary, cold and wet. It stayed cold for most of the month I was there preparing the show and we didn't see a whole lot of sunshine. But as I got to know the city, the local pub, the curry houses and the other artists in the Skinning the Cat mill, I grew very fond of Bradford. And we did see some sunny days!

We worked for a month recreating the show from what it had been the year before and incorporating my skills into it. We rebuilt props and costumes and tweaked the story. The day that we pulled the set (they called it the rig) out of storage and put it up in the parking lot (they call it a car park) was a memorable one for me. We carried large pieces of trussing, scaffolding and staging down the stairs, across the parking area and up the incline and began to drive stakes into the hardest, densest earth compounded by a century of cars and trucks. It was nearly impossible!

The whole process of putting up our set was difficult and exhausting and I really had no idea how I was ever going to make it through a summer of setting up and striking all over Europe. It was torturous! And then they had the gall to tell me that in fact, they looked forward to it when they were on the road and loved that part of the process. I thought they were crazy and wanted to quit and go home. But of course, I couldn't. But I was sure I was in for a miserable time on the road.

But my god, they were right! We six women became a well-oiled machine. We all knew what had to be done and how to do it, and we all took on the jobs that we thought we were good at and knew how to do well. It was beautiful to see us pull into town, find our spot and get to work. We only needed help from outsiders at the moment of pulling the rig up. We needed at least one more set of arms to lift it as we winched it into the sky. And it was fun to see how amazed people were to realise that we were six women – with no man to help us out. We didn't need it.

Being lent spaces unofficially came at a risk. One year, I had worked hard to negotiate the use of a part of Lister Mill, which had been lent to a community group while the building was empty. I don't quite know what happened but the management changed, and on the day we had packed up to go there I had a phone call from a man I had never spoken to before. He said that we absolutely couldn't use the space. No amount of guilt-tripping or pleading would budge him. It had taken me all winter to sort out Lister Mill and I was paying accommodation and rehearsal time for seven artistes for a month. I remember standing on the pavement next to the truck with expectant faces looking out at me. I sent them into the café and returned to the office to ring everyone I knew. Unbelievably, I managed to find a disused car factory; this was nothing short of a miracle.

Getting the gang going in the mornings to rehearse was always a challenge. It is not easy to gear up to working on a trapeze first thing in the morning. We would start slowly with rounds of tea and coffee, long chats and a slow warm-up which seemed to last forever. When we were finally ready to start, people would disappear to the toilet or spend ages looking for their wrist tapes or ankle straps. This used to drive me insane. I felt as though I was the only one who cared that the days were slipping by and we had so much to achieve.

Rehearsal time was a time of the year that I both loved and hated. There was the excitement of putting the show together and the promise of heading off on our travels – but it was also when I wore the most hats. I had to pull the team and the show together while running in and out of the office, trying to finalise tour dates. I would invariably develop a dreadful cold or stomach bug by the end of it.

We had two regular outdoor spaces to put our rig up to rehearse. An artists' agent whom I had met at my college degree show had become interested in my work; he ran his business from a large house in Aberford, which was surrounded by parkland and fields. It was very grand and I always thought that we made a bizarre spectacle arriving in our trucks and caravans, driving through the park gates and down the tree lined drive. I think there must have been novelty value for him, having a bunch of women practising a trapeze show in his large garden. There were constant comings and goings of business men in expensive cars alongside our rig and equipment. At the end of rehearsals, the business men would have a barbecue and watch our dress run.

The second place we used, when we had smaller shows to practice, was my friend Julia's garden. Joolz, with whom I used to house-share, was now married to Mark from the circus workshop and had two young boys. The two boys sacrificed their football space and all the neighbours came to watch.

Julia, friend and ex-housemate – It happened in springtime, same time every year, to the wonder and maybe horror of our neighbours: the evangelical Christians on the left; the Mormons on the right; the Catholics across the road next to the Muslims. We became known as the Pagans on our street, because at this particular time of year, along with the daffodils and crocus, the garden would be filled with mystical-looking structures, giant coils of rope and huge black blocks, transforming the back garden into a stage set. If it wasn't for the 'hippy convoy' van sitting out front, scrawled with 'Skinning the Cat', no one would have been able to have put a name to this annual event.

My two young boys were both thrilled and terrified by the fortnight's entertainment, eagerly pressed up behind the safety of the French windows looking out to the back garden. Yes, the spring fairies had arrived, to practice their dancing, flying skills and magic. We were so lucky they chose here to play.

A flicker of fear triggered by a stray sequin on the carpet, 'Do they come inside the house too?' asked the boys. Only when it's raining, to eat and talk through their next moves. Each morning we would leave the house, boys in the car ready for nursery, clutching their lunch boxes, knowing that shortly our space would be filled by our daily visitors. The house would vibrate expectantly as the diesel truck ground up the road. In they would come, boots off, jackets and bags slung, kettle on.

Don't get me wrong, it wasn't all tinsel and fairy dust. Some of the team looked pretty tough, in particular the roadies and techies. It was more apparent when we came back from work and there, just inside the door, lined up were giant Doc Martens the size of my son's bedroom. Every mug was out on the side containing half-drunk builder's tea and soggy biscuits. They would sit shoulder to shoulder round the kitchen table and, from the back, the heavy duty leather jackets seemed to merge into one large mythical beast, topped with strands of wild pink and orange tufts of hair.

The worst days for everyone were the rainy days. Stuck inside, the performing team would find a room to do their warm ups. Coming back unexpectedly, I had to step over outstretched Lycra limbs and coils of rope the size you find on ships, with the air smelling of warm exercise.

The days of sunshine meant the garden was filled with spring activity, ghetto blaster blaring and extension cables dangling through propped-open downstairs windows. Neighbours and stray boys would sit expectantly around the garden while dangling and twisting flips were rehearsed up and down the ropes, feathers and glitter paint transforming moulded scenery and props and the air filled with purples, pinks, greens, blues and sparkle.

It was a very special period for us, one we knew at the time would pass quickly, ephemeral and magical. A secret in our garden.

I had experienced a stomach upset following a dodgy prawn curry, and just could not seem to shake it off. We were rehearsing 'Chameleon' in Mark and Julia's back garden. I felt exhausted all the time, could hardly bring myself to stand up and had a recurring desire to crawl under a duvet and never come out. On the final day, our invited audience waited for the dress rehearsal as I retired to Mark and Julia's spare room and couldn't seem to move. Somebody called the doctor and I have the dreadful memory of sitting in bed talking to her as I could hear the show music start up outside.

Whether I could perform or not, we needed to run the show to check the timings for lighting and rigging changes, At the time, I was doing several different routines, including catching the doubles trapeze. So there were a lot of times when the spotlight just focused on some empty rigging.

Following some tests by the doctor, it turned out that I had caught Campylobacter, a sister bug to Salmonella. It took me two or three months to get rid of it properly. We went on tour and I forced myself through the shows. The shows didn't look good and I was permanently on the point of collapse.

It was horrible to be driving across Europe when all I wanted to do was curl up and sleep in my own bed. I spent a lot of time lying on a mattress, trying to direct the rigging without having to walk around. We were doing a week's run in Germany and I felt bad for the event organisers, who were so keen to have us and found themselves with half a show. We padded out bits of extra routines and I struggled through some cut-down ones. There was just nowhere to hide: I was permanently on public view and it was awful.

On the way through Belgium we stopped off in Brussels to stay with Lucie's family. It was heaven to be in a proper house with her mum caring for me. It was Lucie's mum who sorted me out eventually by recommending a two-week cleansing diet. I could only eat plain boiled rice and boiled carrots, no salt and pepper, oils or sauces. It was pretty dire but I was getting desperate and it worked. I have never felt the same about boiled rice and carrots since!

CHAPTER 28

Costumes

> **Gazelle** – This trapeze move creates an elegant leaping shape. Sitting sideways and tucked into the corner of the trapeze, bend the leg next to the velvet around the velvet and brace it with all the weight on so that, keeping the other leg straight, the aerialist can lean backwards under the trapeze with free hands.

The costumes and the performance characters were central to the uniqueness of Skinning the Cat. Because I was both a trapeze artiste and costumier, I was in a good position to experiment with pushing the boundaries of the average trapeze costume. Costumes take a lot of wear and tear on the ropes and must survive hundreds of shows. My first attempts were made from t-shirt fabrics appliqued with swirling patch patterns because, at that time, it was impossible to buy Lycra on the roll. This was not satisfactory, as the patchwork fabrics reduced the stretch of the t-shirt fabric, which was already not stretchy enough. Consequently, I was either unable to move properly on the trapeze, or had to make the costumes slightly baggy. Luckily, Lycra soon became more readily available and I developed a technique which has continued throughout my aerial costumes.

I cut the base from Lycra, then create shapes and decoration using very thin strips of leather. I find that this is the best way to achieve clear lines, also leather is the only material which I have found is strong enough to survive the wear and tear from performing on the ropes.

If I conjure up a pattern with the embossed gold or silver leather strips and leave enough space in between, the blocks of coloured Lycra retain enough stretch.

Everything must be edged with sequins and any characters which allow for it have feathers. Washing is done carefully by hand – and infrequently. Each wash removes some lustre from the sequins which must be painstakingly unpicked and replaced, dye will come out of the feathers and the leather will lose its embossed finish. So they are often left sweaty: it is fortunate that the audience is not close enough to smell us!

My imagination thrives as I put together different fabrics and the vision clarifies in my head. I feel happy as I work on them; they become my friends, whom I begin to love as their characters take shape. I have learnt that when I love a character, the costume will be successful, but when the feeling doesn't come the costume will just be run-of-the-mill. I do not like making costumes to order.

My costume designs sometimes emerge through the cross-referencing and exaggeration of existing personalities. For me, a ringmaster is not only that: the red coat inspires a devils tail, the top hat its horns, and the ringmaster should reflect this combination by performing as a corrupt sideshow entertainer.

I made myself a glamorous cabaret character, called Petula, all glitter and fishtail; she was Shirley Bassey, Cruella De Vil and Danny La Rue all rolled into one. I used her to introduce our show in my stilted German, inadvertently adding comedy to the mix.

We have a great history of Shirley Bassey in our family. I don't have many of my dad's things but I managed to keep some of his Shirley Bassey singles. Mum loves her, especially the real belters like 'don't rain on my parade'. I love the glittery show biz dresses and her powerful rich voice and charisma. She does a great emotional song. My sisters and I bought Mum Shirley Bassey tickets at the Albert Hall for her birthday; I was meant to go too, but of course a show got booked on that date and I had to give my ticket away. I was gutted.

One day when I was staying at Claire's in London a fellow guest turned out to be teching for Shirley Bassey on her tour. She was playing at a country mansion in the middle of nowhere just outside London that very evening and he had a crew pass that I could have. Excited, I left without hesitation. I got the train to a tiny station in a village I've never heard of and after some difficulty got a taxi to the mansion. We drove around lost in the dark for ages and arrived late, after the show had started.

With my crew pass I could enter the security area between the stage and the audience. I was about two feet from Shirley throughout the whole concert. I stood at her feet transfixed with adoration. She shook my hand several times, not registering that it was the same person who kept reaching out to her. She was everything and more close up: her power and presence, her glamour, her talent. I was so happy, I just stood and cried without moving. This was real goddess worship. When she went off stage, I was round the back within about thirty seconds, confident of catching her backstage. But no, apparently she steps off stage straight into a car and is gone in about five seconds flat. That was efficient, I couldn't believe it!

I suddenly became aware of my situation: stuck in the middle of nowhere late at night after all public transport had stopped, I had been so keen to get there I never gave a thought to getting back. With a confidence born of necessity, I used my pass to get into the mansion house where all the musicians were packing up their instruments. I announced my predicament to the band and asked if anyone was driving back to London. I was lucky: a kind man took me to a convenient Tube and I got home safely. What amazes me now, looking back, was my complete blinkered focus on this. No planning, no thought, except that I must see Shirley Bassey. What a magical night that was!

In the early years, I did every stitch of the costumes myself but, as the responsibilities of running the company grew, my winter time was taken up with planning and office work. I was lucky enough to find a soul-mate costumier in Jan Huntley. I would make a costume for her to finish, or, if we needed a matching set, I would make one which she would reproduce. Later, as we really got onto the same wavelength, I would provide fabric bits, sample sections and scribbled drawings, which she would interpret to perfection. But I did miss being completely hands-on. This was a problem which increased more and more: if I wanted Skinning the Cat to be a successful business, I had to spend less time being an artist.

There is one special costume from our early show *Chameleon* which has been chosen by the Victoria and Albert Museum in London to represent modern circus in their Theatre and Performance collection. The costume itself is the chameleon. It is one of a pair of costumes made for the doubles trapeze. Its partner is a bird. The story was about a woman who, while shopping in a supermarket, found that her trolley was magic. It danced around the stage and bizarre creatures sprang out of it, performing acrobatics around her. The shopping trolley flies into the air, growing wings and flashing lights and taking the woman with it. The show was about escaping mundanity. The chameleon symbolised change.

I chose the colours of the chameleon costume for their reptilian look and because they contrasted well with the colours of its partner, the bird. To make the main body, I cut my pattern into vertical strip sections in order to give the irregular effect of different colours. These were separated by strips of differently-sized 'prickles' in various colours, reflecting the shapes of strange, unknown tropical fruits sometimes displayed at the greengrocers. None of my costumes have any scientific reality.

To make the spikes three-dimensional, I sewed Lycra onto wadding. They had to be Lycra because the spikes frequently got caught on the ropes, trapezes or other parts of the costume. Hence, they had to be flexible and durable enough to survive lots of tugging. I put a strip of Lycra onto the wadding and, using a zig-zag stitch, sewed a row of spikes. Then I went in between these spikes to make a smaller row of spikes as well. I did this partly because it was the most efficient use of fabric, but also because two rows of spikes together are much easier to cut out. Cutting them out was fiddly – if I cut too closely I snipped stitches, but if I left a gap the white wadding would be visible.

Before I sewed all the strips and spikes together to make the body suit, I decorated the Lycra with embossed gold leather, cut into innumerable small u-shapes of different sizes to go up the body and give the scaly effect that I wanted. Amongst these scales, I scattered quantities of coloured sequins, which catch the lights so well and give a slightly wet look. Around the neck, the tops of the arms and up the back, I made larger wadded pieces in the shape of the kind of frills some reptiles have around their necks. These pieces were added asymmet-rically, as I did not want an even appearance. Between them, I gathered some different fabrics, cut jaggedly, to add to the depth of the costumes – a bit like the layered petals of a flower.

This costume has been worn by three different trapezists: if you look inside, you will see that it has been hacked around to fit different people. Many layers of new sequins have been added over the years as old ones dropped off or lost their shine. This has created a rather organic effect. I love this costume especially, as it was one of my early ones and was partner to my bird character, which later became my *Firebird* show. When I visited the chameleon costume in the V and A, I didn't like seeing it in a glass case, worn by a dummy that looked and stood the way no aerialist ever did. It is a bit sad for those two costumes that they are separated now. But it is displayed as part of performance history, next to Margot Fonteyn's Black Swan tutu, so I feel very honoured.

One of the most fun parts of making a show is mixing the music. We worked mainly with Carl from Inner City Music. Completely off-the-wall and extremely talented, he normally worked with rock bands and only at night. He was much in demand. The routines and characters would have to be at quite an advanced stage before I could plan the music. I would often find a sound, or a couple of bars on a CD track which inspired me and I would say to Carl: 'We need trumpet playing, but out of tune' or 'Something a bit windy-sounding here' or 'A bit Tom Waits goes to the circus-ish'. Carl never failed to understand what I wanted. When Helen and I turned up to Carl's studio for a late night session, it was exciting to hear the music come together as I imagined the aerial skills that would accompany each piece.

We found a wonderful singer who had trained in Indian singing. We worked a lot with vocal sounds and recording live musicians, as well as Carl's skill on the drum machine and keyboards. It was wonderful when Carl came to see the finished show and see how the music worked with the action.

One year, we worked with Urban Strawberry Lunch, a group of musicians from Liverpool, whom we had met on the touring circuit. They played bizarre sculptural instruments made out of gas tubing and found objects. Long coils of bright purple of different lengths, hit with table tennis bats, made an eerie thudding beat of different notes, mixed with more traditional instruments and large welded musical sculptures. The instruments were large, so performing was a very physical experience. Working with them gave our show exciting new aspects. It really came alive as they followed our routines – a completely different experience from working to a soundtrack.

Rehearsing was a complete nightmare though: our strict regime of warming up and then going straight into our routines was disrupted when we had to fetch them out of the pub when we were ready to perform. Aerialists and musicians have very different pre-show agendas. Despite this, it was a wonderful experience, but short-lived due to the expense of running two companies for one show. Working again with pre-recorded music afterwards, the performance felt depressingly lifeless.

CHAPTER 29

Post ankle accident

> **Rings** – Two metal hoops, approximately one foot in diameter, suspended from a swivel by two short ropes, the length of which must be the measurement of the performer's inner leg, from crotch to the end of pointed toe.
>
> The swivel can be attached to a fixed point, often the catcher's neck loop or wrist loop.
>
> While rotating, the aerialist holds the rings in her pointed toes and goes into splits, returns to a tuck to increase rotation and extends again in a variety of shapes.

One of my most difficult challenges, while on tour, was being the boss in a small touring company. Sometimes, the situation was awkward for all of us: if I were the boss all the time, then I had no friends. But if I was everyone's best friend, the company became slack. So I shifted between the two roles, which didn't always work and often left me feeling lonely and confused. The year that it was easiest was the year that we did a really small show, consisting of aerialist Claire, technician Helen and myself. They were both long-time members who knew their roles so no 'bossing' was necessary.

The small show allowed Claire and me the space to develop our style and find a different direction from that of the traditional routines. The three of us were extremely close and all very different but symbiotic personalities. We developed ways of doing things, small pleasures that kept us going through the hard work. Claire lived in London and would travel by train to various places where Helen and I could drive with the caravan to pick her up. Without the wider team to look after, we could do things to suit ourselves: stop and cook dinner where there were beautiful views, help each other with our love lives, clothes and social activities

I don't think that the show that we were doing was very good as we were developing a new idea. I had designed a small but more complex rig, which needed some refining and was initially quite limiting.

It was the year following Lou's accident and I was suffering from post-traumatic stress and a resulting low immune system. Lou was still stuck at home, slowly recovering, and this weighed heavily on me. I needed to slow down and should really have taken a year out. I believe that accidents happen for a reason and in the same way that Lou's accident was a culmination of stresses, it was later that year when I fell from the Perch and snapped my ankle.

Following my accident, Lou and I had to try to make our way home. For the first stage of the trip Lou and I travelled together; we were put in first class, where there was more space to elevate my foot. We thoroughly enjoyed all the associated perks and the free champagne. When we changed planes, Lou was on a different route and so I was left to the mercy of airport officials to push me around in a wheelchair. I spent a lot of time stranded in the airport waiting to be collected and pushed off again. When I needed help, toilet, drink or food I had to ask a passer-by to fetch an attendant to get a chair to transport me. This made me aware for the first time of the frustrations of being unable to walk.

When I checked into the English hospital, I was told that the ankle had completely dislocated and, because it was stuck in a sideways position, the first task was to reposition the foot on the leg. This was done over several weeks with a succession of different plasters which gradually and painfully forced the foot around. When the surgeon thought that he had correctly repositioned it, he left the final plaster in place.

During my time on crutches, I did not stop my normal off-season preparations. Organisation for the coming season had to continue. I would get up to the second floor in the goods lift and sit on a pile of cushions in the corner of the office, bossing everyone around. When the last plaster came off, I was left with a balloon of an ankle and a long schedule of exercises. I still could not walk without crutches. My foot was stuck in the forwards and slightly sideways position. No amount of effort by me or the physiotherapist had any effect. The physio's diagnosis was that there was an obstruction in the ankle joint, stopping any movement, and that's certainly how it felt.

I was living on my own at the time and had to develop some innovative ways of moving stuff around the house. This could involve a lot of crawling and pushing plates of food and mugs of tea along the floor to get them from the kitchen to the table. I had to apply hot and cold compresses to my ankle three times a day to reduce the swelling and therefore needed buckets of water and a high stool set up in the kitchen and a constant supply of ice cubes and kettles of hot water surrounding me. I spent a lot of time sitting on that stool with my foot in a bucket. I was waiting for a consultation appointment, to find out why my ankle wasn't healing. I was in fairly low spirits.

Finally, the big day of the appointment with my ankle surgeon arrived. I was pinning a lot of hopes on it. A friend dropped me off at the hospital in Leeds. When I went into the surgeon's office, there were a couple of students watching. The surgeon made a joke about me being a trapeze artist. I am accustomed to this, but when he followed it up by looking at my ankle and adding 'well, used to be a trapeze artist', I did not feel in the mood for tactless jokes.

I had brought a letter from the physiotherapist telling of the work that we were doing and giving her theory about the obstruction. He crumpled up the letter and threw it in the bin. After examining the ankle, he told me that I was being impatient and should just keep going with the exercises. I believed this advice to be incorrect: it was months down the line and my ankle was still painful, swollen and stuck. I wanted another opinion.

It turns out that changing surgeons within the NHS is not easy. I began the long, slow process of convincing my GP, then waited for an appointment. When I finally succeeded, the new surgeon had the joint scanned and, sure enough, there was broken bone stuck in it, as well as a fracture in the ball of the joint, which was pushed so hard against the socket of the foot bones that it could not heal. I needed an operation to correct this.

We were just about to set off on tour. It never crossed my mind to consider not going. I put off my operation until the autumn and we took on an extra artist with us so that my physical work in the show was minimal. During rehearsal time, this artist hurt her knee and, before I knew it, I was upping my aerial work to full tilt again.

The inspiration for the show *Enchantress* came from the unavoidable fact that I was on crutches for the foreseeable future. I could use the crutches to get to the bottom of the rope then leave them on the ground as I ascended. This necessitated the invention of a new character, Enchantress. I had special crutches made with a large light-up eyeball on top and covered with strips of drippy, spooky-looking stuff. I had a set of fangs made and blacked out my middle teeth. We all wore prosthetic pointy ears stuck on. Now, between shows, not only did we have glitter stuck in our eyebrows, we also had glue congealed in the hair around our ears!

Hunching, shuffling and baring my fangs, I could limp into the arena, towing an organic-looking prop on wheels, nicknamed the 'Podmobile' because it looked like some kind of giant seed pod, edged with smaller pods with little lights inside. Technician Helen, who had crewed on a show over Christmas, had got me in free to watch it and, as a result, I asked her to re-create some of their special effects, only on a lower budget. That year I was obsessed with tiny lights: every prop had them in or on it. I made the Enchantress a cloak with a cobwebby cowl around the shoulders and each point of the cowl had a tiny light on the end. It looked magical.

On the small stage, I would cast a spell over a smoking cauldron with Claire hiding inside it, ready to pop out as the result of my spell. Initially, as we could not afford a smoke machine, Claire invented a technique using little metal holders containing pellets normally used to smoke out rodents. She would crouch inside, lighting these pellets and holding them so the smoke came out of the cauldron, while I threw in various props, a prosthetic foot, slime, sparkly powder. Seeing her crouching there with her smokes, it was sometimes all I could do to keep a straight face. Another low-tech cauldron effect was a metal rim with a wick around it. This created a ring of fire and looked impressive – until the time when the wind blew the fire towards the silks on which I was performing. Claire, from her position inside the cauldron, could not see that the end of the silks had caught fire, so she was puzzled to see me descend speedily and hit the bottom of the equipment repeatedly before ascending to continue performing!

I had managed to reinvent my routines so that there was minimal strain on the injured ankle and the weight was distributed on more reliable parts of my body. What was harder was general touring: driving with a stuck foot isn't easy; loading the truck; even keeping up with the rest of the gang socially could be a difficult experience, when they forgot and rushed off ahead of me.

By the time we made *Enchantress*, I had already started moving away from the design of a traditional trapeze rig. My attempt to make a really unusual rig began with the idea of developing one that looked like a tree. It was initially a simple gallows shape which we arrived at through trial and error, with cables supporting the outstretched limb from above and extra branches added by way of decoration. This was a good first stage, but it was small and limiting as there was only one weight-bearing point at the end of the branch.

I became obsessed with looking at cranes. The weight-bearing arm of a crane is counterbalanced by concrete blocks as well as supporting cable systems above. We couldn't carry that tonnage, nor could we have hoisted it into the air on a regular basis, so I developed a system of cables which went down to staking points in the ground. This way, when weight was on the end of one tree branch, the cable above it carried the strain first to a higher central point in the middle of the tree, and then down to the stake on the opposite side. We ended up with three equidistant weight-bearing branches. It was unwieldy to put up because it was very top heavy. It also took a lot of adjusting, because the three branches had to be completely even.

The structure, which was made of triangular aluminium trussing, had decorative branches and a tree-like cover in silver, with creepers, glitter and woody-looking knobbles on it. It was so unusual and created such a lovely centrepiece for events that, even after we had stopped offering the *Enchantress* show, event managers always asked to have the tree. We developed a range of routines on it but eventually got very bored with putting it together. It set a standard for inventive rigs.

I was on crutches for two years following my ankle accident; I needed two corrective surgeries before the foot sat roughly right on the leg again. I never stopped working; I was more comfortable in the air where my foot was clear of impact than hobbling around on the ground.

It was not only pig-headedness that kept me going. As a company, we were on a roll. Bookers were waiting to see what the next show would be like and agents were putting pressure on me. I had worked very hard to get our agents: they were the key to our financial success. I felt committed to providing work for our members and knew I might lose good artists to other companies if I took time out. The yearly cycle could not just be picked up and put down: we were constantly preparing for the next season and had the administrator and office overheads to pay; there were trucks, rigs and caravans to store, publicity to send out.... When could it stop?

The bottom line is that I had to earn my own living and this was the way I did it. I know now that it is recognised that artistic directors can get burnt out and need to replenish energy. It is not unusual for funded companies to give directors sabbatical leave to research and to develop themselves. But we weren't a funded company and it was not possible.

I was in a race against time on two fronts: the women's race and the aerialist's race. Only so many potential child bearing years and only so many athletic years. I did not have a definite plan for either, but both were there at the back of my brain: the next show runs for two years and then I'll be 30; after the next show, I'll be 35...

I had always assumed that I'd have kids some day. I came from a big family so it felt right, but I couldn't quite think where I would fit it in. And, of course, I would have to stop still for long enough to form a proper relationship. My friend Al Dix, artistic director of Major Road Theatre Company, once said: 'You behave like someone who is going to die tomorrow.' I was surprised at the time: did not all artistic directors plan their lives manically? However, he was neither an aerialist nor a woman.

Who would I be, what would I do, if I wasn't an aerialist? It had become normal for me. Even if I had time off I would always have to keep practising trapeze, so I might as well do shows and earn money. These reasons are all genuine. But there are much easier and more financially rewarding ways to earn a living, so the simple fact was that I didn't stop because I didn't want to.

CHAPTER 30

Administrative Support

> **Wagon ratchets** – normally seen on the back of trucks to secure loads, hence the name. In rigging they are used for tensioning off cables.

During the off-season months, I worked closely with our administrator back at base. We went through all the highs and lows and financial worries together; and, when I was away with the whole team, I could call the office partly to find out what was going on and partly for support. We were both the odd-ones-out. The phone calls were sometimes stressful, sometimes hilarious touring narratives. Talking to base provided support and relief for me and enabled the administrator to understand what we were involved in. Administrator Ann Nicholls always used to say 'you must write this stuff down' but of course I never did. I thrived on this manic lifestyle at that time: it was all a big challenge, a game, a good story to relate in the pub when we got home.

Jan, administrator – What I loved were the days when you were in. We had great fun, we worked really hard and we had lunch at a fantastic café which specialised in wonderful soups and fruit crumbles to die for. It was wonderful working with you, though my heart would sink as time and again the budget would prove to be a work of fiction.

I used to work in the office at the Mill. Getting there was quite an adventure. After a train journey and a bus ride I'd start by grappling with the 12 foot high, very heavy, metal sliding doors at the entrance, climbing several flights of worn stone steps which were covered in pigeon shit, negotiating another heavy metal door, then finally climbing a glorified ladder to reach the administrative hub of this international touring company.

The Mill was freezing cold in the winter, autumn and spring. It was my first experience of keeping on hat, coat and gloves in the office – in fact I bought some fingerless gloves specially. I was accompanied in my work by the birds and rats that lived in the walls. Visiting the loo was another adventure. In the summer it was OK, except when the chain came off and the only way to flush was to climb a ladder and lift the ballcock manually. In the winter the water froze; need I say more! That was the downside, and it was soul-destroying.

The visit of the clearly wealthy, perfumed lottery assessor was one of the more cringeworthy experiences. We'd hoped to take him to the nice café for lunch but all that was open was a very dodgy greasy-spoon. We were all laughing and pretending everything was fine, but I knew he hated it and was appalled by where we were based. He remarked in his report that, in terms of access, even able-bodied people were challenged in trying to gain access to the premises. He had a point.

Eventually we moved to the city centre, which was a vast improvement for me. I could get there easily, just a train ride and 10 minutes' walk. There was plenty of space and there was heating, and a café in the same building. We even bought a computer. I was lonely when the company was on tour and generally in a state of heightened anxiety as I was dependent on you calling me. We didn't even have a mobile phone in those days, let alone e-mail. I'd get a frantic call and then have to fax papers through to an hotel in the middle of Europe. And then cross my fingers that they'd got through.

The isolation got to me. I only really liked it when you were in. By this time I had become your confidante; we were very close. That's the legacy for me. In 1998 I was offered a job with another theatre company for 2 days a week. At that point I was working 2, sometimes 3 days for Skinning the Cat and 2 days for an arts management consultancy. Something had to go and in the first instance it was the consultancy firm. Then after a few months the theatre company offered me 2 more days, I decided to only work 4 days a week in total and I took the decision to leave Skinning the Cat. You were about to go on tour and I had to tell you before you left. Somehow the day wasn't working out right and I ended up having to tell you I was leaving as you drove me through Bradford on my way home. It was awful. You stopped the van straight away and burst into tears. In hindsight, I realise that I was someone you had utterly depended on.

I loved the challenge of working in grubby old mills. When the lottery assessor complained about the access, I was surprised. After all, I had been on crutches for two years and I still made it in via the goods lift.

What I couldn't understand about the lottery assessor, with his posh car, designer suit and aftershave, was that we so clearly needed the funding. I mean, if we already had a nice heated building with disabled access, why would we be applying? But he was not impressed by us. A different personality might at least have given us some advice about re-submitting our funding bid. But he really could not get away quickly enough.

I loved Dot's cafe. The Arts Centre café, where we went once a week, was nice. But Dot's was our regular haunt. Grubby, greasy, smelled a bit like an old people's home and full of builders eating piles of bacon butties and slurping mugs of steaming tea. Pensioners could get a meal deal and stay for a chat. We ate piles of egg, chips and beans with extra-cheap white sliced bread to mop up, together with a big mug of tea. It gave us a comfortable warm feeling that enabled us to go back and work in the cold damp mill. Fantastic.

Dot herself was of course the centre of it all. She knew all her customers by name and everybody's favourite orders. On special days, there was jam roly-poly or treacle pudding with custard. We felt rather sick afterwards, but would soon be off to Manningham Sports Centre to work it all off on the trapeze!

We were based at Bradford Art Studios, which was an artists' collective based in another dripping old wool mill, with holes in the roof and a small wood-burning stove at one end of a large communal room. We felt true camaraderie as we huddled around the wood burner, getting warm from tea and packets of chips. There were sculptors, painters, photographers, ceramicists and Skinning the Cat. We had to haul all our heavy equipment up via the goods lift; when it snowed we had to dig the van out of the yard.

It was always great to return to the Art Studios after a tour. We would all go for a curry and to the pub. The Skinning the Cat office was like a shanty town hut in the corner of our storage and making-space. I didn't mind the cold too much: it was what I was used to, I dressed like an Eskimo and was always moving about, shifting equipment and making things. The cold also justified the huge amounts of comforting carbs we liked to eat at lunchtime.

The artists were a co-operative which included some really talented and interesting people. Photographer Lizzie, my house-mate, was one of them. There was a real sense of community. I remember some good parties. We all helped each other with projects, pooling skills, and of course everyone went to the Bavaria pub.

At one time, when we were trying to publicise the art studios, I rigged some equipment from the beam which stuck out from the loading bay, through the wall to the outside of the building. Originally, it had been used to haul wool bales into the upper stories of the mill. There is a picture in the local newspaper of us doing a routine on it, with the studio artists peering nervously out of the open loading bay doors.

Anne, administrator – Since first meeting you at circus workshop, I had followed Skinning the Cat with interest, seeing your shows whenever I could, and as you became more successful artistically I helped set up some basic admin systems. As a 'thank you,' you made me a beautiful patchwork jacket with a hood that I still have and still wear to this day. It's a slightly odd shape, in that the sleeves seem to be facing backwards, but what does that matter when something has been made with love?

One Friday evening in the pub after circus workshop in late '94 you came in and announced that I could leave my job and go and work for you, because you'd managed to get the money together to pay me for a year. In January 1995 I started work full time as Administrator with Skinning the Cat. On a snowy January morning you collected me in the Skinning the Cat van and gave me a lift to the office base at the Art Studios in Thornton.

The rent on the studio space was minimal. All props, rigging and materials were kept there and the view from the office was absolutely stunning over the valley. There were two gaps in the stone walls of the office which were also pretty spectacular – with a little bit of skill I could waggle a ruler through and into the outside world. My previous job had been based in the centre of Leeds, in an office that was equipped with phone, fax machine, IBM PCs, photocopier, franking machine, central heating, a cleaner, an account at a stationery suppliers and facilities such as the bank and post office nearby.

My new workspace provided me with phone, fax and Amstrad computer. The photocopier was based at the grocer/newsagent but it couldn't be used when bread was being delivered because the deliveries got piled on top of the photocopier. Mrs Patel (the newsagent) advised me that the best time to use it was about three in the afternoon, but she used to get a bit cross with me if I went too often as the machine would frequently run out of toner, or get overheated, or 'simply wasn't meant to be used so regularly'. We didn't have a franking machine and I had to remember that the post office in the village closed for lunch.

For heating I had a choice: use a Calor gas heater, which was slightly faulty and a bit gassy, or freeze to death. I chose thermal underwear, fingerless mittens and the gas heater. And brought some heavy velvet curtains from home to put across the door and window. Cleaning wasn't a problem – the office was a bit dusty but who cared. The computer had a beautiful fabric cover over it to keep out the dust, we got stationery supplies from a cheap place at the market, and going to the bank meant going into the city. It was simply a matter of being organised.

Some of the systems in place were fine, others not so. I recall buying a year planner and some coloured dots: a white dot meant an enquiry; a yellow dot meant that negotiations were under way and green meant a confirmed booking. Well, it was comforting for me to be able to see at a glance where we were up to with the various enquiries.

The first day was spent hearing about plans for the year: promoting and booking the current show, *Enchantress*, the collaboration with the Liverpudlian band Urban Strawberry Lunch, and learning about the agents that the company used in Europe. My first meeting with the accountant, who looked just like Bart Simpson, was so funny: he was very anxious to know how long I was going to be with Skinning the Cat. The relief in his voice when I told him that it would be for at least a year was amazing.

At the time, Skinning the Cat had two main vehicles: the 'Pat van' – so called because it was like the van driven by Postman Pat and the 'Cat van' – which was big and white. Big white van needed replacing, and you had been successful in obtaining funds from the Foundation for Sport and the Arts to buy a replacement, which was quite exciting. One day you told me that you'd been talking to a guy called Joe – 'looks like a pirate, you'll have seen him at juggling conventions' – who said he could get us a van for £5,000. I was asked to 'nip down to the bank, get the money, meet Joe in the Java café and give him the dosh.' So I have to walk into a caff with five grand in used notes, hand it over to a bloke who looks like a pirate and I don't receive anything in return; my suggestion that I give him a cheque wasn't seen to be a good idea.

In the end I was worrying needlessly, although my husband did insist on going to the caff as well, 'just in case'. I made him come in a little bit after me and sit a few tables away. He hid behind a newspaper and I think he rather enjoyed playing at bodyguards. Joe did indeed look like a pirate but he was absolutely charming and didn't even insist on counting the notes there and then. And the van, when it arrived, turned out to be okay as well.

On one occasion I was in the office, having sent the company off on a booking to somewhere in Holland, when I received a slightly frantic phone call from you saying that you had arrived in France but the immigration authorities were refusing to let one of the team into the country because, as an Australian, she needed a visa to enter France! This was the first anyone knew of this but, as the authorities were refusing to budge, my mission was to somehow get a plane ticket for her to enable her to fly from 'somewhere, anywhere' in the UK to an airport in Holland where the company were due to perform the following day. As cheaply as possible, of course. There really was never a dull moment.

Those first months were fascinating as I saw the props, rig and costumes for *Enchantress* being developed. The mill, where most of the work was done, was absolutely freezing and while you thought I had a tough time in the office I think I had it easy compared to you, Claire, Helen and Vicki: there were occasions when the glue that was used to stick layers of papier mâché together actually froze.

We worked our way through a few office administrators; the cold and frequent isolation eventually got to them. There was a year when a new administrator was left alone for the summer as we were almost solidly abroad. I became slowly aware that something was wrong as I could not get hold of her and information wasn't getting through to me. On our return in the autumn, it transpired that she had become ill and not an awful lot had been done in the office. Faxes from booking enquiries, not replied to, were strewn around the desk, bookkeeping had not been done and there was no work set up for us – so, no money coming in to pay for administrative help.

Sitting in the freezing cold shanty-town office in the mill I look helplessly at the mess of paperwork, I am exhausted and need an end-of-tour break but it is not going to happen. I pull myself together and crack on with sorting stuff out. The administrator is very ill with an unknown disease and is talking about dying. She is rushing through her marriage, just in case. I think that I am dealing with the crisis calmly and maturely but that night I dream of murder: the victim is non-specific and I am not aware of committing the act, but I know that I have killed someone. I dispose of the body, dreaming in detail of parts in black bin bags.

I am holding a machine gun
I am running away from something in the woods,
I have done something terrible again.

Clearly, I was suppressing murderous anger but I didn't know how to get rid of it so I carried on with the office work and went to her hen night to celebrate with her friends. I felt like a fraud. I went to the wedding too, feeling guiltily resentful. I was so very tired.

CHAPTER 31

Henri

> **Carabiners** – generally used by rock climbers. Aerialists use them on our rigging harnesses. They have a screw gate which can be snapped open and closed quickly when moving around the rig.

We were staying in a hotel in Ghent during a couple of days off in the middle of our first hectic tour of Germany, when Henri first arrived in my life. Ba's knees had become increasingly painful. She could hardly walk and was very depressed. All of us were wiped out from struggling with the extra burden of her work on top of a rather-too-packed touring schedule.

We were in the middle of a crisis meeting about how best to return Ba to England for rest and treatment, and how to get a new technician out to us, when Lou piped up: 'If it makes any difference, I'm pregnant.' That was the first we heard of Henri.

He was due to be born about six weeks before we started rehearsing for the following year's tour. Lou and I planned, without hesitation, how we would take him with us. Lou was very determined to keep on working and I was equally determined that we must be able to support her. I never stopped to think about whether Lou or the rest of the company could cope.

I bought Henri a tiny little caravan which doubled up as a tea room, and we all painted it yellow and wrote our logo on the side. We planned to take a nanny with us, so that there would be always someone to look after him during rigging and show times. We had several different nannies, none of whom were actual nannies: students on placement, company friends and my youngest sister Annaliese. They were paid badly and really must have come because they wanted to. Henri and his nanny became a crucial part of 'us'. It was both a fantastic experience and an incredibly difficult one. It put my relationship with Lou under strain as she was exhausted. It also bonded us.

Henri adjusted amazingly well and was the centre of many of our long-standing 'on tour' stories. There was the time when, needing to leave a site in a hurry, we couldn't find the van keys. We were so busy looking for them that we ignored Henri, who was crying because he needed to have his nappy changed. Eventually Lou gave in – and discovered that he had posted the keys down the front of his nappy.

His routine was non-existent. He played with ratchets instead of rattles and played at driving the van when we needed him out of the way. He came everywhere with us, including late night parties. Many was the time, I am ashamed to say, that Lou would push Henri's chair back to the caravan with one of us on either side, drunkenly using it for support. I eventually ran over his pushchair in the truck – luckily without him in it--and he had to learn to walk! When I asked him recently if he remembered anything, he said: 'A Cindy doll and a red van.' We had a Cindy doll dressed as a mermaid sitting as a mascot on the dashboard of the red van.

Lou, company member – when I found out I was pregnant I was in Holland with Skinning the Cat. I can remember it quite well, I was sharing a room with Lucie and she had seen the pregnancy test thing in the bin. I didn't think anybody had spotted it but that's the thing about Skinning the Cat, everyone knew everything about you.

I went to the Doctors in Holland, I can remember exactly the street, and he said 'you can carry on doing what you are doing now, just as long as it's the same as you normally do'. I thought 'that's fine.' I had an obstinate determination, I didn't want it to interrupt my life. When I came back to the hotel from the doctors and everybody was in the middle of a crisis meeting about Ba's knees so I said 'if it makes any difference I'm pregnant'. Everyone was so happy but I wasn't so happy, I just felt, 'Oh my god what does this mean'. But when it worked out that I could take Henri on tour it was so fantastic. I could do the things I like and have the baby with me. I was able to pass him around the group, which was only really possible because it was all women. He did become quite a group mascot. I look through the photos and I see pictures of people running around with him in a pushchair amongst the trees. I didn't see myself as a stay-at-home mother, because I just don't think I could have done it like that. It was just extraordinary what we did, thinking back, it was amazing how the other members of Skinning the Cat helped with the baby on tour.

I remember once in Germany walking through the door going to the breakfast room and just bursting into tears. I was really embarrassed, but I hadn't had any sleep: he didn't sleep through the night until he was 5 years old. That's partly because of the life we led, but it might also have been the kind of character he is, you can't really be sure. We led such an erratic life, I loved it. I don't like routine and there wasn't a chance of being bored.

Another time in Germany, he'd woken up at 4 or 5, I went for a coffee or a drink in a café and he'd slipped down the side of a wall and sliced open his ear. Luckily there was a surgeon in the next-door house and he'd stitched up Henry's ear. He had 2 stitches in his ear before anyone had even woken up and that was just the beginning of the day.

He was 8 weeks old when we started rehearsing; he went on 3 tours in 2 years. Well it was just nuts really. I believe that the stress of it did lead to me falling, but now I look at the photos and think, wow what an introduction to life. The first time he got on the stage was at *Oerol* festival, he went to the front, it was dark and the lights went on him and then people cheered. After that we couldn't get him off: at the end of every show he wanted to go up on stage and collect the props.

When we were in Italy, one of the aerialists, a French girl, Sylvie, had to go home because her father was dying, and we all had to do extra jobs to cover for Sylvie. Becky's sister Annaliese, who was nanny to Henri, took on controlling the trapdoor in the show so we had to find someone else to look after Henri. We just passed him to complete strangers. When we went to look for him after the show he was in the hands of the most enormous baker, surrounded by elderly women trying to sing English nursery rhymes to him, and they didn't want to give him back. It was just fantastic. But he did put pressure on the rest of the group, I didn't really appreciate that at the time, I was in another world.

I always throw myself into my work; I want to do more than I possibly can in every job. I think it's creative drive, it sounds romantic to call it that but it makes us obsessive, selfish, possessive and single minded. In a way, taking Henry on tour might seem like a very selfish thing to do, but for me it was brilliant. He got socialised, he was used to being around other people, he didn't get frightened by things. He caused chaos to our lives. When I think of the effect it's had on him now, who knows? They do say the first 2 years of life are the most impressionable. He didn't have Dusty with him but there were 5 other adults. Also there had to be rules. As Annaliese took him out of harm's way as the rig was being pulled up, he'd shout, 'no Annin. no Annin. no', but he still had to go. He was a very happy child on tour.

My mum's birthday is in June. I was always away, normally abroad, so we would celebrate some other time. But the year that she was going to be 60, my siblings and I had discussions all winter about how best to celebrate it. Every time we thought that we had an idea, Mum would scupper it by ringing one of us up and insisting that she didn't want anything done, especially not a party. My brother took this at face value, but I wasn't fooled after years of Mum insisting that we should ignore Mother's Day then being chuffed to bits with cards or presents. Mum is incredibly sociable and has many friends.

We eventually took the risk and organised a secret party on a barge, followed by a buffet back at Mum's. We invited everyone that we could think of. It was almost blown by one confused friend ringing Mum to ask if she could stay the night which sent Mum into a complete panic and took a lot of smoothing over.

The main problem was that Annaliese and I were away on tour. She was being Henri's nanny and we were working in Holland that week, miles from an airport. Mum thought that we were just having a family get-together and that only Crispin and Nadya and their partners would be there. After years of being tough with other company members regarding family events, I could hardly call off a show for my mum. In any case, the company needed the money. Poor Lucie had missed her sister's wedding one year: it was just part of the job.

The show was a couple of hours' drive away from Amsterdam airport and there was no public transport late at night. There seemed to be no hope of getting to the party. The night before the party we had to do a show and a de-rig, but at the last minute it transpired that a long-term fan of ours from Amsterdam was coming to visit. I managed to persuade her to drive back to Amsterdam late at night and drop us off at the airport. It was a hair-raising journey. She insisted that I sat next to her as she drove and spent the whole time with her hand on my knee and looking at me intently. Annaliese, sitting in the back, was terrified as we swerved around the road.

We took a night flight and made it back safely. Nadya sneaked out from Mum's house on some pretext and picked us up from Bristol Airport. It was so worth it to see Mum's face when we both walked in for breakfast. She still thought that it was just family, so when we took her to the barge and she saw all her friends she was actually thrilled. It was a brilliant day. At one point, I looked over to smile at Annaliese: she was asleep in the corner of the barge – it was enough just to be there!

CHAPTER 32

Malabar and Salvador

> **Mermaid** – a move underneath the trapeze bar with both ankles together hooked around one side of the bar; the near hand holds the opposite side, with the far hand being free to gesture. The legs are straight and the body leans sideways creating the shape of a mermaid's tail.

In 1990 we were performing at Stockton International Festival. As we were putting up the rig a large group of French performers were brought over and introduced to us. There were so many of them, all very friendly and confident. They were dressed in the French circus/street performers 'uniform' of scruffy black leather trousers and faded black t-shirts. I felt very small, new and young. They were from the company Malabar, who I had heard much about, and I was looking forward to catching their show.

The show started with a parade: first a large, white ship, like a ghost ship, part skeleton and part covered, glided majestically in the streets. The ground became sea as they pumped enormous amounts of white foam out, filling the street with sea spray flying up into the air. Stilt-walkers strode alongside the ship, in extravagant costumes covered in spindly protrusions, skeletal and ghost like to match the ship.

The ship slid eerily through the foam-filled streets, stopping once it reached another group of performers, then all the whiteness merged into blackness. There was a vehicle covered in ripped up materials and welded metal. The costumes now were red and black, scruffy and weathered. Everything was raw-looking with a tremendous energy. The music was hard and fast, upbeat and exciting. The atmosphere became anarchic; at the peak of the energy they arrived at an aerial rig with a wild, fast cloud swinger performing on it. Their simple scaffolding rig looked thrown together and dangerous, and the whole show seemed to be particularly close to the edge. The air smelled of smoke and fireworks which were thrown or held on sticks. There were acrobats tumbling along the ground. I was so involved that I ran along beside them, completely swept along by the strong feeling.

I kept the special feeling of the show with me and was reminded of Malabar again when I was in Paris that winter, having meetings with a potential French agent. I had a couple of days to enjoy myself between meetings so I looked around for the local practice spaces, with the intention of getting some training done and meeting some new people. I found my way to the Palacy flying trapeze school on the edge of Paris and managed to secure myself one of their caravans for the week.

The great thing about being part of the circus scene is that you can arrive in a city, find the hub of aerial training activity and have an immediate bond with the people there. I have found this all over the world. I learn some stuff, teach some stuff and have a whole bunch of new friends. I was just waiting for my turn on the flying rig when I heard a babble of French conversation with the words 'Skinning the Cat' inserted in the middle. I turned around to see a member of Malabar who I'd met at Stockton Festival. This is a joy of working in a small world: you so often re-meet people, bump into an old friend or at least create a bond by discussing mutual friends; sometimes just the name of your company or the skills you do brings you recognition and a welcome.

His name was Salvador, a Spanish man living in Paris and working with Malabar. He invited me to stay at his apartment in Paris, so I dumped the caravan – how could I refuse? He became my boyfriend for a couple of years; we either met at our homes in the off-season or visited each other at different show sites. He was an acrobat and an aerialist of the type I really admire, a purist. He would practise one thing, a somersault or a throw out, to the exclusion of all else; a question about how he was or what he was doing would lead to long explanations of where he was at with these obsessions. I am more of a generalist, seeing a show as a whole, working on different bits of routine, making costumes and organising the tours. He used to get frustrated at the amount of time I spent on the general responsibilities of Skinning the Cat, wanting me to spend the time on the trapeze with him.

Staying with Salvador in Paris always meant training time, either watching him rehearse a show or training together on the trapeze. I found his French friends very intimidating to train with: Continental Europe was ahead of the UK in circus skills and they also spoke so fast that I couldn't understand; after initial attempts to join in with my pidgin French I would lapse into silence.

We always went together to see the circus shows that were on in Paris. French shows often have a bar in the Big Top, which creates a relaxed, cabaret-style atmosphere, and chairs may be set around little tables. In one particular show the whole tent was decorated with fairy lights around a central tree, with real birds flying around inside. I remember one costume/prop which was based on the first aeroplanes, with fragile wings and tensioned wires. The most amazing thing was that their Big Top had a transparent cupola and they did the show at sunset.

Salvador lived in a tiny two-room apartment at the top of a very high building. It had a little balcony with a great view across the Parisian street, from which you felt both part of Parisian life and a spectator. The rooms were set up like living in a caravan, in that the bed had to be put away every day to provide sitting room space, and the shower, which was in the kitchen, had to be assembled for each use by putting a tray on the floor and pulling a curtain across.

Salvador looked very Spanish, dark of course with incredibly sharp cheekbones and arched black eyebrows. He had an acrobat/trapeze artists body, compact with broad shoulders. He was smaller than me, more of a classic acrobatic size than my Amazonian look and height, but traditional stereotypes never bothered me. The nature of my relationship with Salvador suited me at this time; it was exciting and never became mundane. I loved the feeling of being part of a world which was forever changing and re-adjusting, flitting around Europe, in and out of each other's lives.

The summer following my trip to Paris, and the successful acquisition of a French agent, was the first time that we worked in France. I had never been anywhere where artists were treated and paid so well. The French artists were very confident about their rights: if the food, conditions, site or accommodation was not quite up to scratch they were extremely vocal about it. Each event would have a canteen marquee with long communal tables and a larger-than-life French cook dishing out helpings of wholesome food. The conversation was loud and very male, as all the performers overlapped with the riggers and technicians; the boundaries between them are often blurred in the circus arts.

French circus and outdoor theatre is highly respected, funded and organised. They have extensive conferences, networks, publications and high powered committees lobbying for profile and quality. As a result of this the standard of the artistic and physical skills is very high, with some excellent circus schools and training programmes. At the time, artists were well supported by the government financially: their benefits system took into account that an artist must take time out of paid work to train and make shows. The investment is a good one, as the French have a reputation abroad for excellence in this field. The French shows were on a scale that we could only dream of: a story told through a life size pop-up book; a temporary railway line installed; mobile theatrical props the size of a small building; companies supporting as many technicians as artists. It was breath-taking.

Our show was very gentle compared to the French style and for a while I briefly tried to present us more like them, inspired by their productions but also out of insecurity, producing an aggressive poster which didn't suit us at all and certainly didn't work. They seemed keen on us as we were.

When I first saw the French circus Archaos I was completely blown away. It was the first time they came to England; the show was presented in a big top with an internal skin made of rope like a giant web. They had amazing energy and brilliant disorganisation. I have since learnt through my own shows that creating that level of crazy disorganisation takes an amazing amount of technical preparation and rehearsal.

Archaos approached circus from a completely original angle. The cradle for the catcher of the flying trapeze was on a forklift truck, the clown was a butcher, the horses were motorbikes. It was smelly and oily and not a sequin in sight.

As in all circuses, there were injuries and accidents because they constantly pushed boundaries. Part of the reason for circus is to create daring feats which seem impossible to a normal human, but there can be a price to be paid by the individual, who can get left behind when they have worn out or injured their body.

I finally split up with Salvador, as I was under pressure to give up Skinning the Cat and work with him in a duo, which is the only realistic way that circus performers can be properly together. I was not ready for this and, as always, I reacted badly to pressure and backed right off. It was around this time that the pattern of my relationships with men started to change.

The death of my dad and the line crossed by my grandpa are very connected for me. They both left me in a dark place in their different ways, and as the stress in my life was building up it began to manifest itself through my relationships with men. I met a German lighting technician, Andre, during a show in Munich. He seemed nice and we were attracted to each other. He kept calling and faxing me, and after I had returned home he booked a flight to England. I got scared and didn't want him to come. He refused to take no for an answer and arrived. Half way through the evening, as his attitude became aggressive, I noticed that the bottle of gin in the kitchen was almost empty. I holed up in my bedroom.

I wasn't in a good place at the time. I had had another of my stress attacks and felt very vulnerable. Despite my doubts, I began a relationship with him. We had some good times but I don't know what I was doing really. When, on a visit to Germany, we had a terrible row, we made up the next day and he asked me to marry him. I said yes. I didn't love him and I didn't want him: I was scared and I was losing myself.

When I got away from him I cut off all contact but, for all that year, every time we did a show in Germany, he found us and turned up. He gave me the collywobbles. I could not talk about it, so the others thought that I was being callous. They believed in my reputation as a man-eater, unaware that I had lost my confidence and had handed over the power. 'Oh, poor Andre,' they would say.

He's over there sitting on the street bollard, waiting as we put the rig up. I don't like being close to men any more, they seem to expect so much and I cannot give it. I am no longer in control. I want to be left alone.

In the night I go to that dark space where a man has taken me,
I am desperately digging for love in the wrong place,

I go inside myself to feel safe.

I am powerless to stop him and it will end in my pain,
gasping sick pain –
after the man has gone.

CHAPTER 33

Amsterdam and Wanda

> **'Dogs'** are used to splice the end of cables in order to attach them to the rig or webbing strap, clamping the loose end back to make a loop. A metal U goes around the two pieces of cable, which is then trapped by a metal piece slotted onto both ends of the U and firmly bolted. Each rig had a huge number of cables and each end needed a minimum of three dogs, each of which had two bolts. This was a job to be done at the beginning of the tour and then checked once in a while – very boring.

We loved our touring breaks in Amsterdam and had many friends there. I look back on the first time we ever went there and cringe. We had been told that we could buy dope in coffee shops so, as soon as we got to the outskirts of the city, we stopped at the first café we came to. We did not realise that a 'coffee shop' in this context is a specific type of café and not just anywhere that sold coffee. It was pretty embarrassing. After that setback, we nervously sidled into the correct type of coffee shop in central Amsterdam, still embarrassed from our first experience, and asked in hushed tones if we could buy some dope. It was the opposite experience: the woman behind the counter slapped down a huge album displaying every type of dope and grass you could imagine. Taken aback by her openness, and not knowing about the different types, we just chose one which looked nice!

During the summer it can be very hard to find anywhere to stay in Amsterdam, and that first year we didn't know the places for living in vehicles. Luckily, our friend Pino from Stalker Stilt Theatre took us in and we camped on her floor for a few days. She lived in an amazing squat: an old perfume factory split up into separate bedrooms, with large communal cooking and living areas. The Dutch are ingenious at creating living quarters out of any space: a boat, a factory, a bit of a hut on someone's roof, whatever it takes.

We soon started using Amsterdam as a regular northern European base and found a site on the edge of town where we could stay in our caravan. There were several of these types of settlements on bits of waste ground or strung along the edges of dykes.

The Dutch are very efficient and run everything by inflexible lists of rules. Even squats and vehicle sites are run strictly, with committees and waiting lists. Over the years, I spent more and more time in Amsterdam, even moving my big and much-loved caravan 'Wanda' there for a few winters. I found a small aerial training community there where I could earn a bit of money teaching and selling aerial equipment.

It was hard to contact me when I was wintering in Amsterdam in Wanda, and this was the point. I wanted to escape the ever-increasing strain of the Skinning the Cat office. As the shows grew bigger and more varied, we were increasingly under pressure and I needed a break sometimes. I felt very free on my own in Wanda. I loved cycling around the city, mixing with so many nationalities, drinking tea in cafes and shopping at the flea markets.

Living in Wanda meant that my life revolved around keeping the wood-burning stove alight, especially while it was snowing, and knowing where to get a hot shower. I had been inspired to buy Wanda during the time that I had spent in Jim's gypsy caravan at the circus farm. I bought her from a flamenco dancing gypsy family we had met on the circuit. Their daughter was called Wanda. My caravan was enormous, with a separate double bedroom, kitchen and dining area, and so heavy that she needed to be towed by a truck. Outside she was covered in shiny chrome; the inside was lavishly decorated with etched glass mirrors. She had light-up display cabinets all around her interior and I found great satisfaction in hunting around Dutch flea markets to find just the right artefacts to go in them. I upholstered her with gold velvet cushion covers and red-tasselled velvet curtains. Wanda was my pride and joy.

It was during this time in Wanda that I really expanded my crockery collection. I have inherited the passion from Mum who has a dresser with a collection of mismatched blue-and-white crockery. My theme is gold and/or floral, and the more mismatched the better. My obsession was fuelled by the treasures available in wonderful continental flea markets. And I cannot pass a charity shop without checking their wares.

Every available space in the kitchen and sitting-room of the house where I now live displays my finds. I recently acquired a mirrored crockery cabinet in which everything displayed in it reflects and reproduces itself. It of course reminds me of the mirrored cabinets in Wanda. There is nothing like drinking a cup of tea out of a beautifully decorated fine bone china teacup. I bought a perfect little teapot from a junk shop in Hay-on-Wye and get pleasure every time I pour a cup.

The site in Amsterdam was full of transient people from all over the world. I spent time in the evenings in different caravans, drinking hot chocolate, smoking dope and sharing meals. On a nearby site was Feri, a Dutch man who did an act with crocodiles, snakes and spiders. He had a special climate-controlled vehicle that he kept them in, and some impressive bite scars on his face. I had always thought that aerialists have a tough life, never getting much of a break due to the level of training they must keep up. But getting to know Feri made me realise that here was a performer even more tied down by his work than we were. He told me that, as well as having to constantly monitor the temperature of the animals to keep them safe in their special tank, he had to handle them every single day or else they forgot him. Feri was a very cool character and his crocodiles had cold eyes: there was an absence of the warmth normal between trainers and warmer blooded animals.

We had many friends who either lived in or passed through Amsterdam. I have never met people more passionate about their work than Marley and Vincent, the couple who ran the Brazilian/Dutch company, *Corpus*. They were both physically striking, tall and athletic, one dark and one fair. They were acrobats, who later employed me to teach them aerial work.

Marley and Vincent lived in a squat in a rambling old school which was freezing at all times of year. Bedrooms had been built in the old classrooms on mezzanine floors and the only heat came from wood-burning stoves. A wood-burner can heat up my caravan in ten minutes but in this place, no chance. The décor was beautifully eccentric: there were huge old chandeliers and large patterned rugs hung from the ceilings to create smaller spaces and trap some warmth. I often stayed or worked with them. They were very intense; there was no such thing as a casual conversation over dinner, only fiery discussions about circus work and our latest projects, followed by some impromptu acrobatics.

The festival that best sums up the Dutch style is *Oerol* on the island of Terschelling, in the north of Holland. It was one of our favourite places to work. The whole island is taken over by the event. As you approach on the ferry, you see art installations on the beaches and, as you drive to your site, bizarre sculptures in the fields. There are many sites all over the island, covered in big tops and stages. My favourite structure was the Spiegel tent, a German design, big top-shaped but made of wood, and intricately and densely decorated with paintings, chandeliers and etched glass mirrors – rather like a larger version of Wanda!

Among these venues were many different kinds of aerial rigs, side shows and bizarre constructions that couldn't be identified until the show unfolded. On the village streets, an extensive programme of weird and wonderful theatre and walkabout acts took place. The costumes and characters that were devised for the streets were the most inventive I have seen anywhere. Festivals like this always attracted the best of the best. It was always exciting for our company to go to this festival. It was a point of pride to be booked on the main programme, and we would meet up with old friends and make lots of new ones. It was inspiring to see as many shows as possible, some of which had taken weeks to set up. Often the most beautiful were the smaller shows, lovingly made and performed by dedicated artists.

Ba, company technician – I really loved this festival; I had a near-religious experience in a natural amphitheatre in the pine woods. But best of all was being told not to worry about the weather: they would tell us when the rain would stop. They pointed up to the sky, saying 'We get weather reports from up there.' It seemed like they were suggesting God, but it turned out they had a helicopter up there to give them a weather report!

CHAPTER 34

The Show

> **Ankle straps** – made of tough stretch bandage or laced-up leather. These protect the ankles from rope burns and sweat slippage while on the ropes.

The relaxed atmosphere of rigging day would disappear as we neared pre-show time. This is what we called the two hours prior to the show and involved putting on make-up, costumes and doing our stretching exercises. First, we would sit round the caravan table, or, if we were lucky, in a more spacious dressing room supplied by the booker, chatting as we did our make-up. This took up to half an hour – but, at a push, I could do it in fifteen minutes. I used bright colours, gold and silver swirls inspired by Balinese dancers. It was always bold and bright, to match the patterns and style of our costumes, with plenty of coloured glitter to catch the lights. We glued red sequins to our eyelids so that, when we blinked under theatrical lighting, our pupils appeared red and added to our other-worldliness.

Next was our warm-up. This was very important for protecting the body from the strains of the show. At least half an hour of stretching was required. If the weather was warm, we would unroll the big gymnastics mat outside the caravan, arousing local interest. I also used this time to start focusing my brain on my performance.

The final part of the transformation was when we all crammed in the caravan to put on costumes. After the costumes came headdresses, then ankle straps and wrist tapes. Then finally the cry of: 'Where's the resin sock? Who's got it?' Resin is the sticky stuff from trees, dried and ground to a powder, with which we covered our hands for gripping. We always had several of these resin socks positioned around the rig but, somehow, one was never to be found in the caravan before we went on. Finally, Helen would put on our upbeat pre-show music and there was the inevitable last minute rush to the toilet before we took up our positions for the entrance.

One frustrating part of doing outdoor shows is when you work all day rigging and the show is rained off. It can also happen the opposite way round: rain all day while you are rigging, then suddenly stop just before the show. In common with everybody who works outside, we have the best job in the world – and the worst. During the show, a backdrop of scudding black clouds, sunsets or fantastic moonlight is a special effect that you could not buy.

Our show was a night time spectacle and that's what we planned for. But often we were booked for daytime events. The worst thing was sweltering heat: the show did not look good and it was hell for us to work in. An engagement that I always thought looked good on our list of shows was our grand opening of the Channel Tunnel. But actually we were rained off! Most of the time performing outdoors really suited me, but sometimes struggling with wind and rain just got too much.

We often spent our pre-show preparation time, when we should have been warming up our muscles, racing up and down the ropes, putting tarpaulins on and off the rigging, which must not get wet. Or it could suddenly start to pour down in the middle of a show. In those circumstances, we had an understanding that the first artist to feel her grip going would slide down to the ground and that was the cue for the technician to fade out the music and make an audience announcement. One time in France, when Jo panicked about having to make an announcement in French, she couldn't remember the word for rain, so she just used the English word *rain* at the end of her French sentence. The audience hung about in a slightly puzzled way, and we were told afterwards that it had translated as 'we will have to stop the show because of the Queen'. They were unsure whether to expect her arrival or if it was just some strange patriotic English tradition!

The show followed a formula dictated by the nature of aerial routines. The average routine lasted four to seven minutes and between each one was a rigging change. The rigging changes could take about one minute, so this is where a fire club routine, stilt walking beasts, a character sketch or special effects would take place. In the early shows, I did five aerial routines: corde lisse, cloud swing, doubles trapeze, doubles web, solo trapeze and fire clubs. By the final show before I retired, I did one routine!

The beginning of the show is very important. We would often start with a special effect. For the show *Enchantress*, I entered with purple smoke. Occasionally it would fail to set off and my entrance would fall rather flat. One of the most embarrassing things ever to happen to me on stage was when I was meant to perform a wild and whirling fire club display to cover the rigging change going on behind me, but the stage manager was unable to get the lighter to work, so she passed the fire clubs to me unlit. It was hard to be wild and whirling with a couple of unlit sticks. The memory still makes me cringe.

The hardest times to perform were in extreme temperatures. When it was very hot, make-up used to drip off the end of my nose onto Rachel, swinging beneath me, and it was a struggle to hold the bar with sweating hands. Or when it was freezing cold: when we played outdoors in Edinburgh on New Year's Eve, my hands were so cold that when I tried to catch my trapeze partner, I was unable to feel her.

The best shows were outside at night on mild evenings with a slight breeze and the moon behind the rig like a free special effect. I really felt like part of the elements, standing on the platform up high on the rig, surrounded by darkness and the black shadows of people and trees behind the spotlights.

Straight after a show, all we really wanted to do was to wash, get changed, relax and chat to the people who came to meet us and have a drink. Unfortunately, there was always rigging, props and electrics to be put away and, if we had to leave that night, the whole structure had to be de-rigged. The least popular part of our work was loading the truck. It was heavy work and frustrating at the end of a long de-rig. There was a lot of waiting around and passing stuff up to the people who were doing the packing.

We always had more stuff than space, so the packing was quite an art form. Claire became obsessed with filling gaps: she would crawl around in the tunnels between tightly packed equipment, growling if anyone put something in before she'd filled a space. It was tough on a small team to have to remove costumes, put on a harness straight away, climb up the rig again and get all the rigging down. Our preferred option, whenever possible, was to throw tarps over everything, invite our friends into the caravan and open our bar.

CHAPTER 35

The Fire

> **Block and tackle** – pulleys assembled together to form blocks, with rope threaded through them so that one block is fixed and another moves. This system removes the load from the arms onto the blocks and amplifies the force applied when lifting.

It was the first show of the season. We had rehearsed with a new member of the company, Australian Zoe. The site was in Dumfries, Scotland. I'd done a site check there earlier in the year and we were to set up in the main square of the town.

It started badly. Before we had even arrived, we were pulled over in a random check by the police to weigh the trucks. We were, of course, over-laden. This cost us some time, but luckily Lou was back at base and able to borrow an extra van from Dusty and come and relieve us of some weight so that we could proceed. We must have decided to rig the day before the show, probably as it was the first of the season and we were working with a new member.

At the end of the day, as we often do when feeling vulnerable in a city centre, we parked the truck within the show arena so that it was cordoned off and the security guards could easily keep an eye on it. The truck was full of props, lighting and sound equipment. We loaded the costumes and pyrotechnics into a smaller van because we wanted to keep them near us. We left the caravan on site, behind the rig, and drove to the hotel. We rarely stayed on site for a city centre show as nobody would get any sleep there.

I was in the heaviest part of my sleep, about 3am, when in a haze I heard the sound of police walkie-talkies and then a knock. I answered the door still half asleep. The police kept asking whether there was anyone sleeping in our caravan. Then I heard that something had burnt down. But it was a few minutes before I realised that it was our rig and caravan, because the police had no clue what the pile of melted metal had once been.

We all piled into vehicles and were taken to the site. Some vandals had hidden behind the caravan, out of view of security, and set light to the bottom of the rig. This must have been pretty difficult as it was fireproofed. But they must have persevered. As the rig had burned, the webbings which were attached to the cables burned through and the structure had fallen, burning, onto the truck and caravan. Not a lot was left: only half a smouldering truck and caravan. The aluminium rig had melted and all but disappeared.

We just stood and looked at it. There was nothing to be done as the fire had been put out. It was a great relief that we weren't in the caravan, that the gas cylinder hadn't exploded and that we had taken the pyrotechnics and costumes with us. All the relevant people were notified and we returned to the hotel.

At the time of the disaster there was a sense of crisis, even of excitement, that carried us through. Then followed a lost and aimless feeling: our core had been removed. The next day, we went with the loss adjuster from the insurance company to the compound where all the debris had been taken. We became like excited prospectors striking gold as we pulled each damp and half-blackened prop out of the truck. The pile of melted and twisted metal was the saddest. Our beautiful rig.

Feeling numb, I got on with the business side of things: police, insurance, press, cancelling shows, dealing with the guilt-ridden booking agent. It was new member Zoe who seemed most visibly upset: she hadn't even got to do the first show.

Jan, company administrator – Saturday morning, and bleary-eyed I answered the phone. Your voice sounded really wobbly and you told me the news. Someone had burned the rig down. I remember sitting on the bed beside Dave, tears in my eyes, gutted. Would I go and check the insurance on the rig? One unspeakable horror was replaced by the thought of another. What if I'd stuffed up, what if the insurance wasn't valid? I was utterly silent as we drove to the office – sick, quite literally, nauseous with worry. I'm SO careless. Then the relief, waves of it, as I found the up-to-date insurance certificate and passed the information on.

Initially, I didn't know what was going to happen next. That was it. With no show we couldn't fulfil our tour schedule and pay off the overdraft which we always accumulated during the rehearsal period. The loss adjuster was surprisingly enthusiastic and helpful. He was determined to sort out our claim in double-quick time and get us back on the road within the month. This kicked me into action although, with hindsight, taking the insurance cheque and going on holiday might have been a wiser option.

We then had the month from hell back in the office, cancelling shows, itemising equipment and costing it up as fast as possible.

Jan, company administrator – Days passed. A birthday, mine or Dave's, I forget, spent working late typing up all the items, an endless list for replacement. By then, the fire had turned from disaster into an opportunity to replace the rig with a better one, to enjoy shopping for new carabiners and all those other bits and bats of rigging. To enter into a shopping frenzy, retail therapy for an aerial theatre company. Budget? But I must have these gold-plated sequins!

Of course, we turned out to be under-insured. The cost of specialised equipment when you build it up slowly over the years is one thing, but the cost of it all when you need it in a hurry, is a whole lot more.

It didn't stop raining all summer. We didn't have time to fit out the new truck properly so we had to bunk in rows on the truck floor and cook on a camping stove.

Miraculously, and madly, we rebuilt the show in a month and re-launched at Glastonbury festival.

CHAPTER 36

Founder of the RSPCA

> **Skinning the cat** – the name of a trapeze move. Hanging underneath the trapeze bar, holding with both hands, swing the body through the arms and continue until the body is hanging at full extension almost, but not quite, dislocating the shoulder joints. Return.

It was the same summer as the fire. Because we had had to remake the show from scratch and hadn't replaced all our facilities, the tour was feeling like extra hard work. We were playing in Birmingham in the grounds of a cathedral. We didn't think too much of it when we first noticed that, in the programme and on the posters, we were billed under the show name rather than, as was normal, our company name.

It turned out that the organisation who had booked us were trying to keep our name a secret, but they hadn't realised that all our vehicles had 'Skinning the Cat' written on them and that there were banners on the rig bearing our name. We have never been ashamed of our name and we didn't choose it to be controversial. It is simply the name of a trapeze move. In the main, it did not cause any problems. People who did not know it was a trapeze move assumed it was something esoteric.

That said, I have had the odd weird experience. Following one of our mail shots, the phone rang and a cross voice said: 'It's disgusting what you do to animals.' And there was a time when one of the company had to bring a kitten with her, as it was on regular medication, and it sat in a basket beside us as we rigged. Someone called the authorities, wanting to know what exactly we were going to do with the kitten...

The cathedral where we were playing turned out to be the final resting place of the founder member of the RSPCA. The booker, who had been keen to get our show, had not mentioned this to us, hoping to hush up our name in case it caused offence. Of course, the papers got hold of the story, which led to my one and only experience of being trapped in a hotel with the press trying to reach us.

Sometimes, we were asked to make special shows, specific for a certain event. I enjoyed doing these as it made us think a bit differently and increased the scale that we worked on. On one occasion, we were asked to tender for Newark's 'Year of the Artist'. They wanted an artist or company of artists to work with community groups in the city to produce a site-specific event based around their castle. I proposed to put several rigs in the grounds, including a central castellated one, which would be placed so that it framed the view of the castle and on which we would perform. As there was a moat, I planned a boat to sail past, carrying giant puppets; giant flowers would inflate on the battlements, and hanging from the castle walls there would be an enormous decorative banner. Working with community groups, we would make the costumes, props, puppets and the banner, which would be paraded between spectacles to link them together.

We were there for weeks. It was a large-scale, challenging project and, while I was directing it, other bookings had to be fulfilled. I loved it. I had booked a large camp, just out of town, where we could all stay. But when we arrived we saw that it was worse than basic. Disgusting, in fact. We could not face weeks there. We found a local B and B which accepted lots of extra mattresses on the floor and we all crammed in there. The couple who ran it were artists, and quite eccentric. They became involved with us and added to the sense of organised chaos in the making and rehearsing of the show.

The day of the show was exciting and unexpectedly funny. I was co-ordinating the extensive space and large numbers of people, with only an unreliable radio set. There were men waiting on the top of the castle to drop the banners and inflate the flowers; a decorated barge hovering behind a bridge, awaiting instructions; teams of community groups and aerialists stationed around the site. Overall the show was successful, but it didn't go without a hitch. It was a windy day and the men on top of the castle had a struggle to prevent the flowers and the banner from flying away. Finally, they had to drop the banner in an unplanned fashion and then, at the moment when the flowers should have reached full inflation, they had to turn off the blower, creating rather a flop – otherwise they would have taken off. And, to crown it all, there was a considerable delay after I had given the barge its entrance cue. This was because the driver, a local man, had spotted some sheep in the water. Quite rightly, he refused to continue until he had hauled them safely out. This was a true community show, sheep and all, and a very good example of why the show should not always come first.

CHAPTER 37

Spain

> **Web rope** – a single rope suspended from a swivel, which must be firmly attached to a static point. Cover a loop of webbing (about half metre circumference) with something soft, such as velvet. Thread the loop through the strands of rope at a height which allows the aerialist to sit up on it with her head remaining lower than the swivel (approx. 2 metres from swivel). Place one end of the loop through the other and pull tight. The loop, now known as the web loop, has a leather keeper around it which then pulls down to trap the aerialist's hand, foot or neck in the loop.

Spain was possibly our favourite country to work in. Certainly, after a stint in Germany, we craved a bit of Spanish wildness, though after a stint in Spain we were desperate for a bit of German efficiency.

Anything went in Spain. I was often booked there with my solo act and was able to rig up my cloud swing much more randomly than in other countries. The narrowness of some Spanish streets lends itself to my favourite rigging technique: choosing two sets of high-up windows close together on opposite sides of the street, feed a cable around the pillar of wall between each set then string a cable up between the two, across the street. I would attach my cloud swing to the taut cable. This made a very bouncy swing, but in the wonderful chaos of a Spanish street event, top technique was not called for. The Spanish loved having an apparently half-crazed aerialist swinging above their heads, while other performers, wearing wild and outlandish costumes, ran amongst them with hand-held fireworks. My Firebird act was very popular in Spain.

Festivals and fiestas in Spain can often run, back to back, all night. It was not unusual to find that, as we were de-rigging from an arts festival, someone else would be waiting to use the space for a beer festival. We would fall into bed at four in the morning, desperate to get some sleep in order to perform again the next night, only to find that the rest of the town didn't have the same concerns and would continue their loud party outside the hotel window. At one time, this got so bad that I had to arrange to stay with friends out of town, just to get a night's sleep.

We worked mainly with the Spanish agency *Free Art*, run by Pilar and Carlos. Unlike most agencies, they understood their acts properly and toured with them to make sure everything was all right. We all loved them. They worked with a select band of companies, all of whom we came to know. After driving or flying long distances it was always a treat to arrive and see their familiar faces.

Arriving in Spain after a three-day drive in a hot truck, we would get taken immediately to a Spanish restaurant: nothing fancy, just long trestle tables and good down-to-earth food and drink. While we ate and drank, Pilar would have long, animated Spanish discussions with a succession of men who would turn up from the town hall or whatever organisation had booked us. This was such a treat for me as I was normally in charge of such things. But Pilar took it all on and had a good understanding of our technical requirements. The discussions would be about the placement of the rig or the position of underground gas pipes and electric cables which our stakes might hit. These conversations went on for ten times as long as they did in other countries, while we relaxed happily and fed our faces.

Eventually, I would go off with one of these people to look at the site, normally a market square, and lift a cobble or a paving stone to test the ground for getting the stakes in. We learned to keep the sledge hammer and a stake handy, after having to unpack the whole truck to get at them one too many times. If we were working in a city centre or market place, the fire service would turn up to check that we would not be blocking any fire engine routes with our rig. They were not officious, just relaxed and Spanish.

We would become a temporary part of the market place activity. There was always a bunch of elderly people who spent the day there, chatting on the benches or playing pétanque. They would watch us with polite interest as we invaded their calm space with our alien look and equipment. In the evening, this informal audience was joined by throngs of strolling young people and families who arrived to watch the show. But it was the old people who stayed on the bench, dressed in traditional Spanish black, with caps and head scarves. Only they saw the whole story.

The main problem with rigging in Spain was the heat. Our schedule never seemed to allow time for a siesta. Working outside all day was a killer; often, by show time we would have mild sunstroke. We wore the skimpiest shorts and vest tops with our rigging boots. I wonder if our dress was offensive to the locals? If it was, they never showed it.

It was in Spain that we played to our biggest ever audience, at an important festival in Tarrega, which attracted groups from all over the world and thousands of bookers and punters. We were popular at this festival and were sited on a square which was like an amphitheatre with steps all around it. The audience was estimated to be three or four thousand, and we felt like pop stars. Our outdoor show was what was called a 'spectacle', which means that it is normally shown at night as lighting effects work best for a large crowd and from a distance. We were often used as the finale of an event, followed by fireworks.

Meal times at Spanish events were very special, with huge catering tents for all the artists and crew. This was very sociable and an opportunity to take a break from members of Skinning the Cat and meet other people. Food would also be served after the late night shows, then we would move en masse to a bar. We loved to meet people and have a few, sometimes too many, drinks.

CHAPTER 38

Russia – St Petersburg

> **The web sitter** – At the bottom of the rope is the web sitter who controls the rope. This job takes a bit of practice to do well. The aerialist climbs up to the loop and, once the hand, foot or neck is trapped in position, the web sitter starts to turn the rope. The web artist performs a number of different positions. With the body in the tucked position the aerialist will spin faster and, when outstretched, slower.

My trip to St Petersburg was organised by Slava Polunin of the Licedei Cowns. Slava has been famous in the UK for many years for his beautiful *Snow Show*. He is the best clown I have ever seen: not a slapstick clown, but a proper mime-based clown, beautifully tragic and deeply moving. He communicates tragedy through his every look and movement. He can change from breaking your heart to childlike play with the blink of an eye. The *Snow Show* is also lively, fun and inclusive, culminating with the audience jumping out of their seats to throw enormous inflatable balls around the auditorium.

I arrived at St Petersburg airport, a grubby, rather depressing, beige-painted building, it was freezing cold. We were herded past stern-faced passport officials as though we were potential criminals. There was nothing at all welcoming or friendly about my arrival, apart from an extremely chatty American clown who got off the same plane as me. We were both picked up and loaded into a battered car by some unsmiling comrades, sent by Slava.

The drive from the airport, through a never-ending grey expanse of ice and snow, seemed long, probably due to the devastating bleakness of the landscape. We were taken straight to our lodgings, an extravagant palace with turrets and golden gates and snow, snow and more snow piled everywhere around it: the Chinese pavilion. Despite its stunning exterior, inside the palace was painted dirty beige and completely bereft of comfort. Our rooms were massive and freezing, with small iron bedsteads and a set of drawers in the corners.

I was to work in the Leningrad circus, but I was lodged with a group of international clowns, brought over by Slava for a festival of clowns. They were a friendly bunch, especially Hilary, the clown who had arrived with me and who had not stopped talking all the way from the airport. It turned out afterwards that she had thought that I was shy – but I simply had not been able to get a word in edgeways.

That first evening, I was taken to see the circus in which I would perform. It was an enormous, old, purpose-built circus building, the type where circus history was made and embedded in its walls. Sitting on the tiered seating inside, I looked up but could not see the top of it; they worked very high, with the rigging points way up in the darkness. I felt sick as I watched the acts: all the Russian artists were of such a high standard and their style was very traditional. What would they think of me and my rope act, dressed as some kind of crazy bird with my Balinese-style make up?

The next day, I had to do a technical run with my equipment. I rigged up my ropes and warmed up. The whole circus had turned out to watch the English girl. No one smiled, spoke or made eye contact; they just stood around the edge of the ring and watched silently. I felt completely intimidated. I found the Russians initially suspicious and not prone to polite displays of friendship or small talk. I found them cold and unfriendly. I could not have been more wrong.

At the palace, things were rough. We had a Russian houseboy to look after us. On the contract, we had been told we would be provided with morning and evening meals, but we had not reckoned on what this would actually mean in Russia. For breakfast, I was provided with boiled rice with the water left in, sloppy and gruel-like, and for dinner, strained boiled rice – dry, so it stuck in the throat. Mmm, lovely! I had brought some tea bags with me. They felt very precious. I got them out hospitably after our meal. Our houseboy put one in each cup and poured on hot water, one for everyone. Most people left them to grow cold. My heart sank: tea is my lifeline and we had used up half the packet.

Communication was difficult with our Russian boy. I had a strange experience one night, when I was woken from my sleep by him sneaking into the room. He approached the bed, lay down and tried to kiss me. I made my disinterest clear and he was not forceful. He sat down on the end of my bed and cried, then shuffled quietly away. Nothing was ever said. The next day, I wondered if I had imagined it.

I felt sorry for him. God knows what was behind this desperate act; we certainly hadn't bonded or flirted beforehand. When I was packing at the end of my stay I found that my emergency cash, which I had wrapped in my socks, was gone. As the bedroom doors were locked, it can only have been him who was able to go through my stuff and help himself. I wasn't too upset about it as I was sure his need was greater than mine.

At that time in St Petersburg, Russians were queuing round the block for bread. Hilary and I roamed the streets, thinking that we would be able to find a café in which to spend our American dollars. We could not find a single place to eat, so we asked our interpreter to take us to one. It turned out that Russian cafes did not have 'fronts'. They were in ordinary people's homes, so you had to be in the know to find them. There was a small counter and a couple of little tables with Russians eating foul-smelling soup. On the counter were a few small plates with, for example, a stick of chewing gum on one, a cracker or two with some bits of dried fish on another. I assumed that this was a display of what was on offer and tried to order plenty of what looked the least disgusting. But it turned out that what was on display was the entire stock. Once again, we went hungry.

The lack of food became an increasing problem. I have a healthy appetite and, especially when doing shows, need to eat regularly or I become light-headed. Searching for other sources of food, we tried eating at one of the international hotels. But this was not practical on a regular basis because it was very expensive, pompous and time-consuming. And the food was disgusting anyway.

I finally discovered a black-market stall, which was a man standing at the roadside with a small glass case on a stand. This contained a few precious items, typically bananas and Snickers bars. It cost the equivalent of a Russian's weekly wage to buy one of these items but, fearing for my safety in the air, I guiltily spent my money.

This lack of food presented a very sad situation for the circus lions. There was not enough food for them and the hungry and bad-tempered animals were making the lion tamer's job increasingly dangerous. The lion tamer was a broken-hearted man because the word was that they would all be shot at the end of the season.

Although poverty was obvious everywhere, the circus was full every night. I began to settle in. Gradually, the other artists started to greet me and I was overwhelmed with pride when one of them asked if he could film my act. There was a big family troupe of acrobatic horsemen in the show, consisting of the parents and their grown-up sons. The act was exciting and dramatic. They galloped at top speed, bareback, round and round the ring, somersaulting on and off the horses and shouting to each other in Ukrainian. For the finale of the act, the mother was winched off her horse into the air to perform a stunning trapeze routine above the wheeling horses.

I have not done much horse riding but what I have done I have loved. So when they offered me a turn, I seized the opportunity. They set up a lunge line from the centre of the building and I galloped around it, holding on for dear life. It was brilliant, but for a week afterwards, I could hardly walk.

The horse troupe father invited me to dinner in their quarters. They spoke a tiny bit of English, so we muddled along sociably. I was completely knocked out by the tradition of toasting: vodka was poured into shot glasses and someone would make a wordy Russian speech in honour of the occasion. It was about the union of circus families from around the world, sharing love and comradeship – which grew as the vodka shots increased. Then we would all toast enthusiastically, knocking back the vodka. I made a speech but have not a clue what I said. By then, I was carried away by vodka and enveloped in the warmth and camaraderie of their family.

Later that evening, when I was happy and sozzled, the father offered me a choice of his strapping sons for a husband. I extracted myself politely. With one more vodka shot, who knows what I would have agreed to? Thinking about it the next day, I realised that the turn on their horses had not been so much of a friendly gesture as an audition. The mother was getting older and probably hoping to retire from the trapeze when a suitably skilled daughter-in-law could be found.

I came away from Russia with my ideas changed on some important points. Firstly, that while it is clear that animals are best left in the wild, training them for circus can be done lovingly and humanely. I am not anti animals in circus, just anti cruelty to animals anywhere.

Secondly, being a vegetarian is a luxury reserved for comfortable countries. It would have helped me greatly if I could have eaten meat, because what little food was available was usually meat stew. The smell of it repulsed me and I found that I had given up meat too young to change; I could not eat it even when I felt that my health was threatened. This was a surprise to me, as I had always thought that, if I had to, I would eat meat. I came back to England determined to practise meat-eating.

Lastly, all Russians wear real fur coats. Of course they do. In a country as cold as Russia, you would die of cold in fake fur. They all wear big, bulky fur coats and hats – making huge cloakrooms essential in every building – while we froze in our fake furs. I realise now that there is a time and a place for lifestyle choices and moral judgements.

CHAPTER 39

The pantomime

> **Keeper** – a small leather loop, about the size of the circle made when thumb and finger tips are put together. It is placed on a half-metre webbing sling and pulled tightly down to trap the ankle, wrist or neck, so that the artist can perform safely suspended.

It was the year after my ankle accident that I agreed to do a pantomime the following Christmas. We were to be 'The Flying Carpets' in *Aladdin*.

In the first half, we appeared as assistants in Widow Twankey's carpet shop, performing doubles trapeze while we helped fetch down the carpets. Later, we had to rescue Aladdin from the baddies on our flying carpet, which was a bizarre contraption invented by me. It was constructed across a swinging trapeze and we stood at opposite ends of the carpet and swung, facing each other. It was a cumbersome article, with a tendency to swerve all over the place if the swing wasn't perfectly even, and the moves we could do were limited due to having a carpet between us. But I hoped that the general effect was impressive enough to override the lack of skills in the routine.

We carried the carpet onto the stage and attached it to the cables of the electric winch. As the winch took us up, we started swinging, performing from the centre of the auditorium, right above the heads of the audience. While this was a great dramatic effect, it was a nightmare of safety lines (each controlled by a crew member) and winch cables. The rehearsals with the crew took a lot longer than we had anticipated.

I had already put off my corrective ankle surgery in order to do the summer tour and it was shortly after the tour finished that the new surgery date came through, for that autumn. I was still hobbling around on crutches and couldn't put it off again. The surgeon instructed me not to work on it at all for three months after the operation. Unfortunately, there was only six weeks between the operation and the pantomime. I thought that would be plenty.

I remember coming around from the general anaesthetic as the nurse was saying my name and instantly bursting into floods of tears. The poor nurse was worried something had gone wrong, but I think it was simply that I had been carrying a huge amount of pain and stress for such a long time with this injury, and it was the relief of thinking that it was over.

They had removed the bit of broken bone that had been stuck in the joint and drilled some space so that the fracture in the ball of the joint could heal. Hooray. Mum had come up to look after me for a few days' post op. This was a mixed blessing. as she is not a very patient person and soon got bored with me lying with my foot up.

I was soon up on my crutches again, and a friend would pick me up to take me to the gym to keep up my upper body strength while my ankle was out of action. I remember being irritated by a member of the gym commenting on how impatient I was being and that I should not be back there yet. I always was a very similar personality to my mum.

Rachel was in Thailand doing another show so I was to work with Misha, an aerialist I didn't know very well. I went into pre-panto rehearsals with Misha about a month after the operation and initially all went well. I was a very strong catcher and actually the month off had rested my muscles and I felt great.

The decision to ignore the surgeon's advice seemed fine at first. It was when we moved from rehearsing the routines in our own training space to driving to the theatre rehearsals every day that I started to feel the strain.

Rigging the flying carpet was a big and complicated job. The kind of challenge that I relished. Wakefield Opera House had recently been refurbished, and it was a delicate job to drop the suspension cables from the roof beams through the decorative ceiling as there was now only about an inch in which to manoeuvre – then we had to attach the spreader bar, with the extremely heavy electric winch sitting on it.

The spreader bar was tensioned off with cables and wagon ratchets attached to eye bolts in the side walls. The eye bolts had taken months of negotiation to arrange with building control, but I had sorted that out in advance. Then we had to attach each lunge pulley and flying carpet line in the correct place. There was a lot of running – or hobbling – up and down to the roof, shimmying up and down ropes and endless tiny adjustments to be made. At the beginning of the rigging I was off my walking crutches; by the end I was back on them.

It was a strong show with a good cast and crew. Our lunge controllers were Skinning the Cat members, so we felt comfortable very quickly. The problem was that to push that carpet, with its air resistance, and keep it in a straight line, involved a lot of lower body strength, knees bent, up and down on tiptoes, pushing. This was too much strain for my ankle and it was gradually weakening, so my recovery started going backwards.

This problem was exacerbated by other strange symptoms that developed. I remember a meal out after a show one evening with the whole cast and crew. I just suddenly started crying uncontrollably at the table. Everyone looked concerned and the director whisked me out for some fresh air. We all put it down to tiredness. Everyone had been working exceptionally hard to get the show up and running and we were all looking forward to settling into a repetitive routine. We did two shows a day, which for us meant four aerial spots: hard work but not unusual. Despite the increasing strain, I initially enjoyed many happy moments, feeling at home in the middle of a good run.

I kept thinking that my ankle would settle down, all I needed was a good night's sleep and a day off. But I was finding sleep increasingly hard to get, partly with ankle pain but not just that – I literally could not get to sleep. I was feeling depressed and emotional and this was leading to some more distressing symptoms, and it was getting worse and worse...

My ankle is painful, I can't sleep. it feels as though my mind is gradually moving onto another planet. Panic attacks, ignore them, tell myself that I can do this show in my sleep. Normal body functions are starting to shut down. I can't eat, I feel sick all the time and my throat feels tight and closed. Consumed by constant panic about nothing and everything, adrenalin courses through my body at all hours of the day and night. I am weak and drained.

Throughout this time, I continued to make it to the theatre and perform my four spots a day. A friend was giving me lifts into work as I was by now unable to drive. Once there, I hid in my dressing room, unable to walk to the shops or socialise in the Green Room. It became difficult for the other members of Skinning the Cat, who were so sociable and wanted to go to the bar after the show. I desperately wanted to get out as soon as possible, but we had to travel in the van together. I felt reclusive, unable to chat casually or relate to people on a normal level. I would sit in the bar like a killjoy at the party, desperate to go home. I lay awake at night fretting. I just did not understand what was happening inside me.

I don't understand what is going on. Do I have a serious illness? Am I going to die? Before each act, I hobble up to the stage and summon up the energy to perform from my deepest reserves.

It was an unsustainable situation. By this time, my crutches were supporting not just my ankle but my whole body and I had lost a stone in weight.

I had a meeting with the management to talk about my worsening condition but was unable to communicate the seriousness of my symptoms. I was confused and my brain felt foggy. I was told that our name was on the posters and people would want their money back if we weren't in the show.

I went to see the doctor who gave me some anti-sickness tablets. She also said that it sounded as though I was on the verge of a breakdown. Her advice was to try to carry on with the show as normal, because, in her experience, it was when people stopped working that a breakdown takes hold.

But this is a trapeze show, not a normal job...Can't think straight, must do as I am told, must 'pull myself together'. I am consumed by a deep fear which has no particular focus. I have heard people talk about 'panic attacks' in a way that suggests they have a beginning and end: blow into a paper bag and it will pass. My life has become one endless panic attack.

It was about half way through the run and it was almost Christmas Eve, when it all finally came to a head. I remember Helen, visiting me just before I left for the theatre. I was trying to eat some plain rice, had a mouthful and threw it straight back up. She looked extremely concerned. I was trying to convince myself that this was normal. It had to be – how else could I do the show?

We used to climb high up in the flies for our entrance into the carpet shop scene and sit on small loops of rope, waiting for our cue to slide down the ropes onto the trapeze bar. We were sitting in our loops when I started to feel light-headed, blood was rushing through my ears and I could only see black. I was still clinging desperately to my rope. By now, Misha and I had devised a backup plan: she had some idea of my problems. This involved her solo routine instead of our doubles and me just slithering down the rope and posing beside her. Somehow, we got through this. But now it was clear to me that I could not go up again.

Obsessively, I check myself for symptoms, my mind constantly circulates my body, looking for weaknesses, pulsating adrenalin, breathlessness – fear.

Terrifying invisible illness,
crawling naked down the hall,
no one can see it but me.
Cover up and carry on,
force myself through the day.
Immoveable howling pain rising through my stomach,
I cannot trust myself,
I cannot make decisions,
even if I'm right I'm wrong.
Just keep going.

I felt incredibly guilty for having let people down. I lay like a wrung-out rag under a blanket by the fire at home. The set designer came to see me and said these comforting words: 'Don't quote me on this, but it's only a pantomime.'

Jan, company administrator – I'd only been working for Skinning the Cat for a couple of months. Becky had been on crutches when I first started, so when my family and I went to see the panto in Wakefield and she wasn't there, I assumed her leg was bad. Well, maybe I already knew. I can't remember when I learned that she had pulled out of the show. I'm pretty sure it was Helen who told me. I felt I shouldn't ask any questions. There seemed to be an air of mystery surrounding her withdrawal. I wasn't able to contact her. It was a very strange, slightly unnerving time.

I went to stay with Mum, to recover. My sister Annaliese was living with her while she trained to be a midwife, so I had the family support I needed. It was hard for Mum: she wanted to see me well and kept trying to cheer me up, when all I really needed was quiet and rest. I just wanted to hide at the bottom of the duvet, I felt like a complete failure. I tried to explain to my mum and sister how I felt, but it was extremely difficult as I really didn't understand myself. By this time, my anxiety symptoms had faded. I was just depressed and crippled.

Both of my falls had far-reaching repercussions which I didn't understand at the time. I experienced extreme physical pain, followed by inconvenience, and then recovery. But I shut off all emotion. This enabled me to get back to my customary way of life at top speed. I have since learned that there is a long-term price to pay for not taking time to heal properly.

I had asked Sam to pick me up at Manchester airport when I arrived back from Switzerland. He laughed when I was pushed out in a wheelchair, probably thinking that I had twisted my ankle and was being over-dramatic. I don't remember it, but he tells me that I was very angry with him for laughing: the phrase that he uses is 'incandescent with rage'. He says he has never seen me like that. I have absolutely no memory of this, and I can only imagine that it was my first chance for an emotional outlet.

I first shut down my feelings in this way on the morning that I found out that Daddy had died. We were summoned from our beds by my grandparents, who had been staying since he went into hospital. The scene is vivid in my memory. We all sat on my mum's double bed, on the patchwork quilt she had hand-sewn with tiny stitches from small octagonal shapes cut from the offcuts of all the clothes she had made us – I can still identify each dress.

I can remember exactly where I sat, exactly what was said; the scene is vivid in my memory, but no emotion at all. We all carried on exactly as normal. I went back to school the next day. They had told the children in assembly that our dad had died and to be kind. This resulted in my standing silently in the corner of the playground surrounded by a gang of kids saying 'Are you the girl whose dad died?' I got frozen in that place for a long time. We didn't go to the funeral and there was no headstone to stand weeping beside. We didn't know how to let it out.

CHAPTER 40

Debt

> **Tempo** – we use this term to describe the movement of the body where it reaches in the opposite direction from the ultimate one, to give momentum to the move.

Now that I didn't have to go on the trapeze and was surrounded by nurturing, I regained my strength amazingly fast. Within two weeks, I was back in my own home and feeling strong enough to attend the party at the end of the pantomime. Going back to that theatre was not easy, but it felt important to make an effort to see all the people with whom I had worked so intensely. I still needed crutches, although by then I should have been free of them. I had a horrible feeling that all was still not well in my ankle joint.

I went back to work in the Skinning the Cat office. We had a tour to organise and Jan was still fairly new and could not have done it alone. I didn't talk much about what had happened. I put it down to the extreme stress of going back on the trapeze too soon after my ankle operation and put it behind me.

Stuff the lid back on the can of worms, whatever you do don't actually look into it. Stiff upper lip, keep up the public front, keep working, keep in self-denial, what else is there to do?

Despite our work abroad, Bradford remained our base. I had good friends in France and Spain, where we would be able to rehearse outside, which would remove the problem of having always to find buildings with high spaces. Also, there were places where there were a lot of creative people and conditions for artists were much easier. But by this time I was too attached to Bradford. I believed in it and in the things that happened there. We had become part of the scenery and had great support from the home community. There was no real choice.

The artists were the hard core of the company, but in Bradford we had an extended body of characters who were involved in their many different ways. Bradford is full of amazing and fascinating characters.

> **Ian, community member** – Skinning the Cat became part of my Bradford cultural landscape alongside the development of Bradford Festival. Their unforgettable aerial magic was seen as part of a unique local and international festival. On so many September nights I watched enthralled as stunning women defied gravity in fabulous costumes, lighting up the night sky with sequinned wonderment. I had no idea that they were becoming an international touring company. Most memorable was when I saw them at the touring parks events. Instead of curating a smug metropolitan festival, the organisers took far-out ideas to a range of scrubby parks around the city outskirts. Alongside the hot dog van, Skinning the Cat rose up to weave their inimitable flying dreams watched by dog walkers, teenagers sharing cigarettes, and me. I never tried to follow the narratives, just got immersed in the spectacle.
>
> I had met Lou, one of the group, as a near neighbour and parent of Henri who attended the nursery where

I was a teacher. She was recovering from a fractured skull, a fall from the trapeze, highlighting that there is no safety net in this form of performance. I asked her to come in to show the class some of her costumes. She drove the van into the playground, the 3 and 4 year old children were fascinated by the bunk bed alongside the rail of costumes, wanted to know about life on the road and were awed by the chance to look at sweat-stained feathered jump suits. I still look at the photos of that day.

As part of our off-season work, or sometimes as part of a festival package, we often taught trapeze workshops. These took many different forms. Sometimes, we would work with groups of school children or young people with social problems. These weeks were very intense and hard work in a different way from our own training and touring. Anticipating, I always groaned inwardly, actually, and outwardly. They were so draining. Also, I am essentially a selfish artist who likes to create work for herself. But, by the end, I always felt really good about what we had done, mainly because the children with the most problems in school and society were the ones who responded best to the trapeze.

The very best workshops I ever did were with visually impaired children at Temple Bank School. In preparation, their teacher, Graeme, came to our training session and we worked on the trapeze wearing special glasses that mimicked different types of visual impairment. I had always assumed that there were just different levels of sight from 'good' to 'blind'. But it is not nearly as straightforward as that. The glasses not only impaired our sight but confused the brain by making things appear repetitively, or split up, or through a tiny hole. Trying to cross the road or judge where the trapeze bar is much more of a challenge than I had imagined.

We also visited the school and I was shocked when I realised there was another way in which the children had become vulnerable. Many of the children in the school suffered from what Graeme called 'floppy baby syndrome'. They appeared to be completely physically disabled, unable to use their arms and legs for the simplest of tasks. Apparently, they were not disabled but had not learnt to use their bodies as they should, due to fear of moving and reaching out. The work that the school did with the children was wonderful. They started them off in a secure environment, a box with nice things inside to reach out for and feel. Gradually, their environment would become bigger as their muscles got stronger and they would start sitting up and throwing balls.

We worked on the trapeze with lots of safety mats. I hung on the trapeze and held their hands, then I swung them underneath me. They loved swinging from my hands completely in space, with nothing to bang into. I learnt a lot through doing those workshops. Graeme was completely devoted to the welfare of these children. I was gutted when, some years later, this very special place was closed down.

My ankle was still not functioning well. It was much better than before the operation, but when I moved it the ball and socket grated on each other. I went back to see my surgeon and he scheduled in another corrective operation. This time it was simply that so much scar tissue had grown in the joint that it needed 'sanding off' for a bit less friction. This time I went to stay at Dusty and Lou's to recover. My own impatience is bad enough to cope with without having to deal with Mum's as well.

Following this second operation, I was, at the end of the 1999 season, worn out. My memories of the previous two years are a haze of hospitals, crutches and walking sticks. I can't even remember how and where I fitted in the second operation.

Increasingly, I was experiencing small episodes of what I was calling my stress illness. It kicked in whenever things got extra stressful, interfering with sleep, eating and energy, lurching from one *'must do'* thing to another and seeking for ways to deal with it all.

I write lists to help my flagging brain to cope. Some are simply lists of things to do that I cannot keep in my head. Some are lists of situations that I find stressful. I try to work out solutions to get me out of commitments, jobs, social events. Can I get out of it? Can I hand it on to someone else? Do I have to go? I am overwhelmed by my lists.I feel like an old donkey who just keeps on going until it drops.

> *Fretting about everything,*
> *I worry about worrying,*
> *I don't know what I'm worrying about any more.*

I had had enough. I decided to go and live in Wanda in Amsterdam for the foreseeable future, work as a solo artist and close down Skinning the Cat. When I disclosed this to the rest of the company, it prompted an emergency meeting of company members. They proposed that I should go off to Amsterdam for the off-season, and that Helen and the administrator would do the winter work of planning the next year's tour. I felt hopeful that this had brought us to a turning point and the responsibility could be lifted from my shoulders.

When I returned in March I found that very little had been organised by way of a tour and a debt had been accrued to run the office. Organising a tour is a skill which often involves personal relationships with bookers and agents and I had not been able to pass this knowledge on effectively. This increased my feeling of not being able to delegate properly; I never understood why.

This situation had caused us to go into overdraft far earlier in the year than usual. Helen and I went to see the bank manager and explained the situation. We all decided that the company should stay running on minimal costs. The office would move into my spare room; Helen would share financial liability; we would only accept well-paid corporate entertainment jobs until the debt was repaid. Then the company would shut down.

It was while we were carrying out this plan that we got offered a good contract of work at the Millennium Dome. This meant regular money coming in and gave us the opportunity to develop our performance on a small mobile rig that we had made the year before. This turned out to be quite successful and, buoyed up by the fact that I was now sharing responsibility with Helen, far from closing down Skinning the Cat went back into full swing.

CHAPTER 41

Off-season

> **Heel hang** – the back of the heel rests against the trapeze bar as the aerialist hangs below. The key point is that the legs must remain slightly bent: the strength of this position is in the calf muscles, as it is the position in which they hold the heel that maintains the hold; the heel itself is on too steep an angle.

Ever since I started Skinning the Cat, we had been lobbying the Arts Council to recognise circus as an art form. 'Circus is entertainment, not art', we were told whenever we rang up to try and apply for funding. We made many forays, hiding ourselves under descriptions like 'aerial dance' and 'aerial theatre', but they rumbled us every time.

Martin Burton, proprietor of Zippo's Circus – About 35 years ago when the Arts Council gave the impression that you weren't 'proper' without their funding, we felt under pressure and spent six months putting together an application for £11,000 of revenue funding. We were devastated when Southern Arts turned us down, as we had been on the dole while we were preparing the application and felt the time would have been better spent earning the money on a building site. Furthermore, we lost the next six months work as the tour had to be cancelled. We complained bitterly and were sent to make an appeal at the Arts Council's head office in London. This is a very grand building and offices.

We were kept waiting for some time and eventually summoned upstairs to be told 'If we had any money we'd give it to you'. At the time I was running a tiny little office and I looked round the Arts Council and saw expensive electronic equipment and furniture which looked like it was worth more than my whole circus. I was extremely pissed off. On the way out I saw a massive oak reception desk and thought 'well, they said if they had the money we could have it so we'll take that'. Unfortunately, the way out of the building was a revolving door and it was while the desk was stuck in it that the police arrived.

I didn't speak to the Arts Council for 10 to 15 years, then when the artistic climate had changed they asked me (by this time proprietor of Zippo's circus) to be chairman of the Circus Advisory committee. At the very first meeting I remarked that they obviously didn't know what happened last time I was there. To which the Head of Theatre replied 'yes we do and that's why the reception desk is screwed down'.

I too was invited onto the Arts Council's Circus Advisory Committee. They needed help in finding their way into the circus community. What a big breakthrough. It was in Skinning the Cat's fifteenth year that we finally were awarded some Arts Council funds. Circus was finally an art form!

The money was to create a new show, which we planned to fit into large-scale touring venues as well as our normal circuit. We still worked on a skeleton administrative staff, which this project would put under strain. But we were grateful for what we could get.

Off-season was not only a time for organising but a time for me to get some stability in my life and spend time with trusted friends and family. I had met Emma in 1988 when I was just setting up Skinning the Cat. She accosted me in the street and asked for a job on the cabaret show I was putting on at the Bradford Festival. She was a bouncy and energetic character with plenty of initiative and creativity and we became friends immediately. She worked with me as stage manager and was part of the early planning of Skinning the Cat.

After we went our separate ways work-wise, our friendship became more intense. We were each other's confidantes and, to make sure that we had space for each other in our busy lives, we set up a tradition of taking turns to cook for each other once a week. Emma normally cooked as I was so often coming and going from tour and also because she was the more enthusiastic (and better) cook. From time to time, we would take a day off together and she would spoil me with a luxury picnic in the countryside.

Our friendship was based on a detailed knowledge of each other's lives and the people we knew. We could support and advise each other about relationships, family and work, and were always on each other's side against the world. When I was touring abroad and feeling isolated, a phone call to Emma was my mainstay. We led very separate lives but often said that something had never really happened until we had talked it through together.

> **Emma, friend** – Tall and dressed like a Christmas tree; thick curly red hair, often pinned up with an enormous clip of feathers, flowers or sparkly material; clothing equally embellished, mostly handmade with a liberal scattering of leopard print and sequins. Skirts made chopped-off denim with layered skirts of fabric and netting.

I was always so proud of you, especially every time I saw you perform your throw-out on the cloud swing. Our friendship at the time was conducted mainly on the telephone: our calls were full of life on the circuit, the shows, parties, clothes and conquests.

20 years on, the sparkle is a little diminished. We have had a privileged position in each other's lives, never a player but always an intimate confidante looking in from the outside. Perhaps it is this distance that enabled us to maintain such a strong friendship; for so many years we shared every high, low and secret.

Despite all its success Skinning the Cat was always plagued with crisis: constant money concerns, staffing problems, logistical difficulties, accidents, arson attack, you dealt brilliantly with each crisis as it arose but it all took its toll on you eventually and injury and stress became a feature of your life. Alongside this ran a series of difficult relationships which added to your growing instability.

Frightened at what was happening to you, you did the only thing you knew, you continued with Skinning the Cat. It soon became apparent to me that this cycle of events was destroying my best friend.

CHAPTER 42

Rubicon

'**Crossing The Rubicon**' – To pass the point of no return.

I sometimes felt as though I wanted to stay on tour forever. This was the part I loved: travelling, performing and living outside. The adventure began the moment I left home. But when I returned to our base in Bradford, the office work could be overwhelming.

After a long tour I would fantasise about long days in bed, or a holiday perhaps. But the reality was that I had to start work on the off-season treadmill: enquiries, post, phone calls and emails, funding reports and applications, new publicity for next year's show, touring schedule, a worldwide mail-out of our new brochure. It had exciting moments and was sometimes fun, but I was always running behind myself and trying to work out how I could squeeze in a break before the next season consumed me.

Rubicon was the most exciting show I ever made. I had enough experience to know what I was doing and this show was bigger and more technically challenging than any yet. We needed an opportunity like this to increase the booking fees we could charge.

The Arts Council funding gave the company new confidence. It gave me the chance to create new routines in a more experimental fashion. Over the years, we had re-hashed every different aerial routine in every different way that we could think of, so it was great to have the time to start using my imagination afresh.

I wanted to take the skills that I had learned and use them in experimental ways, to use experimental rigging, to create new stories in the air. I did not want to be flying people on trapezes any more. I wanted to re-imagine everyday objects, which, given the correct strengthening, could become experimental aerial work. This was my opportunity, but of course it made the show more technically complicated.

The most exciting purchase that we made with our funding was an electric winch, which we used during the routines, as well as every time we needed to get equipment to the top of the rig. We began to wonder how we had managed without it: all that climbing up and down ropes – how very old-fashioned! Unfortunately, winches are very expensive and our budget hadn't stretched to a high speed one. Consequently, the dramatic effect of aerialists whooshing up into the air that I had planned was considerably modified…

My *pièce de résistance* was the 'flying bicycle'. This was a bicycle on which the heroine rode along a tightrope above the audience's heads. It had a trapeze suspended beneath it. The danger in this piece of equipment was not in the riding of the bicycle, since my weight on the trapeze counter-balanced that of Giselle on the bicycle above, but in rigging it safely.

This single item could take as long to set up as the whole of the rest of the rig. Firstly, it was very high up and secondly, the weight of two people and a bike put the rigging under a lot of strain. The stakes securing the wire at either end could pull out during the show. Or, as happened frequently while I was testing it, a whole chunk of earth with several stakes would come away altogether, depositing the bike on the ground.

The opening of the show was frequently held up by a few minutes as we had to put Giselle (a tiny aerialist) inside a giant balloon and suspend her. We had to put her in right at the last minute as she would have a limited air supply. The problem was that if the first balloon burst as three of us wriggled her into it, (as it did frequently, especially in cold weather), we would have to start again. This was hard on the 'stretch twins' who were also pre-set into their piece of aerial equipment, a Lycra hammock, which was not very comfortable. But you have to suffer for your art!

The story of the show was loosely based on a simple tale an American clown had told me when I was working in Florida. It was about a caged bird that the clown wanted first to capture and then, with a change of heart, to free. It was beautiful and simple when he told it, using a lighting effect and his mime skills. The clown was happy for me to take this and develop it into a more complicated plot – hopefully still beautiful, but certainly no longer simple.

I became increasingly isolated from the rest of the company during the *Rubicon* season. I was completely caught up with promoting the show, doing business and networking. I raced between rehearsing with the group and attending meetings relevant to future work.

Constantly, I carried in my head our bank/overdraft balance, how the tour was shaping up and all the organisation work that surrounds making a show and getting it on the road and – oh! – I must fit in some training or I will never get through my routine. I was so tired all the time and didn't socialise much with the company. More than ever before, I was in the role of the 'boss'. For me, the group feeling was gone. A 'party group' developed within the company which excluded some members, including me. For the first time, I wasn't involved in the company vibe and there was a division.

A problem with receiving funding after such a long struggle was that, rightly or wrongly, I felt that we had to prove ourselves as an art form by achieving something amazing. The show had outgrown the company.

We had always had to do our own rigging but now the show was so big it was clear that really it was too much for us. We needed more crew. There was some moaning about working conditions and I was constantly trying to justify pay and workload to the team.

This situation peaked during Bradford Festival. We had a site behind the Midland Hotel in Bradford which, unbeknown to us, flooded in wet weather. There were three days of heavy rain. My gang of hardy, wiry athletes shivered as they waded through water to de-rig and load the truck with heavy equipment.

At the same time as rehearsing and touring *Rubicon*, we were preparing for a large and complicated contract that we had for the Commonwealth Games in Manchester. There was a special enclosure called the Sponsors' Village, where each sponsor of the Games had a little chalet to entertain their friends and clients with food and champagne. We were to create a private opening and closing ceremony for them.

I have never been involved in an event which was more work and complications. For over a year before it, there were meetings, proposals and ideas. Budgets had to be changed and tweaked countless times. I could be in a field in the middle of nowhere, rigging for *Rubicon*, when a call would come, changing the budget again. I would have to leave the rest of the team and rush to an online computer. The contract was not actually signed until the last minute, by which time we had invested months of work and could not afford for it to fall through. This was not a good financial bargaining position.

Once the show was planned and the contract signed, they started the security planning. This involved knowing by a date well in advance, exactly which trucks with specifically what equipment were coming and going on which days. Each artist had to have a police check – there was no option for an injured artist to be replaced after this. And everything that would be carried in by hand had to be specified – and, of course, we were carrying paraffin and fireworks and sharp tools for the show. This caused great controversy.

We had to do the on-site rehearsals in the middle of the night, partly for secrecy, and partly as they had not allowed room in the building schedule for anything else. This meant the performers didn't get much sleep the night before the shows. I was furious with the production company's lack of care for our safety. There were about 100 artists involved in the ceremony show, plus crew. For a small company like ours, this was a tremendous feat to pull off. We earned good money but had sweated blood for every penny.

At the end of the show; all the extra artists cheered and clapped me as director. Unused to this appreciation, I felt tearful. But it made me realise how far removed I had become from my own company. I had got so obsessed with survival that I had forgotten to appreciate our achievements.

By the end of the season, we were successful but too burned out for it to be satisfying. The company was now in a high-profile position. We had interest for *Rubicon* in the following year and the Commonwealth Games had led to an enquiry to make a show to tour in the Middle East. This seemed to be the only way to make more money: to have different shows touring at the same time on a more commercial circuit than we had been used to. I should have felt pleased with myself for pulling it all off. But the financial strain continued and I had a gut feeling that all was not well with me.

> *Sick and tired of holding it all together.*
> *Fear of contracts –*
> *fear of not getting contracts,*
> *fear of people who don't listen to me,*
> *fear of not listening to myself.*
> *Holding my breath waiting for it all to go wrong,*
> *emotions are physical, shivering and cold.*
> *There's an oblong shaped steel sheet of chilly, grey fear*
> *embedded in my chest.*

That autumn, as we started the normal off-season cycle, small things started accumulating and upsetting me more than I would have expected. One bad review; some work, upon which we had been relying for the winter, falling through. Nothing unusual, but I was so completely drained, I was at the end of my tether.

I had been trying ignore my stress problems since pulling out of the pantomime – no, actually, further back than that – since the struggle to continue after Lou's accident, I had never properly taken the time to sort myself out. Working on the trapeze need not always be dangerous. But it can be. And once you have fear in your head, it takes incredible self-control to continue. I would go through periods where I trotted out my routines twice a day, effortlessly. But there were other times, usually during some kind of a Skinning the Cat management crisis, when I would fear for my safety.

I was sick from a sense of responsibility, from worrying about my own and everyone's safety, I had started out with a beautiful creative dream and, fifteen years on, I felt worn out and trapped. I had failed to delegate. I had failed to get anyone else in Skinning the Cat to take management initiative. There was a constant barrage of people from outside, presenting ideas that I was expected to facilitate.

Rushing to trapeze practice – never feeling fit enough. Rushing to get funding – to prove that I can. Rushing to recover from injuries – but still being broken. Rushing to sort out office admin – but there's always more. Rushing not to be ill – no time to be ill. Rushing to get my personal life together. Rushing to have time to stop not having time. Just feeling so wobbly.

Too much to do.
Always short of time.

CHAPTER 43

Closing down

> **Shackles** – used to attach parts of the rigging together.
>
> **Bow shackles** get their name from their wide-bellied shape which allows them to be tensioned off from three different points.
>
> **U shackles:** with straight edges, the U shackle can be tensioned from two points, as when the rigging is being tensioned in a straight line.

There were two key events which made me realise that I *seriously* wanted to close down Skinning the Cat.

The first was a phone call from Martin Burton of Zippo's circus. He was offering me the position of aerial director with his circus. It was an exciting prospect, with the possibility of re-shaping his whole aerial programme. We both acknowledged that the job was too big for me to do at the same time as Skinning the Cat. It was not the first time that I'd had offers of other work but it was the first time that I knew I wanted to take it.

Secondly, in order to break the cycle of our pre-tour overdraft, Helen and I had made a big effort to raise the funding to pay an extra administrator for six months, specifically to develop a winter programme of workshops. It eventually transpired that for various reasons not one single booking came out of this work. I felt a drop in my stomach, like an off switch in my gut that could not be turned on again. I remember this as the first moment I actually said, and meant it, 'I've had enough'.

There followed lengthy discussions, over a period of several months, about the possibilities for the company. Many ideas were thrown around to dissuade me from throwing in the towel, but we had tried them all before. I was just going through the motions for everybody else's sake; once my mind is made up, it's made up.

Even the glimpse of more financial support did not change my mind. This was not only about money – that was only part of the stress. I wanted out of the whole situation. I wanted my health and my life back.

> **Jackie, company member** – This was the year everything in my life changed: my seven-year relationship ended, I had to move house and couldn't find anywhere to live, and Skinning the Cat, which I loved, ceased to operate. It was a very hard year. I thought that the company would reform in some guise or other; I didn't really believe at the time that it had finished forever. I thought that there would be the odd job, and this would lead to more projects and you wouldn't be able to say no. Then we would all start working together again. I miss working with the company and having adventures. I found that the loss of working with Skinning the Cat hit me harder later, when I realised that this was not going to happen.

We had an office, a huge mill floor where we stored about five different rigs and shows, racks of costumes, sound systems, lighting systems, a yard with caravans, a mobile stage, trucks... I'm glad that I was acting instinctively: if I had stopped to think about the practicalities of closing the company, it would have been completely overwhelming.

I felt like I was shafting my whole family, letting the team down. They were my closest friends, and the way we were together and the way we did things was everything to me.

If you can imagine a combination of divorce and having to move from a mansion into a one bedroom flat, that is how it felt. Plus, I was on a major guilt trip;

Was it simply that things have a natural life and then they finish? Was it that I was no good at delegating? Was this because of my overinflated sense of responsibility, control freak, perfectionist? Was it that I never got the right management team around me? Was it that I tried to be both aerialist and director? Was it that I was unlucky with the falls? Was it that I was too soft to be a boss? Was it that my past issues would have brought on an emotional crisis whatever I did? My mind swam with questions, self-criticisms...

The problem was that while I was ready to stop, no one else wanted to. It was not their natural stopping time, but it was mine and this caused a lot of upset, especially with Helen.

Jill, Mum – I was very excited and interested when you set up Skinning the Cat, although I knew almost nothing about trapeze. And proud, too: you were embarking on a very brave venture. As time passed, I became more proud – and surprised – because I knew of so many people who had set up theatrical companies of one sort or another, which fizzled out after a few months or – at the most – a few years.

Over the years, from the collapse of that first rig to the triumph of Rubicon at Circus Space, I felt emotionally involved with all the disasters, struggles and triumphs. The first time I saw a performance was at Glastonbury, Annaliese was with me. It was very hot and the ropes were slippery with sweat. The sight of my eldest daughter taking such risks was more than I could bear and I could not watch some of it. Neither could Annaliese! However, I was impressed by the standard of the work and also by the costumes. It must have been about that time that I started nagging that the beautiful costumes should be treated with more care – it was years before anybody took any notice!

You assured me, often and often, that all the moves were fully rehearsed and the rig carefully tested for safety etc. And that you did not take risks. After a while, I began to believe you and then, when I directed the show a couple of times, I got so involved in trying to put on a successful production that I did not even think about the dangers. Those women were impossible to direct, by the way! Too many axes to grind, no clear, overall structure to the piece they had devised and were devoted to. But the show was always so spectacular, so skilful, that, mostly, it did not matter. Over the years, I watched shows all over the place and dragged along all my friends. I was never uncritical.

The responsibility was always yours: emotional, physical, financial. I don't know whether this was because you were not authoritative enough, or unable to delegate, or if it was because you were never able to recruit the kind of people who would take responsibility for the areas you did not have the time, or the expertise, to carry out yourself. Even those company members who loved and supported you, forced you to use up time and energy on their personal and professional problems. Perhaps you were just not ruthless enough.

I remember being furious when you had your accident and yelling over the phone: you stupid cow! Or something like that. I was angry because it need not have happened. You did not need to be doing what you were doing at the time. It was peripheral. And of course I was worried and upset. As time went on, the worry and upset increased. I still wonder whether that was the point at which you should have started to concentrate on your own brilliant art work.

You were a young woman in a hurry, always pushing back the frontiers, always at the creative cutting edge. And you will be again, in whatever you decide to do. Only this time, you will have experience and knowledge to support you.

My mum is both my greatest fan and my strongest critic. She came to shows whenever she could, we'd spot her arriving from the other side of the field, dancing towards us waving a home-made cake, often with a bunch of friends behind her. My sister Annaliese once told me that she was surprised that Mum had any friends left, she talked so much about Skinning the Cat. I was proud that she was proud of me but this could also be a pressure; she believed in the 'the show must go on' ethic and told me: 'You die on stage', which means that there is no excuse not to perform.

Mum had morphed from the actress of our childhood into a director and playwright. When I was a second-year art student in Bradford she had a commission to write a play on mixed cultures, and chose to bring herself and Annaliese, now eleven, to live in Bradford for three months to research it.

I was given the task of finding them a room, which I did: a small attic in a shared house full of African men. My sister started school in Bradford and my mum took on voluntary work teaching Asian children and women to speak English. She fitted in well with the African household, Annaliese coped with the temporary school change, Mum wrote her play, and my college friends and I sponged as many free meals off her as possible.

I can see now that I get my *can-do* attitude from her: she just does stuff she wants to do, with purposefulness. Without this example, Skinning the Cat may never have existed.

Mum decided to move to London. Just at the age most people retire to the country for a quieter time of life, *my* mum wanted to be where more was going on. She felt that she had done Bristol and wanted to be near better theatres. Mum is a keen cyclist. She has three bicycles: one for riding around London – cheap, because it might be stolen; a good one for cycling holidays, and a fold-up one to take on trains.

She got a job running the Round Chapel in Hackney, which is a kind of venue and community centre. She had the same effect there as she had had at the Bristol Craft Centre, and when she left some of the artists made models, pictures and paintings of her, beautifully capturing her personality and interests. A model of her in her red jump suit on her bike going to Greenham common; a painting of her with her bike outside the craft centre; a cartoon of her in the Round Chapel office. One Christmas long ago, I painted a picture of her standing on the roof of our house waving a bottle of whisky – not that she drinks *that* much, but we do like to have a shot together sometimes at bed time.

CHAPTER 44

Mad woman in the attic

> **A mental breakdown** is an acute and temporary mental disorder that affects a previously functional individual to the extent that they are unable to function on a day-to-day basis.
>
> A breakdown is often closely tied to psychological burnout, severe overwork and sleep deprivation, which may combine to overwhelm a person with otherwise sound mental functions.

It was during the conversations about closing Skinning the Cat that my stress illness symptoms began, insidiously at first, so I thought that I was imagining them and tried to carry on as usual. My head filled with fog. Driving into Bradford city centre, I became completely lost on roads which were familiar to me. I felt depressed, tearful and dominated by fear. There was no point in asking 'what am I scared of?' It was not rational.

Part of my brain is missing, there is nothing there, nothing to hold onto. I run through the things that I have to do, I tell my brain that when I've done these things it can relax but it does not accept this information. It invents stress, determined to hold on to every small detail, finding anything and everything to fret about, I have lost control of it.

I am waiting for a bomb to go off.
When will it be safe to let go?

Eventually, I had to give up trying to pull myself together and went to stay with Dusty, Lou and Henri. Living alone was not good for me at this time. At their house, I had continual love, support and sympathetic ears. At the peak of the crisis I did not sleep one wink for two weeks. My brain had gone into hyperactive mode. Adrenaline coursed round my body incessantly. I could not eat: my throat had tightened up and food could not pass down it. Dusty cooked me consommé soups and we joked that we could trace my progress as we moved on to thicker soups.

> *Trapped inside my head,*
> *I go back to the circus farm.*
> *Happy ghosts,*
> *freedom,*
> *energy.*
> *Was that ever me?*
> *This broken down machine that I am now?*

I was very weak. Lou would come up to my attic bedroom in the morning and, after listening to my overnight waking nightmares, she would coax me out of bed to do some stretching. She understood that my nature was so physical that, even when I was hardly strong enough to go down stairs, I needed the stretching. It helped me to survive. I refused all contact with the outside world. When I was at my worst, if some friend called at the house, I would disappear off to the attic. I really feared that these symptoms would never go away: I would be forever the mad woman in Dusty and Lou's attic.

As if all the life and energy has been drained out of me, all hope, all courage. As if I am empty and having to start again. As if all my personality and strength has left me, as if there is something terribly wrong and I will never be safe again. As if my body has been invaded by fear in a physical form which creeps into all my

269

*joints like a thick black fog causing pain and discomfort in every
part of me; as if someone has plugged electrical currents in and
left them running through my body so I can never find peace.*

*As if I am utterly unlovable, completely alone, as if no-one could
possibly understand and help me, as if I am of no value and my
friends will find me a pathetic, weak pain in the ass and give
up on me. As if I am in a nightmare to which there is no end.*

*I am at the bottom of a steep-sided dark hole and as I try to
crawl towards the surface something keeps pulling me back.*

To support myself, I used to write, reassuring myself that it's
okay not to want to go outside, to speak to anyone, to have no
energy. I told myself: well done for getting through the minute,
hour, night, day, week... I wrote kind things about myself to
counter the cruel criticisms inside my mind. I would plan one
tiny task at a time to see if I could do it. I told myself, over and
over, to hang on in there, it would pass. I wrote lists. Lists of
lists. Lists about lists. I had boxes of lists.

I was trying to work out my mental state. To find out what was
causing these feelings and, hopefully, untangle and ease them. I
tried to trick my brain by finding different ways of approaching
things. I tried to pretend that certain things had not happened
or that I was just seeing things in the wrong way – strategies
for coping with memories and future commitments.

I wrote down what I was angry or scared about. I was terrified
that the panic would never stop. I explained to myself why
various things will never happen: there is no performance,
nobody is going to fall, no scary man, nothing to fear – I did
not have to climb into the terrifying blackness. But the fear
was too embedded.

No commitment or pressure was acceptable to me. Skinning the Cat must go; relationships must go; friends must go; arrangements must not be made. Because my raw brain always conjured up the worst possible outcome of any given situation, there must be nothing in my life. The last lists I made were an attempt to appease myself: if this has to happen, how can I benefit from it? How it will make me stronger? More in touch with myself? Take me nearer to normal?

Nothing worked. The only way to get through this time was to retreat inside myself, to the safety of personal space. I reacted strongly to this space being invaded. I did not like people around me. I needed silence and peace. The worst thing for me to do was nothing – yet to do anything was so very hard. Dusty took me for a walk around the block. Facing the outside world made my legs feel as if they could not support me. I felt that I would keel over and pass out as soon as I moved away from a solid object. I held on to Dusty's arm and we staggered around the block as he talked reassuringly to me.

Feeling my way along the garden wall,
moving away from solidity – vehicle, house, person – holds
untold dangers.
legs stop working, so heavy like wood,
adrenalin starts rushing
panic racing
nausea
failure
humiliation
I am weak
I am pathetic

Lou, company member – There was one night where I was freaked and I think we rang the doctor, as I thought maybe you were suicidal. I was really frightened for you because you had this feeling of dying. It wasn't suicidal but I didn't understand. I was scared for you, that you would die. That's the ultimate fear. I was scared that your heart was going to stop or that you were just going to go to sleep and not wake up. Looking after someone who's a bit nuts, it's hard to judge, you don't know how nuts they are. You were obviously frightened but you were kind of lucid, you weren't *nuts* nuts.

I cannot state that after this or that period I got better. It was imperceptible – often one step forwards, two steps back. After the initial really hard-core bad weeks, I started having bearable days and bad days, ranging from hope and optimism to depression and despair.

Their house is next to a large park and, as I got stronger, it became an important part of my day to walk around it. I seemed able to think more clearly as I walked.

When I was quite young, I once asked a friend whose brother had had a breakdown how they knew when it had happened. I had never experienced anyone having a breakdown and was interested. He said, 'he walked into town in his pyjamas'. So I waited for this stage to happen to me: 'am I having a breakdown?' I never got to the stage of walking into town in my pyjamas: I remained painfully and annoyingly aware of every action and emotion. It was undramatic and rather disappointing.

Dusty set up a small practice trapeze for me in the attic. Henri and I worked together on it every day and we developed a pretty passable doubles trapeze routine, considering that I was nuts and he was only ten. Making things helped me through my despair: however bad I was feeling, I forced myself to sit at the sewing machine. I was making a new coat. I gritted my teeth and told myself that every seam I sewed took me nearer to normality.

Along with the support I was getting, it was self-discipline that kept me going. I finished the coat and moved on to a sculpture that I had made years ago and which Lou had kept. It was a huge reptile which climbed up her sitting room wall and needed some serious renovation. Luckily, the attic was very large. I had my whole small world up there. The little practice trapeze on the ceiling, the sewing machine in the corner and a large sculpture on the floor, surrounded by the tools of my trade: glitter, gold paint, glue and sequins.

I was getting all the way around the park and even managing to speak to the frequent visitors that came and went in their house. Some days, Lou would come home from whatever arts project she was busy with, and find me in a bad place. She was so brilliant at talking me through myself and keeping me going, always so positive about how well I was doing and making me feel worthwhile by saying how much she admired me.

It was Lou who said that we must give my illness a nice name. I cursed it all the time, this thing that had evolved inside me and was stopping me living the life that I had enjoyed. Lou said that we must stop cursing it and give it love and nurturing. So the first thing we must do was to give it a nice name. I said 'Petal'. From then on, that's how it was known.

Petal says 'NO', no to shows, no to travelling, no to boyfriends, no to socialising, crowds, excitement or new experiences. Petal wants peace and space; to lick her wounds, to cry, to be held by close friends. Most of all, she wants silence.

Petal is my alter ego. She is everything that I have always hoped that I am not. She is scared, isolated, agoraphobic, depressed and unlovable. No one, especially me, has ever bothered to listen to her needs.

I force her back onto the trapeze after falling off it, I give her no space and no sympathy. The endless shows have been like a punishment for her. I have developed a life style that makes me feel so alive that I can ignore Petal when she starts crying. Petal feels responsible for keeping the aeroplanes in the air and the trucks on the road. Whatever I do, or think, along comes Petal, carrying an extremely heavy suitcase.

CHAPTER 45

Dissolving Skinning The Cat

> **Silks**: a length of fabric normally about twenty metres long and two metres wide. The fabric must be synthetic with Lycra content, but not pure Lycra as it overstretches and tears. Double up the fabric by choking it half way along its length through a ring or large shackle; suspend it from this point so that the two ends hang free, with at least a metre resting on the ground. The artist ascends the silks and wrapping, turning and twisting the two pieces of fabric around different parts of the body creates a fluid aerial dance routine.

I was beginning to cope – as long as I didn't have to deal with the outside world. I had cancelled everything that I had been committed to previously. I ignored the phone and relied on the help of trusted friends to sort things out for me. The office had been packed up by Helen. But there was still a yard full of vehicles and a mill floor crammed with equipment.

The management company of the mill where we were based went bust suddenly, and all the companies in the building were given two days to get out. Now I had to face the outside world. There were some pretty big companies in that building. The surrounding streets were clogged with removal vans and people were struggling to carry computers and furniture down the narrow staircases. The electricity had been cut off, so the goods lift upon which we were dependent to move our equipment, could not function. It was pitch dark. We procured torches, floodlights and a generator, then tried to decide what to keep and what to leave.

At the beginning of the day it seemed an impossible task. Helen stood in the midst of all the heaps of stuff, holding an empty bin bag and looking helplessly at me. We did not have the option of just walking away from it all because there was some expensive equipment there, and there were loans to be paid off. Also, I had no idea of the future direction of my working life, and therefore was not sure what I might need.

I found a smaller, cheaper mill space and we set about ruthlessly binning and transporting. It was heart-breaking to have to take an angle grinder and remove the beautiful set dressing from the *Rubicon* rig. It took up a lot of space and, as the rig was saleable but the set was not, it had to go. If Helen had thought that I still might change my mind, witnessing this carving up of my beloved rig must have brought reality home. The trucks, caravans and stages were dispatched around Bradford to yards belonging to friends and contacts, to await sale. The rest of the equipment was passed down through the windows of Woolston Mill and hauled up through the goods entrance of Prospect Mill. These few days were pretty sad.

CHAPTER 46

Physio exercises

> **Complex post-traumatic stress disorder** (C-PTSD) an anxiety disorder which may be diagnosed in people who have repeatedly experienced traumatic events, either as a child or an adult. Traumatic memories seem to become 'locked' in the brain in their raw, distressing form, without going through normal memory processing.

With Skinning the Cat gone there was no normality for me. I was in no man's land. I was not ready to get on with a new career and had not tied up the loose ends of the old one. I found myself repeating my old patterns of behaviour, basing my days around trapeze training at Manningham Sports Centre, but unsure why I was doing it.

Increasingly, I had to miss training because my back or hip was too painful. My problems confused the specialists: should I be sent first to the back man or to the hip man? The hip had been damaged by years of over-extending in straddle and splits. But was the bad hip aggravating the bad back or vice versa? Or was it all compounded by years of walking slightly off-kilter on my dislocated ankle?

As I was able to do less and less trapeze, my problems got steadily worse. It reached the stage where all I could do to ease it was to lie flat on the ground on a special mattress, with my head flat. Simple movements, such as sitting, became big issues. Going for walks on the moors, which I so loved and which helped to clear my head, made the pain worse.

Struggling on my own with my physio exercises, I began to wonder if the past twenty years had really happened. It seemed that maybe this was all there ever had been. I began to dream every night about my routines. I would go through them in exquisite detail, wrapping my foot so, twisting, pulling. I could feel the trapeze like an amputated limb.

The dreams were sometimes happy: I was back in the air, doing what I was meant to do. If I could only just get up there again, my back would be cured.

But there were nightmares too. We would be trying to rig in a venue that was too small and there were no rigging points to attach to; or the team would be setting up and I was not allowed to be involved; or Rachel was late and there was not enough time to rig before the show. Whatever the problem, I felt that I had lost control and was the only one with any sense of urgency.

It always ends in the same way – Lou is slipping away and the nurses are not taking me seriously. It will be too late.

I visited many different specialists, osteopaths, hospital consultants and physiotherapists, waited for MRI scans and ultrasound appointments, always hoping that this one would help me. That there would be a magic special exercise, explanation, treatment, operation: anything to take me back to normal living. Physiotherapy is the most boring form of exercise. The months dragged into years. Results were very slow.

On the exercise trapeze in my kitchen, I carefully stretch my spine – this provides the weightless traction that is a relief from pain. I move slowly, partly so as not to shock my body, but more importantly not to kick my collection of decorative flea-market crockery beside me on my dresser!

Some years before, I had visited Sarasota in Florida, the winter quarters for the Ringling Brothers' Three Ring Circus. It is here that they have the circus hall of fame, the Hollywood of the circus world, packed with serious circus aristocracy. I found there a community of retired performers. They still lived their lives through circus: there was a community centre where they regularly met for meals; their homes were packed with circus memorabilia; their lives revolved around circus meetings.

I visited La Norma, a famous aerialist now in her seventies. She spent her days making beautifully detailed models of circus performers, which she made to order and sold to the industry. She still had a trapeze rig in her garden and commented that even now being up on the trapeze feels like home as she had spent so much time up there. I really related to her.

There is undoubtedly an element of relief in stopping a career which can be life-threatening and hard on the body. But my own experience showed me that it was only after stopping the trapeze that I felt what I had done to my body. I followed a path similar to that of many other injured athletes. This slow and frustrating process is part of our life story. A combination of yoga, a persistent osteopath, and advice from many different specialists finally gave me the tools I needed to manage my injuries and move on.

I had gone from a high flying aerialist touring the world to a crockery trapeze artist using the small trapeze hanging in front of my kitchen dresser to stretch my spine. So life changes!

Lucie, company member – One of the things that I found wearing about being an aerialist and a performer, was the irregularity of work, I never knew where I would be or what I would be doing in 3 or 6 months' time. I was a lot less sensitive to that problem when I was twenty. Of course I was also conscious of the freedom and pleasure that comes from this job. I got a lot of pleasure from the exchange of energy with the audience, from moving around in the air and swinging!.

I don't have the same drive for the trapeze any more. I don't have the energy to challenge the pain and the fear, or not as much. When your life depends on your body and you get injured, you never know how much you are going to recover and if you will be able to do the same again. After two months with crutches, I had a phase of depression. But injury teaches you to be patient with yourself, that life is not all about performing (I sewed a lovely blanket for my godchild), that performing can be different, that your body is a great machine and that you can build again and get stronger, even if differently. It is also a special time where one is in touch with what being weak or disabled or old can be about, which with a healthy body one cannot realise. I remember sitting in the Tube being so scared that anyone would touch my bad knee, or having to depend on friends and family to go from place to another, and shopping, and realizing that I would not be able to do much if I was hassled in the street. I am well aware that I feel really bad and heavy if I don't train. I know I don't have the energy any more to train for the hours it takes to be really strong and good, so sometime I know I will have to let go but it is scary to let go of the skill you mainly rely on to earn a living with.

When I injured myself, after doing the physio someone introduced me to Iyengar Yoga to strengthen and open and balance my body. And Yoga is great for me, it has really done a great job regarding my injured knee but also all the other parts of my body that compensated for the weak joint and somewhere along that also for my head and my heart. I know that I will always have to keep doing some sort of regular physical training.

I had time to focus on myself during this empty time and made some important discoveries. Although I clearly had suffered a breakdown, I was diagnosed with the ongoing condition of Complex PTSD, where recurrent trauma has not been processed. I have realised that while there is a time and a place for the 'stiff upper lip' approach, it is not always sensible to bottle up emotions. At some point, it is time to be brave enough to face them.

I realised that it can sometimes take more guts to walk away from something than to carry on battling it. I have learned that if something gets too hard, *I mean really too hard*, stick two fingers up at it and walk away, even if you are walking into terrifying nothingness. I also understood that despite everything that most books on the subject told me, anxiety is not just a habit to be ignored: fear is there for a reason. Anxiety *appears* to be irrational as it kicks in at inappropriate times, but the original reason for the panic is completely reasonable: there are real roots to it; it is not just a silly embarrassing mistake.

Another discovery I made at this time was that some of the physical symptoms that had been worsening since early childhood were caused by a high intolerance for gluten. Mum had taken me to the doctor as a child but at that time gluten was not widely recognised as a problem, and the doctor just said that the pains were 'tiredness tummy-aches'. This phrase added to my feeling of being a bit of a pathetic specimen. I grew up feeling that I had to prove myself.

I also now understand that abuse in childhood programmes guilt and inferiority into the brain. I picked up guilt and responsibility like it was all meant for me. I had developed a strong urgency to escape from places and situations, which was a feeling that I had first had when leaving my grandpa's house. I understand now that my problems grew from a combination of relationships and events which all fed into each other.

CHAPTER 47

Selling Equipment

> **Eye movement desensitization and reprocessing (EMDR)**
> is an approach that seems to 'unblock' the brain's processing,
> so that traumatic memories become ordinary ones. It is a
> fairly new therapy, one of the treatments for post-traumatic
> stress disorder (PTSD) recommended by the National
> Institute for Health and Care Excellence (NICE).

When I felt ready to face the world again and came out of Dusty
and Lou's attic I felt good: plenty of good food, love and no
stress had done its job. Unfortunately, as I tried to get back to
normal life I found that everything I tried to do freaked out my
anxiety symptoms. I don't mean extreme things, just normal
life stuff like moving in with my boyfriend, social events and
taking on bits of work. Everything was a big deal. I was getting
requests for teaching, directing shows, designing rigs; I forced
myself to do these things but I kept feeling so ill, it was as if
I had become allergic to life. Any perceived stress at all and I
slipped back to my frightening space. I began to feel that I was
a social misfit, beyond help; techniques which worked for other
people were not helping me.

If you think of mental health problems as a place, somewhere
that you have got stuck, then something has sent you there at
the outset. Throughout life, the links to that place are made
stronger and stronger if more traumas are added. Each time

I went back to that place I felt worse, and condemned myself for it. My problem was that having compounded the situation so many times, I found that I could not get out of this place. I tried counselling, CBT and hypnosis. But for some reason nothing helped.

I finally found help in an amazing process known as EMDR: Eye Movement Desensitization and Reprocessing. My unscientific explanation of it is that normally we process everyday events in our sleep, that's what dreams are for, and the rapid eye movement (REM) part of sleep processes trauma, which is why it is so important to have a healthy sleep pattern. But when a trauma is buried too deep, or maybe just been repeated too many times, normal sleep cannot deal with it.

EMDR recreates REM while at the same time the psycho-therapist gets you to think about the traumatic events, and this finally and properly neutralizes the memory. What this felt like for me was initially a kind of letting go, followed by a really raw emotional feeling for about twenty-four hours. Then in the next few days the emotions would fade. The result is that when I think of the memory, I can still remember the details of the event just as clearly but the pain that I associated with it has been rubbed out. Brilliant.

This has been an amazing relief. Very slowly, unravelling memory by memory, I have worked to clear the habitual pathways that my brain had got stuck in. We went round and round in slowly decreasing circles cutting the links to the dark place. It was exhausting, but it gave me my life back. It was so wonderful to let go of these things that had become so much a part of me that a lot of the time I was not even aware of what they were.

I had built up a fear of men, a fear of stress, an obsession with doing exciting things to keep myself feeling alive... The list goes on and on, and these beliefs were completely subconscious. I began to make sense of the career that I had chosen, the pattern of multiple boyfriends, my ultimate feeling that every time I got stressed I must go back to the dark place.

It all sounds mad in the cold light of day, but as I traced further back into my subconscious I realized that the panic I had assumed was irrational was attached to completely rational original sources. I would have found it fascinating if it hadn't been me that had to go through it all.

During my journey of recovery and change, one of the hardest things to deal with has been the sense of shame that I felt about succumbing to stress. I have hidden the extent of my vulnerability from as much of the world as possible, terrified of what people would think of me. I have felt like a fake: posing as a strong-minded, creative woman while secretly battling to become 'normal' again.

These understandings have helped me to begin to forgive myself for the car crash that my life became.

None of my recovery events happened in a neat chronological order but as I waved goodbye to my demons there were key people and experiences that helped re-build my confidence.

One of these experiences was teaching trapeze to Sophie and Zahara, initially because I liked them and I needed the money, but increasingly because I became fond of them and cared about what they were trying to achieve. Neither of them was very good, and for a long time they continued to look like a couple of sacks of potatoes on a rope, their hands sticking out with all the elegance of a couple of spades. As these two determined women slowly developed into professional artists, they became very important to my life. My mobile continued to ring with booking enquiries for Skinning the Cat, so I was able to pass on work to them, which felt liberating after years of panic in case there would not be enough work. I loved telling people that we were no longer available but I could highly recommend a new duo, Arabesque. The girls were so grateful when I made them a rig and advised them how to start their company. But for me it was therapy. Their enthusiasm and passion was helping to heal me.

Sophie, aerialist – The first time I saw Skinning the Cat, I must have been about 11. Some of my friends and most of my family were heading to Lister Park for the Asian Mela. That day and evening remain one of my most memorable experiences of Bradford.

In Lister Park under the hot sun I remember trying my first vegetable samosa. I ended up scoffing another two, sitting watching a band playing amazing Bhangra music. I remember looking out and seeing a sea of different faces, sitting, dancing, eating, chatting. It was a brilliant feeling of unity.

For me there was a certain atmosphere that summed up this time in my life. It was in the early days of the rave scene and the music was trance-like, all about reaching another place. Skinning the Cat encapsulated everything that was special about this time, they created a magical surreal world unlike anything I had ever seen. Seeing those colourful and bizarre creatures dancing in the air provoked something in my imagination. It's funny to think that moment changed the course of my life.

They also represented an alternative way of life, travelling in caravans, they had an air of mystery. Also they were open to everyone, in the spirit of the Mela that day, not just those who could afford or would think to buy a ticket.

Since that day I had always secretly dreamed of being a trapeze artist, although it seemed ridiculous as I was never very gymnastic and always quite shy. Unbelievably though, over 10 years later I met Becky and was given the opportunity to leave my life in Brighton and start training on the trapeze in Bradford.

During this time I was also trying to sell the Skinning the Cat equipment. The bulk of it was in the storage space and, without the company's income, finding the rent was a struggle. We also had vehicles and a mobile stage stored with various friends and businesses around Bradford. Gloria, the biggest truck, was parked at a local fire station. I had to move the vehicles around frequently, as the parking offers were often short term. Although we had some valuable equipment, it was highly specialised and therefore difficult to sell. It felt like the past still hung over me. I received initial help from the rest of the company to move everything, but now I was on my own with the problem. Helen and I were feeling very angry with each other at the time, because she had never wanted the company to end and I was angry to be dumped with all the aftermath. I seethed as I spent time and energy doing up and advertising vehicles for sale to pay off our joint overdraft. It took me two years to sell everything, but as each of the large items sold I felt a little lighter.

The last big piece of equipment to be sold was the *Rubicon* rig. I was relieved when it was taken away. It was bought by Deborah from Urban Angels, a small Leeds-based aerial company, and we fell into a very easy and supportive friendship. She needed to be taught how to put up the rig but I felt uneasy about having anything much to do with rigging; I had completely lost my confidence. She never pressurised me, but the following year she still had the rig in storage and casually asked one day whether I might be ready to teach her yet.

> **Deborah, Director of Urban Angels** – Right from the start, the relationship between us was about more than the handing over cash for kit. She was very clear about the responsibility of owning a rig and I was very aware that the sale of this equipment was an important shift in Becky's career. Becky had spoken about her injuries and the effect of stress as the Artistic Director of Skinning the Cat. I listened to everything she said and learnt that there was a lot more to running a show on an aerial rig than putting the right piece of metal in the right place. So when she delivered this lovely curved rig I was aware that putting up the rig together could be stressful for both of us.
>
> The purchase was done on credit with no contract other than a few notes made on the back of an envelope. She generously slipped in a few extra pieces of equipment. I remember saying to her that it was more important for me to be able to pick up the phone to ask advice than to quibble over prices. I've done quite a lot of picking up the phone.
>
> With each transaction, we have had that same mutual respect and empathy and this has proved the basis for a friendship. This is a good way to do business and ultimately, to make circus.

I decided that I did feel up to the challenge. Not only that, but I felt I was on a roll and reclaiming my old confidence.

The first job was having a look at the rig which could have been damaged while in storage. So, one scorching hot day found

Deborah and me laying out the rig at her lock-up. I slipped back into my old role; sorting through the equipment, making lists of missing parts, piles of soft rigging to be strength-tested, stakes that needed straightening, re acquainting myself with the shape of this rig. I felt so at home in my old rigging boots and grubby leather waistcoat.

Waiting for the train home, I was aware of a happiness and peace in myself, a feeling of everything being right. I felt more normal than I had for two years.

With all the equipment mended and tested, we planned the day of rigging. I was both excited and nervous and determined that is should happen, swiftly sorting out a field with a farmer when Deborah's venue fell through. There was no option for postponement. I had missed working outside, laying out the rig, banging stakes in, bolting, shackling and laying out cables. Pull-up was a bit nerve racking, until I saw that of course everything was going fine and all the concerns were in my head. The whole day went like clockwork. It was wonderful.

I was still training on the trapeze whenever my injuries allowed it. But I became apathetic as this was without purpose and my skill level just slipped backwards. I decided to film myself doing some silks moves. After warming up, I set up the camcorder and tentatively executed a few moves. I then checked to see how it looked, went back up on the silks again for a few minutes, then checked the recoding again, all the while very conscious of my injuries and fearful of causing further damage.

The video illustrated what I already knew: while I was still able to perform the movements, I had lost the ease and grace that I had considered my trademark. As I drove home, it dawned on me, with relief, that I wasn't in love with the air anymore and I could stop trying.

I can finally breathe,
sounds of running water soothing my brain.
I am drinking in the peace and saturating my soul with
sun,
wind on skin, smell of pink heather.
Storing up light for darker times.
It is wonderful to not be broken any more, just cut loose a
bit sometimes!

CHAPTER 48

Albatross

There are two types of ropes used by aerialists: three ply and woven.

Three ply – the most common, has three strands twisted together. This takes various forms of width and lay, depending on its use.

Woven rope – multiple smaller strands woven together. This type of rope, which has a very much stronger pattern, is used when a rope is likely to become untwisted. It is used, for example, when the aerialist is spinning.

Lay of the rope – the tension with which the strands of cotton are twisted together.

3-ply cotton rope – Each of the three skeins is made up of many different lengths of thin cotton. The rope factory feeds together lengths of cotton to make strands of the required thickness and the three strands are twisted together on a rope walk. which has to be twice the length of the finished rope. An aerialist's rope must be just the right width for the hand to hold and each strand must be the right width for the toes to grasp. The lay must be tight enough to prevent the rope from untwisting, but not so tight that the rope becomes inflexible.

I always kept a close friendship with Jan, the Skinning the Cat administrator. She has been enormously instrumental in helping me deal with the pile of crap through which I had to wade in order to move on. When Skinning the Cat ended, I could hardly turn on a computer. I had always refused to learn the necessary skills and had simply dictated information to the office staff. Now that became my main problem. Jan patiently sorted out the many defects on the old Skinning the Cat laptop and sent me on a computer course. When I was ready to look for work, it was Jan's idea to write a list of all the things that I could do. This ran: teaching aerial skills, teaching art, directing shows, artists' agent, rig designer, rigger, truck driver, costume designer. Also, I could, like many of my colleagues, develop my stilt walking and do corporate/shopping centre entertainment. I started working my way through the list.

My phone still rang frequently with requests for artists and shows and I passed on so much work to other artists, mainly aerialists, acrobats and stilt walkers, that I thought I might as well do it officially and charge commission. This involved innumerable phone calls, contracts and paperwork, mainly office-based, which is not to my liking, so after a few months I started passing on the work for free again.

I was asked to direct aerial shows, and undertook a couple of them. I did enjoy it but it was just too similar to Skinning the Cat.

I tried long distance truck driving but found that it had a terrible effect on my back.

I spent some time walking round and round the yard on stilts but could not stop thinking about friends who had smashed wrists and knee caps falling off stilts. I felt that my body had been through enough.

I was going to have to find a whole new way of earning a living. I wanted to be connected with circus but did not want to go back to performing in it.

I designed several aerial rigs for different companies. Rig designing is an exciting mix of creative challenges to meet technical specifications. The work allowed me to live the outdoor life while teaching people to put up rigs. I particularly enjoyed working for a show called *Albatross* and toured with them as their rigger. It was great to be part of a company and not be the boss. I had my area of responsibility and if anything outside that went wrong, it was not my problem. I could take a tea break and join the rest of the company in blaming the boss. Liberating! And, beautifully, it gave me the opportunity of working with Lou again.

Initially, Lou came along just to support me as she knew my confidence was low, but, being the live wire she is, she was given the job of stage manager and ended up as a crucial part of the team. Lou was up on the rig with me at every opportunity (although the surgeon had said she should never again work at height). We were back where we were happiest together, on top of a rig.

I added rig design and installation to my developing patchwork career, but not the role of rigger. Although Lou and I had both loved the experience, this type of work was not sustainable for either of us: we were both too damaged in our different ways. I carried on working my way through my list.

> **Lou, company member** – I don't talk about Skinning the Cat that much now, but I kind of make jokes to kids in schools that I work in, or I drop it now and again that I used to be in the circus. It's like a dream world that I used to be part of.

Skinning the Cat was outdoors, it was physical, and no day was ever the same. It was a challenge, because you had to react fast. Putting up the rig was a satisfying job to do, because it was so impressive, it was macho, using that sledge hammer to put the stakes in and all being self-sufficient was really very satisfying. You weren't dependent on anybody at all: you could arrive on site and ask the right questions, which meant we could just get on with it, and people would watch while we did a job really efficiently, and then do the show as well. Being on the road was hard but I loved living very intensely with people, because you had to work at it; there would be crises left right and centre and it would always be just as you were going over a border or in a service station or something. To me it was a dream job; I'm probably too old for it now. It was the most fantastic time of my life. We were living life to the full, seizing the day.

I accepted work teaching on weekend courses at a circus school. I loved the contact with circus performers and initially was happy enough teaching, but I ended up with a stiff neck from looking upwards, concentrating on controlling the lunge lines and saying over and over again: straight, push, tuck, and point your toes! I found that I wasn't passionate about teaching trapeze, now that I wasn't doing it.

It was holding the lunge line as I was teaching that I finally understood something which had been bugging me for years. I had always felt confused about issues surrounding Lou's accident and my own. I had felt guilty that the company had worked so close to the edge that Lou's accident had been able to happen. There was so much baggage surrounding both our accidents: was my accident my fault for taking Lou to Switzerland too soon? Or was it Lou's responsibility for not pulling the lunge line when I fell? It dawned on me while I was teaching at the circus school that, regardless of her head injury, I had not taught Lou how to work the lunge line properly. It is a skilled job which involves a high level of concentration. I pretty well just handed her the line and expected her to pull it at the right moment. I realised that, through my own slackness and the pressure to create her a role in the show, I had caused my own accident and I have had to live with the consequences.

Lou, company member – In hindsight you look for answers, and how I think about my accident now is that it was culmination of events. I carried on working like a lunatic during pregnancy, had a child, and then continued touring. Henri didn't sleep and I was leading a crazy life. On top of this, the stress of coming off tour to a different lifestyle caused me and Dusty to have a big row. I'd also sprained my ankle a few weeks before and it felt really weak. I remember what the venue in Holland was like and that I was really unhappy with the rigging of it. I felt really nervous, partly because I was knackered, and then running up the stairs to rig in such a high space, it felt very unsafe.

The TV show was like the Dutch Oscars. There was a Production Manager putting pressure on us and you said to us, come on, you all need to stop now, go for a cup of tea, just calm down, and I said yes I'll come, but I didn't and I spent the tea break running up and down the stairs because I really thought I could sort it out.

Then we went into the dress rehearsal. There was the moment when I had to drop in the trapeze and climb over the top of the rig and get onto the rope: there was too little time to do it in and I knew that. It's difficult to know what I really remember and what I have been told, but I remember waiting for that bit and climbing over in a rush. My sprained ankle weak and blood sugar very low, and just not feeling safe. The next memory was being taken out of intensive care, though I didn't remember being in it.

The strongest thing I remember about the day of your accident is you being very pre-menstrual. That was a really strong thing, at one point you were in tears because you kept overbalancing. I could see your obstinacy because you walked out of the room to recover and when you walked back in, you went up again, then we had the accident. You were determined; you felt you ought to be able to do it.

This might be a bit hard for you to hear, but for a long time afterwards, I thought the accident was your problem, not mine. I thought it happened because you were pre-menstrual and you weren't in touch with yourself. I know now that wasn't true: it was our accident, and the fact was, I failed on the safety line. I remember after you'd fallen I pulled it tight so that you wouldn't see it was slack, because I suppose I was feeling guilty.

That night the agony that you were in was just awful.

CHAPTER 49

Calm Space

> **Back balance** – the aerialist lies across the trapeze; the bar must be positioned at the top of the buttocks rather than the lower back.

Inside my house it is peaceful. I feel a sense of relaxed control. It is a bit messy but makes sense to me, my comfort zone. Bright colours are everywhere, a mish-mash of fabric, rich velvets and flashes of leopard print on cushions. Embroidered gold swirls on hangings, on masks, on circus posters; faces look out from pictures, horses gallop and ladies parade on elephants above the fireplace.

I sit in my conservatory, spinning my dreams: costumes, masks. Strings of sequins twist to make the coloured shapes on fabrics and characters begin to form.

Sometimes I am joined by my small daughter; working beside me she places her favourite toy rabbit on some fabric and cuts around it. The rabbit regularly gets new outfits, little coloured trousers, a jacket... and a sequin headband with a feather in it!

My conservatory is the same size and shape as my caravan, Wanda, with the patterned rugs that I once had on her floor. I am surrounded by windows and light. Outside, my garden rambles its unkempt way to its low stone wall and my eyes skim over the bungalows beyond and up the steep, green hillside.

From this calm space I plan my sculptures, costumes and circus projects while watching the changing skies: grey and overcast or pink, deep red and gold as the sun sets. I love the shapes of moving clouds, so many different colours as the light bounces off, through and around them. There is a great expanse of sky outside my back window. I depend on it.

Mum wrote me another poem.

For Rebecca:
Spinning dreams
with quick, bright threads
that loop and swirl
through long white fingers,
casting cobweb shadows
on your still face.

Spinning hopes
that fly up, curving
across the moon, weaving
walkways that glitter
through the cold air
to the stars.

Sweet spinster,
spin strong: fast and
tight cast your light
silver net where sardine love
can slip safe away from
stormblack seas.

Jill Truman

Yesterday, I sat on a rock on the moors for an hour, drinking tea from my flask, gleaning the last rays of the November sun, facing up to the sky, shoulders back, my body open and relaxed. Today, on the same moor I hunch in the icy fog on a damp log, crouching over my flask cup for warmth. I gulp down the hot tea with my neck tucked into my headscarf and, move on as quickly as possible. I need to stride out, breathing in the scent of earth and heather, to gain some height so that I can look across the valley to the sky. This satisfies the same part of me that needed to swing up high on the trapeze. Inside my head, in my body, I feel the silence in the air, in the view, in the light space around me. I drink it in.

I love the smell of bracken when it's warming in the sun.
As I walk on the moors I rub it between my fingers so that
the green juice stains my skin and releases its scent.
The cack, cack of pheasants and the thin tinkle of
moorland streams punctuate the wind as it races around
the contours and crevices of the hills.
I imagine the wind like a random overture: starting low
like a distant sea as it chases through the dry reeds, then,
building to a crescendo, whooshing and roaring as it hits
the twigs on the leafless treetops.
The weak but welcome winter sun is on my face.
There is nowhere that I would rather be.
By myself with my thoughts, silent and peaceful.

CHAPTER 50

The Grande Dame

> **Life-casting** – the process of creating a three-dimensional copy of a living human body, through the use of moulding and casting techniques. The most common life-casts are of torsos, pregnant bellies, hands, faces and genitalia; it is possible for an experienced life-casting practitioner to copy any part of the body. Life-casting is usually limited to a section of the body at a time, but full-body life-casts are achievable too.

When I was eighteen and in my first year at Art College, we all struggled to add depth to our work. We had to borrow substance by researching other experienced artists, trying out their styles and themes. We tried to imagine that we could engage with their issues, their politics, their suffering. But of course we couldn't. Our work was just an experimental shadow of what it would become. Now, I have a lifetime of experience to play with. The richness of my experience as an aerialist continues to feed me.

A young aerialist once referred to me as the 'Grand Dame of Aerial'. Initially, after my retirement from the trapeze I felt uncomfortable when people still introduced me as a trapeze artist, but now I think that when you have done something so completely then you are always that thing. Cut me in half and I will have aerialist written all the way through.

I used to think that my work was very shallow: all sparkle, bright colours and showbiz flourish. I thought that to be a proper artist, the things that you made had to be black, academic, wordy, overtly political. But now I see that I was telling a story all along and that, in itself, is enough.

Through a series of chance events, completely outside of my attempts to re direct my career, I developed a passion for life-casting. I had been trying so hard to reshape my life and one day I got a phone call offering me work which led to my training with mould-making and life-casting guru Martin Hanson from Madame Tussaud's workshops. There was no way that my list of career options could have anticipated this turn of events.

I loved the effects, materials and experimental possibilities that life casting opened up for me. I seem drawn to skills that combine practical work with creativity: life-casting gives me the same satisfied feeling that I get from rigging. By taking moulds of people's bodies which capture their muscles, ageing lines, calluses – all the physical elements which develop throughout our lives and tell our personal stories – I create a three-dimensional portrait. I use it like a physical snapshot in time that I combine with my other skills to make sculptures, masks and costumes which capture the images and emotions of the circus.

I sculpted the life-cast faces into masks after an inspirational trip to the Venice carnival. Wandering around the narrow streets and squares, I spent a lot of time visiting different mask shops. Some were very commercial, mass-producing for tourists. But once in a while I would come across an artist's workshop where stunning and highly individual masks were being made. I related to these artists. There was a similarity in our style. My imagination was fired up.

In the past I have always said that I won't make costumes for people outside of Skinning the Cat. The few times that I had tried it had not gone well, as I must follow my own way and my designs are quite over the top. But as a more experienced costumière I have found that I can be fussy about my clients and only chose people who will allow me creative freedom. This has allowed me to involve costumes in my new combination of work. When people ask me how I earn my living now, I say that I am an artist and that everything I do is linked to the circus. I make rigging, costumes, sculptures, masks, films – all of them for and about shows, and sometimes all of them mixed together! I have found a role as someone who is *about* circus. There is so much to learn and pass on from an industry which supports Olympic-standard athletes working in such a tough environment. When I visit my friends' shows, I now see the lifestyle more objectively and I am in awe of the commitment that a travelling show takes.

The great thing about being an artist is that you never stop. You never wake up one morning and think 'I'll give up being an artist today'. Okay, so I stopped physically being a trapeze artist, but making things, for both pleasure and work, will only stop when my hands, brain and heart seize up. If you get bored with one sort of art, you find your way to a new idea.

I suppose that, for me, art is like religion is for some people: it makes all things possible. It makes me believe in life. My religion is beauty. I don't mean it has necessarily to look beautiful but, when you are creating it, it must feel beautiful, or do something beautiful, or be part of something beautiful.

Post script

I arrive at the Netherlands national circus with a gang of my daughter's school friends. We are welcomed in and do not pay for tickets. The children queue for drinks and candy floss, again no charge. Tony, the circus proprietor, offers them programmes and light-up whizzy toys to hold; Romana finds this all completely normal.

Tony and I sit discussing a project we are scheming together at a table in the foyer tent. We drink tea from Styrofoam cups which I nurse to keep my fingers warm. As we talk, the Big Top is flapping like a wild animal; they put it up in a storm last night. He needs me to lend him some pulleys for a rope that is getting frayed, he must run off and get more heaters – the audience must be kept comfortable. It is freezing cold and muddy and I think guiltily of my warm cosy house that I will soon return to, where the generator doesn't keep cutting out... There are many things that I miss about this life, but oh my god today is not one of them!

My daughter has been to more circuses in her ten years than most people would go to in a lifetime. She has become something of a circus connoisseur and likes to compare the new programme to that of the year before – and she can be very scathing if an act is not up to scratch! After spending time on our kitchen trapeze, she has announced that she doesn't like going upside down. Good. It's dangerous.

Acknowledgements

Thanks to Jill Truman and Jan Scott for trolling through the grammar and making sense of it all, with additional thanks to Jill Truman for permission to print her beautiful poems.

Thanks to Lin Webb, my editor, for her diligence, enthusiasm and encouragement.

Thank you to everyone who has written pieces to add richness to the experience of Aerialist.

Thanks to The Arts Council and to Bradford School of Art for the financial assistance that has helped make this book possible.

Photo credits

Front cover: *Firebird* Split Image

Inside front cover: *Millennium* Unknown photographer

Inside back cover: Lizzie Coombes

Back cover: *Portrait* Harvey Dwight